0309

TRIBE WANTED

VOROVORO, FIJI

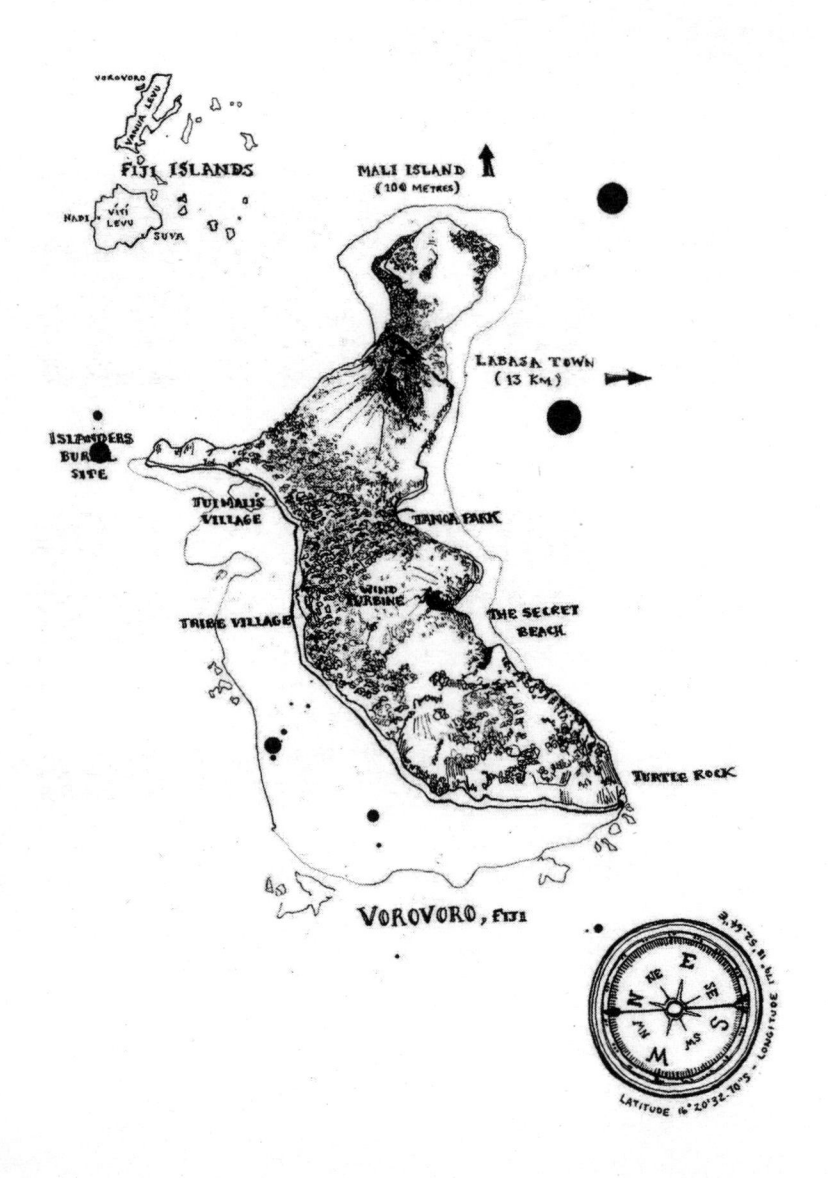

TRIBE WANTED

MY ADVENTURE ON *PARADISE OR BUST*

Ben Keene

EBURY PRESS

1 3 5 7 9 10 8 6 4 2

Published in 2008 by Ebury Press, an imprint of Ebury Publishing
A Random House Group company

Copyright © Shine Limited, 2008
Illustrations on pages 2, 13, 131 and 267 © Lisa Cresswell, 2008

Ben Keene has asserted his right to be identified as the author of this Work in accordance with the Copyright, Designs and Patents Act 1988.

All rights reserved. No part of this publication may be reproduced, stored in a retrieval system, or transmitted in any form or by any means, electronic, mechanical, photocopying, recording or otherwise, without the prior permission of the copyright owner.

The Random House Group Limited Reg. No. 954009.
Addresses for companies within the Random House Group can be found at www.randomhouse.co.uk

A CIP catalogue record for this book is available from the British Library

ISBN 978 1 09192 162 0

The Random House Group Limited makes every effort to ensure that the papers used in our books are made from trees that have been legally sourced from well-managed and credibly certified forests. Our paper procurement policy can be found at www.randomhouse.co.uk

Project editor: Steve Tribe
Typeset in Helvetica Neue, Destroy and Palatino Linotype
Printed and bound in Great Britain by Mackays of Chatham plc, Chatham, Kent

To buy books by your favourite authors and register for offers, visit www.rbooks.co.uk

CONTENTS

Prologue: 'The world will come to Vorovoro' — 9

I. FINDING A TRIBE

1. The sunny side — 15
2. Dreaming from Devon — 19
3. Google: Islands for sale — 28
4. Fiji! — 33
5. Bartering for paradise — 48
6. Bula or bust — 52
7. Revolutionaries — 65
8. Breaking America from our back garden — 76
9. Tribal gathering — 85
10. Taking the tribe to New York — 98
11. Decision time — 108
12. Scam artists — 114

II. BUILDING PARADISE

13. Figuring out Fiji time	133
14. Countdown	146
15. First feet 1/9/06	164
16. Tribe life	179
17. Fire	188
18. Building a Great Bure	199
19. Chiefly challenges	209
20. Trapped	219
21. Coup	229
22. Consolidation at Christmas	239
23. Enter the Tikinas	246
24. Goodbye, Dan	251
25. Cyclone	255

III. THE COCONUT EVOLUTION

26. Sunshine after the rain	269
27. Living the dream	277
28. The future fishermen	291
29. Tribewanted 2.0	300
30. 'Nothing hard in this world'	306

Acknowledgements	314

For two tribes: the Yavusa of Mali and the global Vorovoro Tribe, you worked and lived together to realise the dream.

PROLOGUE
KO VURAVURA ENA QAI YACO MAI VOROVORO
'THE WORLD WILL COME TO VOROVORO'

For twenty-six years, a Fijian chief lived on water and not land. He sailed the world – London, Sydney, Hawaii, New York – working aboard the *Guardian Enterprise*. In 1987, he returned to his small island home to bury his father and inherit his chiefdom. The next fifteen years passed without incident as, under the title of Tui Mali (Chief of Mali), Ratu Apenisa Bogiso lived the quiet life of a sailor, fisherman and gardener, interspersed with visits to the local villages to make sure his people were happy in their lives and work. He became Tui Mali, or Chief of Mali, carried out his duties and lived as his father had done. He expected that this was how it would be for the rest of his life. He was wrong.

On a dazzling dawn, as the sun crept over the dramatic headland that jutted from his island home, Tui Mali walked slowly out of his house and took the few steps down onto the empty beach. Looking out across the flat water of high tide, he could just make out the distant breakers on the outer reef. He could even hear the quiet roar as the swell met the coral wall and created lines of white water over the turquoise platform. But he could also hear another noise that morning. It was coming from down the beach, and it was clearly the sound of a machete slashing its way through tall grass. Slash. Slash. Pause. Slash. Slash. Pause. He knew his good friend and keen gardener Tevita was staying on Vorovoro, and it was probably him. But why was he cutting grass further down the valley away from his home, his garden and the two-house settlement where he lived? Tui Mali walked the hundred metres towards the sound and ducked under the trees. Tevita, a tall, well-built man, stood feet astride, dressed only in a pair of muddied denim shorts, and leaned into the head-high grass, swinging the blade back and forth. Tui Mali wondered again, why was he clearing space all the way down here? Surely, he thought, if we wanted to extend the garden we should be doing it closer to the house?

When Tevita saw Tui Mali walking towards him, he stopped what he was doing, wiped his hands on his shorts and threw the machete into the nearest log so that it stuck like a dart. He took two steps towards his Chief and shook his hand, bowing slightly as he did so. He said good morning: 'Yadre sia'. Tui Mali greeted his friend and then looked at him with his deep, luminous eyes. Tevita didn't need to hear the question to understand what his friend wanted to know. He knew that Tui Mali would not understand why he was cutting grass this far away from the house, people didn't come down here. Apart from family and friends no one ever came to this remote island. He looked at his friend, his Chief, and decided to tell him simply and directly the reason behind his actions. He knew it was a big statement and he knew the consequences could change the Chief's future, as well as his beloved Vorovoro's, forever. Tevita looked Tui Mali dead in the eye, his eyebrows raised as sweat poured down his face and said:

'Ko vuravura ena qai yaco mai Vorovoro.' ('The world will come to Vorovoro.')

Tevita let the words sink in before continuing: 'Me da vakarau.' ('We have to get ready.') Tui Mali nodded slowly and turned

'THE WORLD WILL COME TO VOROVORO'

away, walking back towards the beach. He knew of Tevita's ability for prophecy, and he knew that what he had just heard was big news. Big news. He began wondering what it all meant. He turned, thinking he might go and question his friend. But Tevita had turned too, his back glistening in the morning sun; he was already swinging his machete again. Slash. Slash. Slash. There seemed to be a real urgency to his work. 'The world will come to Vorovoro,' he repeated carefully in his own mind. Tui Mali knew this was an important day. Maybe his and his island's future wouldn't be quite as quiet as he had expected.

I
VAQARAI NA YAVUSA
FINDING A TRIBE

1
BABASIGA
THE SUNNY SIDE

I was floating. Silky, warm water was breaking gently over me as I breathed in the aromatic atmosphere. But this was no opulent five-star spa. This was the natural wonder of Vorovoro, a small island in northern Fiji that a friend and I had leased for three years. Along with the local community and visitors from around the world, we were now living a reverie. And at that moment, with the morning sun bouncing off my English winter skin as I lay in the shallows of the crystal lagoon, it was perfect.

Vorovoro is one small place, a Google Earth coordinate in the world's ocean, but the ideas surrounding this adventure are global and immediate. It's about living more sustainably, about where our current communication technologies can take us as a global community. It's a wild idea but I liked it from the start, and I wasn't alone. We are, apparently, helping to initiate a 'revolution in tourism', combining community driven eco-tourism with online social networking, pursuing paradise with a purpose.

But we weren't the only ones taking risks. The island chief, Tui Mali, had gambled his legacy as the hereditary leader of his indigenous tribe by betting on us, hoping that we would be the people to bring work and a better life to his island communities. This small Fijian tribe had thrown their cards in with the internet generation and on Vorovoro the experiment had begun. Now Fijians who previously didn't have much of a voice began to educate, entertain and embrace the world, or at least those who chose to go to Vorovoro.

'I will stay on Vorovoro, because here I can teach the world.' Tevita, the man that foretold to Tui Mali, that one day many people would come to his small home, was now leading community development. Vorovoro, despite being at the opposite end of Fiji to the tourist hub, was a place where Tevita felt he could make a real impact. His horticultural skills, his extraordinary knowledge of ancient Fijian traditions and his boundless passion for life made Tevita an ideal candidate to pilot the project. If Tui Mali was the all-seeing general, Tevita was his intuitive captain leading from dawn to dusk.

And then there was the internet tribe. Aged six to sixty-seven, from London to New York to Tokyo to Lima, from lawyers to engineers to artists and students, they had joined this ambitious outfit. Many had subsequently visited Vorovoro like Andy, Farrel and Peter, who were all young energetic lads from the UK. They spent their island days building a tree house at the far end of the village out of scrap plyboard and driftwood washed up in cyclone. Chasing girls aside, I don't think many lads could imagine a better way to spend a week, given total freedom to design and construct a real tree house on a genuine tropical island.

Two airline pilots from the US, Geoff and Josh, came to Vorovoro to spend ten out of their eighteen days of annual leave collecting firewood and constructing a poker table out of odds and sods. They could have afforded a comfortable island resort in Fiji but they had chosen to come to Vorovoro and, in their hammocks or running free, they were having the time of their lives.

Vicky from Somerset spent her time reading, hiking and taking some of the most amazing photographs I've ever seen.

THE SUNNY SIDE

She was the first person to swim around the island in one go, but not the last. Matt was an American graduate who was going to be representing Estonia as an Olympic swimmer. He swam the circumference of the island, finless, in a rapid hour and ten minutes. Meanwhile, Gigi, a sprightly 67-year-old, taught yoga in the Great Bure to Fijians and tribe members alike as the builders looked on. saying 'We saw this on a television once.' Eight-year-old Jacob was our first junior tribe member on Vorovoro who, with Stone-cold Steve, his enthusiastic, kava-swilling father, made the island feel even more like a family home.

The combination of communal showers, hammock hang-outs, footy matches, building projects, Fijian ceremonies, reef trips, school visits, island exploring, gardening, tai chi, snorkelling, spear-fishing, feasting, dancing, coconut Olympics and crab racing all made for a fantastic, fulfilling Pacific island life.

Later, as I sat in a hammock in the Great Bure looking towards the beach, watching happy island life evolve around me, I picked up a book lying on the mat on the floor entitled 'Tales from Nowhere'. It was a Lonely Planet publication which one of the tribe members had left in our ever-increasing library, stacked up on hand-hewn bookshelves. Some handwriting on the inside back cover caught my eye. The few paragraphs had been written by Peter Coe, one of the tree-house trio, a 24-year-old former ice-cream van driver. I copied down the words the second I finished reading.

'If you are reading this you've made it to a certain type of nowhere. How you got here or how I got here no longer matters, we both made it. Build it and they will come.' How true those words are, people worldwide being drawn by an unknown source, that sense of adventure, to come here, a tiny island in a giant ocean both physically and culturally. Never have I felt so at home, yet at the same time so far away from my life, everything I know and love is thousands of miles from me. But do I miss them? Do I hell! Good company, check. Good food, check. Beautiful environment, check. And, most important of all, freedom, check. What more do I need? Nothing. It may only be a few short weeks, a blip, a drop in the ocean of time, but the memories will last forever. The legacy of this project can change the world, if you let it.'

2

TATADRA MAI DEVON
DREAMING FROM DEVON

The journey that took me to that same beach on Vorovoro began in Devon on a cold, grey Boxing Day afternoon in 2005, when I got an email from someone I had never met, called Mark James Bowness.

I was sitting at the old kitchen table, my 'boardroom', upstairs in the barn, reading on BBC online about the Asian Tsunami, one year on. Mark's message popped up on the bottom right-hand corner of the screen. I clicked on it. He was looking for a partnership and, although I was not a great choice at that point having just invested everything I had in my own online start-up, there was something in his request that made me want to learn more.

He was suggesting a project involving the creation of an online community with a shared interest in seeing the world by following a real-life journey. In short, he wanted to create a global adventure from a bedroom in the Wirral. He had found me through careerbreakcafe.com, an online magazine I had recently started to promote gap years for everyone, not just for those between school and university. It was a free source of inspiration and advice for those who wanted to put the brakes on their busy lives for a while. Obviously, our ideas were running along parallel lines and, with a bit of a nudge, might converge. I emailed Mark back saying I liked his idea but was already committed and added some thoughts about how it might work in reality.

He responded immediately, revealing that his proposal was in fact only the tip of the iceberg of other plans he had. I was intrigued and within hours we were in a full-scale email dialogue about his visions and how they might function. I had never had such an intense email exchange before and it was kind of weird but, at the same time, exciting especially as the content of our discussions fascinated me. We spent the next week hurling emails back and forth, brainstorming, debating and modifying some of our more ambitious ideas as we tried to thrash out a credible plan that we both believed in.

We had similar motivations. Since my second year of reading politics at university, I had known that the kinds of jobs open to graduates in London were not at the top of my list of things to do next. Although I was having a good time, I was pretty much disillusioned with the vision of being suffocated in the arms of corporate Britain so I turned to something I knew I loved: travel. Purposeful, adventurous, sense-assaulting, unpredictable travel. Being a tourist was not enough. I'd been sure of this ever since I'd had a conversation with a Tanzanian guide called Abel whilst scrambling down the steep screed slopes of Mount Kilimanjaro.

It was 1998, I had just finished my A levels and my dad, my brother and I were attempting to reach the summit of Africa's highest peak. We had always taken on challenges together and this was the biggest yet. Dad had run an event in Tanzania the previous year and was excited about the possibility of climbing Kili with us. So, after an intense fortnight celebrating the end of school with my mates, I flew straight to Tanzania and ten days' trekking. Perhaps two weeks partying was not the best preparation for altitude and after three days on the mountain I was pretty sick.

I struggled to the top, the spectacular Uhuru point, and collapsed on the icy summit. I was exhausted, nauseous, and hallucinating but I'd made it. Still, I barely had the energy to crunch my way through a frozen chocolate bar. Abel was worried. He quickly encouraged us off the melting ice-cap and down into the vast veins that make up the mountain valleys.

A day later and I was starting to recover, with more oxygen in the air and Abel at my side. Dan, my younger brother by sixteen months and my very fit dad bounced on ahead. I asked Abel about his life as a guide, his family and what impact trekkers like us were having on him, his people, and his country. Although his English was broken (he often switched back into Swahili) I found that we could understand each other. I also enjoyed learning about his culture, perspective and dreams. I wanted to know more and wondered how I could spend time with people like Abel and find out about the way he and his people lived.

It also became clear to me that even Abel, with a good job as a mountain guide, struggled to provide for his family - and he was one of the lucky ones. A thought-engine sparked inside me, one that would quietly tick over for the next few years and lead me to unforeseen adventures and projects. Just a year ago, I found out through a friend who still organises treks on Kilimanjaro that Abel had been killed in a road accident. I had only spent a week with the guy but the impact of our meeting had inspired me. It was a sad day.

In fact, the opportunity to begin further adventures like the one I had on Kilimanjaro came two years later when I met a big-hearted entrepreneur called John Lawler in 2000 while I was still a student. John had taken a year out from his studies to teach in Ghana and broke his leg the first day he arrived in West Africa. When he recovered, he helped fund and build a school in a small village called Shia. To thank him for his work and friendship villagers made him chief. Back in the UK, John formed Madventurer, a company devoted to raising funds for rural community projects focusing on health, education and sport before getting young people out to remote places and sending them on overland adventures – a kind of modern and cheaper version of Raleigh International. I joined him.

Madventurer was exactly what I was looking for, an educational adventure that took me beyond the pages of my political books and into real-life experiences with remote settlements, breathtaking mountains and vast landscapes where I could engage with people and cultures. And so I spent the next few summers leading groups of students to places like Kenya, Tanzania, Ghana, Uganda, Burkina Faso, Mali, Peru, Trinidad, Tonga and, interestingly, Fiji. Joining John and his small team instead of applying for the latest top one hundred grad jobs gave me the chance to see the world and learn about building a business from scratch. I loved it and it proved the perfect preparation for everything that was to come.

My experience with Madventurer also taught me about how the world really ticks. It showed me that the quickest way to learn is to put yourself in situations where you have little or no experience. Whether I was being held at gunpoint at a border crossing, or being asked for 'expenses' by a village chief in the middle of the night, or taking a group of English students clubbing in Ouagadougou, I adapted fast. I had to. Most of all I learned how to think clearly, not to waffle about the possibilities and suggest some compromise solution but to focus, decide, act. All I had was my common sense and the untapped intuition and knowledge of those around me. It was nerve-wracking at times but fun and it gave me confidence in myself and in what's possible.

Despite the harsh and challenging realities of much of the developing world, it also gave me a belief that people could achieve together regardless of culture, class, or race. I remember getting an email from a mate who said that even though he'd been in Delhi for twelve hours he still hadn't 'found himself'. Of course he was joking but it is a serious point. I was never going to be content as that stereotypical traveller, destination unknown, even if I did listen to Bob Marley, dream of never-ending adventures and occasionally wear beads. I had to have a base and something solid to work towards, the influence of my dad, the disciplined entrepreneur, perhaps. But, more like my mum, I also had the desire to work with people to achieve something, to be part of a community or at least support communities that didn't have the opportunities that I did.

In the short time I had been speaking with him online, I had learned that Mark, like me, had travelled and worked in Africa, helped set up volunteer projects – stepped out of his own comfort zone. But while I approached most things from a practical, 'how do we do it' point of view, Mark came more from a 'why don't we try this' perspective. If I needed a base, Mark needed a platform. Not to show off but to leap off.

We met in the second week of January. After all the online conversations we'd had, I thought it would be a good idea to meet the guy. If anything was going to happen we would need to get on with each other outside the safety of our inboxes. When I arrived at Manchester Piccadilly's finest drinking establishment, Mark – hoody, jeans, trainers, pint – was sitting in the corner. Three hours, four pints and one conversation later, when I had to leave to catch the train back south, I had a new friend and business partner. With him came the beginnings of a new company specialising in sustainable, adventurous travel to be marketed globally online and aimed at people from any age or background. I really believed in it. I liked Mark, or MJ as I now knew him. I felt confident that we would be doing something together that we could be proud of and which would, with luck, at the same time provide us with the means to a decent income. So I was a little pissed off when MJ rang a week later to say that he wanted to change everything. 'What do you mean, you've had a better idea?'

'Ben, steady, just listen. This is it, trust me. Where are you now?'

'At my desk. Working on our business plan.' I sighed. 'Yesterday's business plan.'

'Check your emails. I've written it all down. Read it, then call me.'

I opened my mail. 'You have one new message.' I looked at the title. Then I looked away. I fell back into my chair and felt my pulse quicken. I read it again. This is what it said:

THE ISLAND PROJECT – A TRIBE IS WANTED.

Nothing like it had ever been done before. MJ's one-page proposal said we were going to buy an island, build an eco-community on it and thus create a tribe. Anyone could join, from anywhere in the world, and everyone would take part on the internet by voting for a tribal chief or joining debates within the community. And, crucially, each member would have the opportunity to visit the island at some point, to live the dream. All we needed was some money. Oh, and an island.

Hang on a second. Was MJ serious? Perhaps, more importantly, why were we even thinking about attempting something that sounded so ridiculous and how on earth were we going to make it happen? I quickly scribbled down the main barriers but didn't send them to MJ. Instead I just emailed him and said, 'Crazy idea mate, not sure where you get them from. I think I get it, I certainly want to get it, but I have a lot of questions…'

Here are a few of the questions that I asked him. Why did he want to attempt this? How exactly did he get this idea? What did he know about 'eco-community-building' on tropical islands? What did he think the impact would be on the local people of the area and how would we manage that? How would the online community work as a decision-making entity? How would the business model work? Did he have projected budgets for different aspects of the project? What was the 'elected Chief' babble all about? And how did he think we might go about buying an island when two weeks previously we had both agreed that whatever we did would need to be self-funding?

I was a little worried my barrage of questions might scare him off – and these were only half of them. But I needn't have worried. MJ quickly emailed me back. It was clear his zest for and, indeed, his knowledge of current online technologies was something I was going to have to equal pretty quickly if I was going to keep up with him. And he had answers for most of the questions. He seemed pretty clear about how the business model, the marketing and the online side of the project would work. He was certainly not short of ideas about how an online community with a real-world base could be engaged.

As to where the idea itself actually came from, he had been sitting at his laptop, thinking about where online communities might go next, when he had started to daydream. His daydream from a dining table in a house in north-west England in the middle of winter took him to the tropics, to sunshine and a beach. We've all had that daydream. But what if, he pondered, you could connect the two? What if the online community's purpose was to go and live on an island? MySpace with a real space; Secondlife with a real life; Facebook with actual face-to-face meetings? It was a brilliant mental leap, a simple and spectacular spark. I absolutely loved it.

Where his answers were shorter and virtually non-existent was on the 'how it would work on the island' bit. That was where he expected me to come in: 'You will manage the island, the real-world community and operation and I will manage the online community and the marketing.' Why did he want to do it? 'To see if it might be possible; to give online communities a real-world dimension; to make a difference to people's lives.' As to how he would go about finding an island, easy, he said. 'Google'. MJ didn't mess around.

Once I'd got the 'what are we doing' and 'how are we going to do it' a bit more clearly established in my own mind, I turned to perhaps the most important question: 'Why are we going to do it?' MJ had given me his reasons. But when I asked myself the question, I came back with some interesting answers.

The first was purely instinctive – there was something about the idea that had gripped me, thrown me backwards in my chair and quickened my pulse. The email had lit up a grey winter's day like a supernova. I couldn't stop asking questions, couldn't stop thinking that it might be possible. My imagination was on fire. I imagined the island – the beach, the palm trees, the building of a village, the games, the fishing, the singing; I imagined the perfect island community and wondered if we could do it. I didn't believe in the idea of Utopia or in a perpetual paradise. I knew society was flawed. But I was irresistibly drawn to the idea of a community in a beautiful environment alongside a different culture.

The second answer was more rooted in my perspective on the world and my experiences. I loved the idea of building something from scratch that could mirror and embrace the environment. A village that would slot into the cycles of a tropical island's ecology rather than simply building a development that would leave its physical and environmental footprint forever. Would it be possible? I was no expert, but it was already obvious to me that sustainability was going to be an increasingly important aspect of the way we lived and travelled. I understood sustainability as simply a style of living where you complement your environment rather than change it. The first thing that popped into my head was the idea that on a small island there isn't any water except rainwater. How much rainwater could we catch to run an island community? It was a question that would not be easily resolved.

Thirdly, and finally, I considered the possibility of an online and island community participating and communicating to create something new and exciting. The sense that a large number of people would be co-creating in two different worlds simultaneously fascinated me. I wasn't quite sure how it would work but I loved the idea of empowering people online to change a real space. A global village – the great macro online network of people connected 24/7 by an instantaneous and infinite information galaxy, would be focusing its time and energy into a tiny micro island village. The original concept of building paradise on earth was, the more I thought about it, an incredible blend of ideas, current trends and even history. By now my mouth was watering at the thought of what MJ's idea might actually mean.

Outside, the January drizzle and mist shrouded picturesque Devonshire landscape and reminded me why English people drank so much tea. I put the kettle on. The email from MJ had come through at 10am and, as I stood in the kitchen, the clock caught my eye: 3.15pm. Shit, I'd been messaging for over five hours without any kind of break. This was proving a serious distraction from my other big commitment, the London marathon. After running in the fresh country air, I sat down with a cup of tea. I wanted to get a second opinion on MJ's idea. So, in 'Who Wants To Be A Millionaire' style, I decided to use my 'phone a friend' lifeline. I wasn't going to spend hours on the phone to different mates, most of whom I knew were going to laugh at me and tell me to get 'my ass up to London and get a real job', so I picked one friend who had sound judgement when it came to ridiculous risk.

I had lived with Mark McGinn, or Marco, for a year at university and he had become my best mate there. We were similar – loved going out, staying up late talking rubbish about travel, music and sport. Marco is one of life's enthusiasts and, if anyone was going to back me on this, he would. And I was right. 'Oh my God, Benny Boy, that is a crazy idea. I love it.' I asked him if he thought it was possible, if he thought the reasons for doing it were sound and if he thought I should be throwing myself into it when I had just started my own business. Marco, as I expected, was realistic about the challenges. But he was instinctively excited about the potential and, like the good advertising account manager he had become, said it was a unique concept that could inspire people and create change. I got off the phone with another surge of adrenalin running through my veins at the thought of giving this a go. As I settled back at my laptop and opened MJ's next email, alone in dark, wintry Devon with dozens of questions in my mind, I already knew I was being sucked in. A black hole was opening up in front of me and I was going headlong into it.

3

YANUYANU VOLITAKI ENA MONALILIVA
GOOGLE: ISLANDS FOR SALE

I couldn't tell my family, not yet. Although always supportive, this was perhaps one new venture too far and I wanted to sort out some of the most pressing problems before broaching it. MJ and I approached a few potential investors and one, Alex Tew, the man behind the Million Dollar Homepage, responded. MJ had somehow got his attention online and we met the 21-year-old millionaire in a Starbucks off Oxford Circus. It was like a student version of *Dragons' Den*, without wads of cash on the table. If anyone overheard the conversation between the three of us that afternoon they would have thought that we were drinking something a lot stronger than hot chocolate.

In the end it was Alex's belief in Tribewanted that convinced MJ and I that we could go it alone, without investment. We would buy the island with membership subscriptions. Simple. Limit the size of the tribe to the island's capacity. Sell each membership for between £100 and £300. It all seemed to make sense. So, aged 26 and without any obvious means of support, MJ and I, for all the world like the millionaires we so clearly weren't, started searching for our perfect island. Anyone can do it. Go to Google, type 'private islands for sale' and enter a world of sunshine and dollar signs. We looked at islands from Thailand to the Caribbean and toyed longest with a stunning specimen in the Philippines, a snip at one million dollars. We even entered into talks with the government. Eventually, and with the serendipity that already seemed to be following the idea, MJ forwarded me the website of Cheyenne Morrison, a 42-year-old island broker based in Australia. MJ had been emailing him. He had written back asking for some background information. We told him a little and he didn't tell us to get lost. He did tell us that our idea was 'pie in the sky' and that 'island owners don't take hessian sack wearers seriously'. I don't know why he bothered at all. Perhaps sales were a bit slow that day in the islands market. In the end, I called him and took him through our business plan step by step. He listened.

Cheyenne probably knew every island for sale in the world, advertised or not, and suggested looking at Fiji, particularly at the website of the government body responsible for official land sales and leases, the Native Land Trust Board. I had been to Fiji before with Madventurer and loved it – a beautiful place with open-armed people and an enticing, vibrant culture. If I hadn't, I might have been unimpressed when I looked at the NLTB site and saw Vorovoro for the first time. There were only two photographs taken on a cloudy day that showed a small island with three distinct mountainous peaks and a long, narrow strip of stony beach fringed with palms. It didn't look like much, yet there was *something* about it. Crucially, it was for lease and not for sale, which meant if we liked the look of it we could negotiate a much lower price than buying outright. I called the NLTB. They were very helpful but in the end we got bogged down. 'I really need a lot more information before I can commit to anything,' I told them.

'Well, we can't tell you anything more on the telephone. You have to come out here. If you are serious, you must come and see for yourself.' I phoned MJ. 'What do you think?' I asked. 'We need to see it, talk to the owners. There's some stuff you just can't do through the web.'

'I'm with you, Ben. But how much are the tickets?'

'About a thousand pounds each.'

'I haven't got that sort of money, nowhere near. What about you?'

'Nothing,' I said. 'But...'

'But what?'

'But I have got a credit card. And I think it'll just cover both of us. But only once.'

'Vorovoro had better be right then, or we're stuffed.'

I thought of the uninspiring beach in the photographs, the tired sky. It was an enormous gamble. I looked at the telephone, still in my hand, MJ on the other end, waiting for a decision. Should we go? My Young Person's Railcard was about to run out and that meant that I would never be able to get a third off rail travel in the United Kingdom again. Ever. I was about to stop being a young person. Man, I thought to myself, remember what you learned in all those projects in Africa. Focus. Decide. Act. I put the receiver back to my ear. 'Ah, screw it,' I said to him. 'Let's go. Let's go to Vorovoro.'

It was time to break the news to my family. Much later, a few weeks before the first footers were due to land, Tui Mali would take me aside and say: 'It is time to warn the land.' His ancestors were buried on Vorovoro, and he wanted to conduct a ceremony to officially let them and the land know of the noise that was coming. In a smaller way, I now had to do much the same thing. I put down the phone and walked over to the main house from the converted barn. My dad was in the kitchen. 'Hey, Benj. How's it going?'

'Good,' I answered, putting the kettle on. 'Actually, I'm thinking of going away for a few days.' Dad frowned slightly. Though right behind me on most things, he was a successful businessman and he knew what it took. 'The first days are the hardest. Shouldn't you be concentrating on the business?'

'I just need a break. I want to clear my head, get some new ideas.'

'Well, I suppose a few days away from here wouldn't hurt much. Where were you thinking of going?'

'Fiji.'

I met MJ at the check-in desk for Air New Zealand at Heathrow five days later. It had occurred to me on the way to the airport that I didn't really know MJ all that well and we were about to spend twenty-two hours side by side in economy seats on long haul to the other side of the world. Experience had taught me that people you like at home can be very different overseas. But I needn't have worried. MJ was a laid-back traveller and he knew that, faced with a long journey with a relatively unknown companion, the best thing to do was to have plenty to read and to sleep a lot. In between the fine wines provided by Air New Zealand, I was re-reading Richard Branson's autobiography. I found his attitude inspiring and one particular phrase of his stuck out: 'Screw it, let's do it.' That seemed to sum up our venture. We were trying to create something from nothing and we had nothing to lose. Neither of us had a girlfriend. We had no employers breathing down our necks, no mortgages to worry about. True, we had no investors either and, with the last of my credit taken up by this trip, no cash. But the excitement was like a drug and, for some reason, what we were trying to do just felt right.

I glanced over at MJ. He was sleeping, two books on his knees, their covers face up. One was an autobiography of a founder of Google, the other was *The Beach*. Like Alex Garland's idealistic young backpackers we had freedom at our fingertips and we could use it whichever way we chose. The ultimate capabilities of the internet were beyond my comprehension but MJ seemed to have an almost instinctive grasp of what it could be used for, in a positive way. He knew the negatives too, as I did. All around the planet lonely people were becoming lonelier, isolated with their screens and their games or the anonymity of specialist chat rooms. Our plan was to use the internet to unite people. Even in the fast-growing experiential economy, MJ and I agreed that there were still too few opportunities to participate; not to win prizes or momentary fame but to touch the lives of other people and feel a different earth under their feet. The genius of MJ's conception was that we would use the internet to *empower* people. To bridge the gulf between the screen and the dream, and make it real. An online network would be the starting point for an offline, island adventure. *That* was going to be Tribewanted.

We had just arrived in Los Angeles and, with three hours until the next flight, we went to get a beer. Through the shifting haze of smog, I could see Hollywood's famous sign, that archetypal symbol of everything we wanted to escape. 'What do you think of it?' I asked MJ, pointing at *The Beach*. 'Getting any ideas?'

He grinned, his customary faraway look focusing. 'We steer clear of drug barons and secrets, that's for sure. And maybe the perfect beach doesn't exist anywhere. But maybe Vorovoro has something else. It kind of has to, doesn't it?'

I looked at him, a realisation beginning to dawn. 'This isn't just a search for a beach or an island, it's about finding a place that this community can call home,' I said. 'It's up to us.'

We fell silent and I looked out of the window at the huge planes lumbering in and out as we sat in the uncomfortable air conditioning of the bar, drinking Budweiser served in frosted glasses by crisp, impersonal Americans. Our flight was called. Air New Zealand was right on time. 'Smile Like You Mean It' by The Killers was playing as we left the bar.

'What are you smiling about?' MJ asked, waking me from my daydream.

'I didn't know I was,' I replied.

4
VITI
FIJI!

We landed at three in the morning with stiff necks and dry, tired eyes and almost staggered as we exchanged the air-conditioned claustrophobia of the plane for the hot, still tropical night air. An open gangway connected the plane to the arrivals building and, as we walked slowly along it, serenaded by unfamiliar birds, the exotic mystery of Fiji began its magic.

Inside, three men dressed in bright floral Hawaiian style shirts and what looked like black wrap-around kilts played guitars and sang. It's three in the morning, you're queuing for your tourist visa and you're being sung a perfect South Pacific harmony by men built like rugby players with flowers behind their ears.

Our passports stamped with a free four-month tourist visa, we took a five-minute taxi ride to the Nomads Skylodge and crashed out in a dorm full of rucksacks, bunk beds and other sleeping travellers.

As I climbed out of the pool later that morning, I could feel the sunburn across my shoulders. Prickly at first then, within an hour, uncomfortably hot. I cursed myself. MJ and I had spent the last two hours sitting in the shallow end talking, getting to know each other better, laughing a lot about what we were doing and where we were. MJ's creativeness, his spirituality and his typically Northern sense of humour were an interesting mix. Obviously we were different in lots of ways. Understanding and anticipating each other would be crucial in making the partnership work. So maybe the sunburn was worth it. MJ had never been to Fiji before so, in some shade now, I started to tell him the little I knew about the place we had come so far to see.

We were in Nadi, pronounced Nandi, on the island of Viti Levu, Great Fiji. Fiji is made up of thousands of islands lying in almost an arrowhead formation spread out over more than a million square kilometres of the South Pacific, 5,000 kilometres south-west of Hawaii and 3,000 north-east of Sydney. Most of the islands are way too small to support a permanent population and, in fact, as I explained to MJ over a Fiji bitter, only about a hundred are inhabited.

'So why *Nandi*,' he asked. 'It's spelled *N-a-d-i*, isn't it?'

'It's a missionary thing,' I told him. 'From the 1800s, when they were trying to write down Fijian words for the first time. There are lots of sounds that are pronounced even though they may not be spelled that way. If we end up with an island here we'll get the hang of it.'

I told him about the volcanoes, the cannibals and the earliest visitors from Europe, prisons and coups, coral reefs and tropical cyclones; not much, but all that I could remember from my previous visit and prompted by the Lonely Planet guide.

'Sounds crazy. But that's why we're here, I guess.'

I took a swig of the local beer. 'I think there are moments of paradise here, sure. More for us than the people who live here, I guess. But it's fragile, and it's already under threat from mass tourism. And the political stability of the region is, well, not very stable. You can see the weather patterns and changes more easily in this place, especially on the smaller islands, so if we want to communicate a message about living more sustainably and responsibly I think this is a good place.'

'What kind of changes?'

'Well, like I was saying, cyclones. There used to be about one every five years. Now Fiji and this whole area get hit far more regularly.'

'You ever been in one?'

'No,' I answered, looking out over the pool at the motionless palm trees in the still air of the afternoon.

I was about to ask MJ what he thought about climate change but the barman was calling. 'Mr Keene? Ben? Call for you at reception.' It was Solo, our contact at the NLTB. I replaced the handset and gave the phone back to the friendly receptionist before returning to MJ with a solemn smile.

'Who was it? What's happening? Come on, Ben. Don't mess about, what's going on?'

I looked at my new, sunburned buddy and business partner, sitting at a cane table with a bottle of beer in front of him. 'Well,' I said. 'I'm not sure of the exact etiquette, but I think we might have to smarten ourselves up a bit. We're going to meet a chief.'

I was exaggerating a bit, but not much. Solo at the NLTB had just told me that someone called Ulai was on his way to see us, and Ulai was the nephew of a chief. Specifically, the Chief of Vorovoro, Tui Mali, the man who would ultimately decide whether he liked and trusted us enough to let us live on his island with a group of people none of us had ever met from all over the world. So we put on clean T-shirts. I was a little nervous and took a careful sip of the fresh beer on the table.

We clinked bottles, and MJ grinned. 'This should be interesting.'

I don't know what we expected, but it wasn't the guy who turned up about fifteen minutes later. He swept a quick, confident glance round the seating area, acknowledged the barman with a raise of the eyebrows and made his way over to us. 'Ben? Mark? Good afternoon. My name is Ulai. I think you were expecting me?' He looked like Bob Marley's more dissolute younger brother. Average height, medium build, he was wearing a baggy T-shirt, cargo shorts and flip-flops. A brightly coloured bandana kept long dreads away from his face and revealed his bright, intelligent, amused looking eyes. He sat down, and, without being asked, the barman brought him over a beer.

We started talking and Ulai told us a bit about himself, his social assuredness and exceptional English putting us at ease. It turned out he was 38, though his looks and his general demeanour had made me guess about our age, 26. He had grown up on Vorovoro. His father had died when he was young and he was brought up by his grandfather, the chief. I asked him about his English and it turned out that he studied law in Hull (an interesting place to leave a tropical island for) and was a big fan of English culture, particularly English legal history, Shakespeare and Austin Powers. And he could quote all three perfectly. Ulai was obviously knowledgeable but he was also very switched on as well. I could easily imagine doing business with him. From England he'd gone to work in Australia, defending Aboriginal land rights, and had returned to Vorovoro only the previous year. Ulai and his uncle, the present chief, had been discussing the future of the island. They both knew change was inevitable but they wanted to do it right, for the place and the people, and even for the world. They wanted to share it. At this stage I didn't quite know why. In fact, they had placed the advert for Vorovoro with the NLTB less than a month before we'd found it. Like so much of this adventure already, it seemed that something was guiding us.

Ulai looked at our empty bottles. 'Shall we do it again, baby?' asked this Fijian version of Austin Powers.

'I didn't know it was your turn,' I answered, attempting a riposte to the impersonation. I wasn't sure whose impression was worse but it didn't matter, we were all laughing. Austin had broken the ice.

Over the second drink, we did most of the talking and explained the outline of the idea. Ulai got more serious. 'So, guys. First thing is, we could lease you part of the island for two years. My uncle and I don't want to commit for longer than that at the moment, we want to see how things work out.'

This wasn't what MJ and I had discussed. We knew that we needed at least three years to get Tribewanted off the ground as a viable business. I glanced at MJ and saw him give an imperceptible shake of the head and I knew what he meant. This wasn't the time to negotiate. It was too early. This was our first meeting, we hadn't even set foot on Vorovoro yet, and we were still pretty tired from our marathon flight. 'Fantastic!' I said to Ulai, raising my bottle of Fiji bitter. 'Let's see the island!'

The next day MJ, Ulai and I flew to Labasa on Vanua Levu, about forty-five minutes north and west of Nadi. The plane flew low over the sea and we could make out the shadowy shapes of coral reefs and atolls under the blue waters. On the way to Labasa, MJ and I were close enough to the earth to get a sense of it, how the islands were formed, their fragility in the middle of that awesome ocean. As we turned towards Labasa, Ulai pointed north towards Vorovoro. I knew it at once, the three peaks were unmistakable. Still remote through the toughened plastic of the plane's window, but real. I strained my neck to keep it in sight as long as possible. It was an image of the island I would never forget.

Landing in a small plane is great. I love the way you see the runway swing from side to side through the pilot's window as he levels the craft for touchdown. Labasa airport is nothing more than a glorified shed in a field with a strip of tarmac, surrounded by sugar cane and mountains. That's it. You duck out of the plane door, climb down three steps and walk the thirty yards to the 'arrivals hall' to wait a few moments for your luggage to be brought on a trolley to the door. No conveyor belts here, just grab your bags, walk to the other side of the room and out into the car park. No queues, no passport checks, no worries.

Two guys from the NLTB were waiting for us dressed in the smart business attire of Fijian officialdom, *sulus* – a kind of sarong – and pressed shirts. MJ and I were still dressed like backpackers, of course, but as we climbed into the back of the official-looking government 4x4 we felt for the first time that we, and our plan, were being taken seriously. We were being treated like proper investors, people who could buy islands, if they felt like it.

It turned out, as the introductions were made, that one of the government men was Solo, the guy I had spoken to on the phone from the UK. The surprise was that he was also a cousin of Ulai, though as I learned more about the complicated Fijian family structure this came to surprise me less and less. In common with a lot of close-knit communities, Fijians recognise any kind of family connection with the title of cousin, or brother. Ulai and Solo had played rugby together at school and, though they were friends as well as relations, it was interesting to note that Ulai's manner very subtly changed. In the bar the day before he had been cool, jokey and laid-back. Here, now, with these guys from the government he was much more serious and was treated with great respect and almost deference by the two officials. Though still friendly, he spoke with gravitas and his words clearly carried something as the nephew of a chief and the representative of a major landowner. There were no Austin Powers impressions today.

It was a fifteen-minute drive into town through the straggly fields of sugar cane, Fiji's major export. We had to do some shopping. Ulai had explained to us that it was customary to present the Chief of the island or village you were visiting with gifts of food, staples mostly, and, most important of all, *Yaqona* (kava).

We entered Labasa and drove along the main street until, just before the river, we parked next to the market stalls where Ulai said we would be able to get everything we needed. The two NLTB guys wandered off to see friends and Ulai led us into the market. I'd been to markets like this one before, in Africa. At first glance they always seem smelly and chaotic, with rickety stalls piled to the point of collapse bearing all kinds of tropical fruit and vegetables, fish, meat and spices. But after a while you can see order through the mayhem. Stalls that look unattended turn out to have a small child or an ancient woman in attendance, swatting away the flies and constantly on the look-out for custom; to pause was to be assailed. Ulai picked his way confidently through the maelstrom, sometimes nearly leaving MJ and me behind.

It was vibrant with people shouting, laughing and bargaining; a long way from the sterility of a western supermarket. No priority parking here. We bought rice, sugar, fruit and vegetables, crisps, sweets, tins of corned beef and – we checked if this was OK – a case of Fiji bitter.

Finally, we bought a kilogram bundle of kava roots which, slightly to my surprise, was as expensive as the beer. The roots themselves were just that. Straggly, brown sticks with thicker, white feet. They looked ordinary, not like the ancient and enduring tribal currency I would soon learn they had become. But they didn't smell ordinary. A quick sniff would tell you that they had significant aroma that most plant roots don't have. The kava smelt good, I was looking forward to trying it.

We continued across the muddy river, past the court house and the sugar cane mill, on the way to Malau and the coast. It would be exaggerating a little to call Malau a village. There were a few houses, one dusty and ramshackle shop, a sawmill and a jetty where the sugar cane was loaded.

Tui Mali stood on the sea wall. He was wearing shorts, a polo shirt and flip-flops. Ulai's demeanour changed again, his posture was more respectful. He stood straighter and took his hands out of his pockets. Really, the only indication to me that we were in the presence of the Chief was the obvious respect that Ulai and the other men had for this moderately built man in the clean but ordinary clothes of the working people of the island. There was no entourage, he had no retainers. But even to my unfamiliar eyes he had something about him. A stillness, a knowledge of himself and the elements. 'This is my uncle, Tui Mali,' said Ulai, and I looked into the eyes of the Chief.

Then he laughed, his face suddenly illuminated by an enormous smile, 'You've come to see Vorovoro!'

'Yes!' I answered. 'We've come to visit your island! I hope that's OK,' I replied inanely. Hearing my instinctive British politeness made me cringe.

'Good, it's good.' Tui Mali assured me. 'OK, let's go home.' Everybody laughed, I as loudly as any. I felt like a big kid, but in a good way. It was like being amongst your best friends in the world yet we'd only just met.

Ulai started loading the provisions onto Tui Mali's boat, an eighteen-foot long, flat bottomed, punt-like vessel about five feet wide. Painted yellow, it was faded a little from the sun and the salt but well maintained and seaworthy. It had three thwarts, but MJ and I waited till we were invited before getting in.

Once we were all aboard, Ulai picked up a long mangrove stick and punted us gently out of the shallows until the water was deep enough to lower the outboard motor. Then I saw yet another side to this multi-faceted man, his skill and dexterity with the long pole and the overloaded boat showing that for all his studies, his fluent English and his knowledge of western ways he was an islander to the core.

MJ and I sat at the front, the NLTB officials in the middle and Ulai and his uncle in the stern, Tui Mali steering. The day was hot, with a few heavy clouds in the sky as we headed away from Vanua Levu towards the island of Mali, just off the coast. Vorovoro was right behind it, obscured by the larger island. MJ and I settled back.

'Now this is the real adventure,' I thought, as the small boat with its fifteen-horsepower engine edged us painfully slowly across the virtually flat sea. Very soon we would be standing on the island we had come so far to see and then we would know for sure whether our idea had legs. After that it would depend on whether Tui Mali and Ulai and the rest of his family, to say nothing of the NLTB, liked and trusted us enough to let us live among them. If that all went smoothly then we would be able to turn our attention to raising the cash. I breathed deeply. 'One step at a time,' I told myself.

As we came round the edge of Mali, Vorovoro started to appear. I recognised it at once, and what had worried me as I pored over the photographs back home on the other side of the world was obviously not going to be a problem. I had thought it might be too small, but no way. As Vorovoro slid into view my first thought was 'This is a BIG island!' It looked like a mirage. It was then that I took the photograph that ended up on the Tribewanted.com homepage.

The first thing you see are the green hills as they dive in and out of the ocean. I was immediately reminded of the Malvern Hills, where I grew up, a nine-mile rollercoaster ride of peaks and troughs that rise out of the flood plains of Hereford and Worcestershire. Vorovoro looked like Malvern-on-sea. As we chugged round the western tip of Mali, we could see villagers waving from a small settlement, as if they were welcoming us back after a long absence. We approached a dramatic headland jutting out into the sea and, as we rounded the cape beneath its chest-out tower of stone, I began to see the answer to one of our main questions. There it was. Hidden from the mainland. Secret. Unassailable, but welcoming. The beach that looked so lacklustre on my laptop. The internet was made real and the reality was beyond our expectations. I looked round at Ulai and Tui Mali. They were both smiling hugely.

We landed with the tide high up the beach and jumped onto the coarse sand of Vorovoro. Every moment of the next week was vivid and, in the context of why we were there, surreal as well. It's hard to explain but it was peaceful and intense at the same time. Past the beach there was a space between the trees marked by a line of beautifully landscaped plants that led to two houses. The first, a weather-beaten ply-board building, was the home of Poasa, Tui Mali's younger brother, and his family. To the right was a solid-looking concrete house with corrugated roofing and guttering that led to a large water tank behind. This was the home of the Chief. The grass between the two houses was a rain-heavy green and chickens scratched freely for insects in its lush carpet.

We presented the kava as a *sevu-sevu* to Tui Mali, who accepted it with great dignity and gave it to Ulai to prepare. Ulai had quickly briefed us beforehand that the sevu-sevu is the name given to the formal presentation of kava. By placing the small bundle of newspaper wrapped roots whilst kneeling on a woven mat on the porch in front of the Chief, dressed in sulus, we were showing our host respect and asking him to accept us into his home. Before long the sevu-sevu ceremony would soon become a regular part of my life. In the old days Ulai and his brothers would have had to chew the kava and spit the juice into a bowl which the guests would drink but, to my relief, this practice had faded with time. While we waited sitting cross-legged in a circle we talked and MJ and I tried to explain to the Chief our aims and ambitions for Tribewanted.

Though the Chief's English was good, it was useful having Ulai there to translate the trickier concepts. Tui Mali was worldly wise. He had spent twenty-six years on a Cable and Wireless ship and had seen a lot of the world and other cultures. His wide experience combined with his almost intuitive intelligence made him a good and receptive listener. I really did feel like a tribesman at his feet.

The kava was pounded in a giant pestle and mortar a few feet away from the veranda. The impact of the lead pipe landing vertically on the dried roots sent shockwaves to the mat on which we sat. The earth moved. It was like a slow pumping baseline from a dulled sub-woofer, its working rhythm carving out an ancient beat in the utterly peaceful afternoon stillness. Tui Mali and the half dozen other men all clapped in unison as the now finely powdered kava was kneaded through a cloth and water was poured over it into a giant carved wooden basin called the Tanoa.

Three deep thudding hand-claps signalled that drinking was about to commence. I was nervous but it wasn't exactly snake blood. The muddy water from the full bowl was scooped into a half coconut and carefully delivered to the chosen drinker. Tui Mali first, and then the other older men before Ulai knelt to my left and with both hands pushed the small shell forwards. 'Clap,' he whispered. I did, trying to imitate the deep sounds the heavy-handed Fijians had been making. However, my clap was more like a slap on a bare back than the warrior-like sounds made by the others. No one laughed, they simply watched as I took the bowl from Ulai, looked Tui Mali in the eye and sank the contents.

It actually tasted OK, not too strong. Imagine earthy water with a feisty finish, one that leaves a numbness on your lips and soon a growing grin on your face. Its narcotic effect is not dramatic but noticeable.

Ulai leaned over after about the third round. 'Alcohol makes you shout,' he told me, 'but kava makes you smile!' And it doesn't dull your mind.

A few shells later, feeling more at ease, I started trying to explain to the island Chief the complex concept behind Tribewanted, the bringing together of a tribe in virtual space and uniting them in reality on a real island. This was going to be interesting. 'The people of Mali are all connected in some way, through family, friendships, fishing, school or church, and ultimately because they are all part of the *yasuva*, the tribe. Well, the internet community is kind of similar.' I heard myself say this, and then wondered where the hell I was going with it. Was it really similar, or was this just the kava talking? Everyone was looking at me, waiting for my next words, and I needed to impress them or at least make sense. I glanced at MJ who just stared at me, three shells to the wind, eyes wide. I pressed on. 'The internet is a global community of people. The big difference is that with the internet you use a computer to get to someone and here you use a boat.' I looked up after this, half expecting the Chief and his men to turn around and cry in unison 'BOLLOCKS!' They didn't.

Nonetheless, Ulai came swiftly to my rescue and I watched him, eyes and hands full of expression, translating my clumsy explanations. I was relieved to see the circle of increasingly kavatised men nodding and smiling. Tui Mali slapped the back of one hand into the palm of another and chuckled, his great eyes alive. 'So the world can see Vorovoro, even though Vorovoro cannot see the world.' Tui Mali spoke simple English but I soon learned that his words often had more than one meaning. Perhaps this was the source of Ulai's love of linguistic subtlety. I clapped as another shell was passed to me. The internet seemed suddenly very distant.

I showed Tui Mali my iPod and explained that in that little

oblong box I had all my music, over 7,000 songs. He had never seen one before, and was intrigued. The Chief asked for country music, but if there was one genre I was just not going to have, it was Country & Western. Luckily he also liked classical and that was a little easier. I found some Elgar and explained that the composer had lived in my home town, Malvern. Tui Mali put on the headphones and settled into 'Nimrod'. He closed his eyes to the majestic melodies of middle England. Something was making a connection even if it wasn't the internet, yet. I just hoped that the combination of kava, Elgar and the possibility of the world coming to his island would do the trick.

Later, Tui Mali told me that if our negotiations were successful he and his family would leave the island and go and live on Mali. I was horrified. 'No! Please! You must not do that. It is very important to us that you stay, that you are part of this. We don't want to change anything, we want to work in partnership with you and your family. And what we build here will be yours when we have gone. So anything, everything that happens here must be with your knowledge and with your consent. We can bring money to the island, and work for some people, but it's most important for us and everyone who comes here to learn. They will take something back to the outside world about the Fijian way of life. You must stay!'

During our time there, I covered as much of the island as possible. Though only a mile long and so narrow in parts you can cross it in minutes, it took a few days to do it properly. Vorovoro is bigger and grander than you anticipate. It is dramatic as well as beautiful and, as I got the feel of its soft fertile earth and its sharp, hard edges where the bones of the island break through the skin, I felt that it could become our new home. Here the online dreamers would turn their ideas into reality amongst its rough peaks and arching coconut palms. What I liked about it most was the fact that it didn't present, at least from the southern approach, the clichéd, postcard image of a tropical island. No beaches were visible, for a start. The hills were sometimes steep, sharp and difficult to climb, sometimes soft and rounded. They were overgrown in parts with impenetrable looking trees while dense mangroves shrouded their feet. But there were clearings, flat areas for cultivation. Sometimes I would find a tiny, secret beach with fresh water trickling down from the rocky slopes above.

Conversations with Tui Mali had encouraged me, signalled that there was a way forward and that the people were on our side. As I learned more about Vorovoro, a feeling grew inside me that the island itself was on my side, that, silly as this may sound, it would welcome and protect us, become our friend.

I ducked under the low branch of a coconut palm and out onto the sand. I don't know exactly what time it was other than it was just starting to get light. We were leaving the next day and I wanted to get a better sense of the island's layout so I could describe it to people at home as well as grabbing some thinking time before we left. I walked along the beach from Tui Mali's village towards the headland, jutting out into the sea like an angry fist slammed down on a table. Waves reverberated at its base. I arrived at the foot of the rock face, which was steep and overhanging in most places. I clasped at a knot of stone above my head and it came off easily in my hand, crumbling like sand. If I was going to climb the headland, I would have to find an easier route, one that didn't rely on holding on to any rock.

Further towards the point, a grassy bank dipped down between the overhanging cliffs. At the foot of the bank were sloping boulders that I could scramble up. I hauled myself up on tufts of long grass until I was standing on the ridge staring out across to Mali island and the horizon. A few feet in front of me I could see what looked like the cemented corner of some kind of rectangular foundation. As I was about to jump up on the slab of stone, I saw hand-carved writing. I stopped, crouched and read: 'Here lies Tui Mali, Ratu Apenisa Bogiso, Na Tui Mali Sucu 1825–1874.' So this was where Tui Mali's great, great grandfather was buried. What an amazing place to rest in peace, I thought, high on the headland of your own island, looking out over the magnificent ocean and all those who came and went from its shores.

Looking at the crack in the face that led to the pinnacle of the island's most protruding rock, I thought I might be able to squeeze myself up it. The problem was if I got stuck, or worse, fell, there would be no one to help. I turned around and faced back towards the island. The route to the top of the second peak looked much easier. I climbed up the forty-five-degree ridge to the top where it opened out into a mini-plateau of conquered headland. I was standing on top of this rock watching the rising sun spit beams of golden light across the sea and land and it was spectacular. It took me straight back to sunrises I'd seen on mountain tops – Snowden, Ben Nevis, Kilimanjaro, Pisco – and how much I missed that feeling of freedom high up at the start of a brand new day. It energises you.

Straight ahead of me and directly to the south in the opposite direction to the headland I was standing on, was the main centre peak of Vorovoro. It is also the highest of the three rises of land. A steep hill covered in trees that drops off to cliffs on either side before tumbling down to the valleys running east and west. And as I followed the line to the east, another sharp, but smaller ridge rose and fell away before the island's geography climbs gently again to its far eastern hill. Beyond this hill, and only a short hop across the water, lies Mali island and the village of Nakawaga, which I later learned means step across.

From the eastern end of Vorovoro a thick border of mangroves follows the curve of the island back to the foot of the headland. Up and over the headland you look west down towards Vorovoro's main valley. Nearly twenty acres of coconut palms nestle v-shaped, like the line of an open shirt collar, between the island's middle peak and the cliffs that lead to the far western tip. In the middle of the palms you can see a clearing and the rooftops of two out of the three houses that make up Tui Mali's village, the only visible sign of inhabitants on the isle. On this side, the north, Vorovoro reveals its favourite asset; a sweep of golden sand that ducks in and out and round the western headland before diving deep into the Mali channel. The beach must be about half a mile long from start to finish, and it's not the perfect flour-like white stuff of adverts. Vorovoro sand is a mixture of soft sands and thousands of eroded coral shells that, one day, will become soft sands. Did it concern me that Vorovoro's beach didn't fit the tropical island cliché? Yes and no. I mean I would love to say that you could run and roll in the sand without any bother, but then you wouldn't have live coral metres off the beach.

To be honest, the details such as the softness of the sand, the ease of arriving or departing on boats, or the number of blind spots along the cliff tops didn't bother me right now. My heart was pounding at the potential of the place. Could we actually come here with a bunch of travellers, build a village, fish, develop, live? Could we connect this place to a global network, an early twenty-first-century trend that for all we knew could pass by like a boat on the horizon? Could this idyll become our home? Could these people become our family? I couldn't quite believe it but I knew on top of the headland that morning as the sun warmed the back of my neck that this actually had a chance of happening, that the dream might be realised, and I was ready to do whatever it took to make it happen.

I could see the smoke rising from the back of the tiny kitchen in the valley below. I clambered back down from my meditative seat, inspired and hungry at the thought of tea, pancakes and what we might achieve.

But, of course, doubts lingered. One came to me when I was talking to MJ on the beach later that morning. 'Is it right to bring people here, mate? Should we push ahead with this, or just let these guys get on with their lives in peace?'

We didn't know the answer but, before we left, Ulai put us straight. 'Look, Ben. Whether you come here or not, Fiji is changing. The world is coming. If it isn't you, then what? A hotel? A millionaires' playground? Big game fishing? For you it may seem like paradise, but for us, what do you think? That we want to stay away from the world for ever, without jobs, without a future? No. My uncle likes you. OK, you are young, you have no money, but your ideas are good. I think we'll make a deal.'

It would not, of course, be as simple as that.

5
KEREI O PARATAISI
BARTERING FOR PARADISE

Later that morning we flew to Suva, Fiji's capital, to begin negotiations with the Native Land Trust Board. Tui Mali might have given us his blessing but we still had to conquer officialdom. A handshake had been enough for the chief; now we had to convince possibly more hard-headed bureaucrats that we were serious, and capable of delivering on our promises.

We landed in heavy rain, one of the last storms of the season. In a battered old taxi we went to a cheap hotel where we tried to smarten ourselves up a bit, not all that easy after five days on an island with no hot water or mirrors. Finally, shaven, clean and at least moderately smart, we set out for the NLTB, the confidence we had gained in the company of the open friendliness of Tui Mali and his people giving way to the tense feeling that precedes any potentially career-changing meeting.

The head of tourism's office at the NLTB tower in downtown Suva was smart. With air conditioning, flat-screen monitors, neatly cabled computers and comfortable chairs, it was a world away from the conditions we knew on Vorovoro yet the same laid-back friendly Fijian charm pervaded. Having stashed our backpacks in the security guard's hut, MJ and I sat down with Peni Qalo and his boss, Mesake, who went to school with Ulai. The Fijians were business-like but not hostile. Ulai had sent them word that his uncle was happy for them to negotiate on his behalf and, if the numbers were right, to offer us a three-year lease. Now it was up to us to convince these pleasant men whose job it was to draw up million-dollar ownership agreements for people like Mel Gibson that the two freshly washed young Englishmen sitting in front of them were more than just hopeless dreamers.

'So, you enjoyed Vorovoro?'

'Yes, very much. It was great, fantastic. A brilliant place,' MJ and I enthused. Then there was the kind of silence that occurs when nobody is really sure what to say next. I mean, I wasn't sure how island lease negotiations were supposed to go but I sensed that long silences were not the way to a successful deal, so I took the initiative.

'Right. This is the offer on your web page: Fiji $10,000 per acre for a 50- to 99-year lease, with ten acres tendered. There are also a lot of other fees and donations to the community and so on.' Smiles and nods but no comments as yet. I continued. 'As you know, we measured the valley floor of Vorovoro with your northern representatives and we discovered that the total of the flat area is in fact twenty acres.' So far so good. 'Now, we agreed with Tui Mali that in addition to the fact that the area we are interested in is twice that tendered, the lease will be for three years, not the minimum of fifty as stipulated.'

'Mmmm.' Were they listening? At least they hadn't laughed out loud or asked us to leave. 'OK.' I paused, ready to deliver the killer offer which we hoped would win them over, despite the fact that we were ignoring all their contractual requirements. 'We would like to offer Fiji $3,000 per acre for twenty acres. Plus all the fees, of course.' And before they could say no, or arrest us for wasting government time and kick us out of the country, I added: 'This is very much a community project. My business partner and I see it more as a relationship with the people of Vorovoro rather than as a simple commercial transaction, so instead of paying the suggested Fiji $5,000 per year to the village committee on top of the premium, we would like to triple that. We will pay Fiji $15,000 per year for the term of the lease.'

Our hope was that though we were offering just under a third of what the NLTB had specified for each acre, this would be offset by the fact that we were offering to treble the amount paid to the community. We were, after all, only going to be there for three years, not half a century, and there were no guarantees for us that we would be given any extension on the lease should the project prove to be a financial success. Any investment we might make could easily be lost. We wanted to show that we were committed to the people of the island, without undermining the capital benefit to the government, which would be looking to take fifteen per cent. Who knows? Maybe we should have offered a lot less, but I was following my travel-tested bartering technique of offering roughly a third of what is asked and paying no more than half. We also thought that what we were suggesting was fair and that's important when it comes to haggling over anything. Of course you don't want to be ripped off and you need to keep overheads down as far as possible but at the same time business is about relationships and, if they are going to last, both parties need to feel that they have got a fair deal. Anyway, we hoped this offer would make everyone feel comfortable.

Mesake stroked his chin. 'Thank you for this. We need to discuss the matter with the landowners involved. If we agree, we will make you a written offer within thirty days.' He stood up and extended his hand. And that was it. We shook hands all round and voiced the usual pleasantries but a few minutes later we were out on the street not knowing whether we were any closer to securing a deal on our island or not. I looked at MJ, not sure of his reaction to my negotiating skills - or lack of them. 'Well, what do you think?' He looked thoughtful.

'I think we should get a Chinese.' As we sat on some steps by the side of the road eating greasy hoi sin wraps out of paper bags he was more forthcoming. 'So, how do you think it went?'

'I'm not sure. But I do think the friendship between Mesake and Ulai is definitely an advantage. And besides, look at our offer. It's a short-term lease, so even if it doesn't work well they get their island back pretty soon with everything we've built on it. The community benefits, Tui Mali likes us – we think – and it's potentially very good news for Northern Fiji.'

'Yeah, but what if some real investor comes in and makes a better offer next week?'

I shrugged. 'There's nothing we can do about that, if it happens it happens. But if I was Tui Mali I'd bet on us.'

At that point, right then, I think I was trying to convince myself as much as my partner.

6
BULA SE KASURA
BULA OR BUST

Back in the UK after the long journey home, it was time to turn the dream into reality. It was the middle of March and MJ and I were keen to get Tribewanted 'live' as soon as possible. We knew there were a few key things we needed to get in place before we shared our great plan with the world, so with the pictures of Vorovoro, the words we'd written and a verbal agreement on an island lease we got to work, hoping the NLTB offer would land at any moment.

First up, we needed to build a website that was going to be both inspiring and believable. Inspiration was going to be fairly easy, I thought. A good idea plus great pictures would hopefully excite at least some of the people who reached our dot com. Credibility was going to be a bit more of a challenge. If people were going to part with their hard-earned money and even travel to Fiji we needed to convince them that we weren't just throwing this together from a student bedsit before running off to the South Pacific to drink beer in the sun. We needed Tribewanted to look and feel professional. I suggested my old mate Andy Greener, who ran a small web company in Newcastle called Komodo Design. I'd worked with him on careerbreakcafe.com and prior to that on the Madventurer websites. Andy and Simon, his sole employee at the time, had great design skills, and I knew they could make the words we'd written and pictures of Vorovoro come to life online. I called Andy.

'Hi, I've just come back from Fiji and I'm working on this new island project called Tribewanted with a guy called Mark…'

'But what about Career Break Cafe?' Andy interrupted, 'It's just starting to pick up in the search engines.'

'Back-burner for now I'm afraid – Tribewanted is going to be big and I need you to crack on with the site immediately. If I send you through the content, pictures and brief can you take a look?'

'Sure, no problem, send it through. But what's this Tribewanted all about?'

'I can't explain now, just have a look at the pictures. You'll love it, I promise.'

The phone rang the next morning.

'Ben, it's Andy – I've read what you sent through, looks fantastic. I reckon we can get something ready by the end of next week.'

'Awesome, thanks, that's just what I wanted to hear, and it's cool about the payment on this one? We won't have the cash up front, you do realise that?'

'No problem at all. I think this is a winner. Now before you disappear, Si wants a word.' Andy 'put me through' to Simon, who I knew was sitting on the desk next to him looking out of the same window over the Tyne. But the size of their office didn't matter to me. I knew these guys well and it's professionalism that counts whether you're a two-man band or Saatchi and Saatchi.

'How-whey Ben, what have you been drinking?' Si asked me, his soft Geordie lilt full of amusement. 'This guy Mark sure has come up with a mad idea.'

'I know, I'm not quite sure how it happened but it's exciting – what do you think about how it could look online?'

'Well, as you and Mark have said in the brief, the key is to create that unique hook through the name Tribewanted and how the online leads to the real – to the island. It's an inspiring journey and that's what you want people to feel when they hit the homepage.'

'Exactly,' I said. Si had got it, first time.

'Do you have any thoughts on how the word "Tribewanted" should be used?' he asked. 'Because I think that's the strongest part, it's a call to action.'

'Actually its funny you should ask, because I was flicking through a book this morning when an image jumped out at me. You know the graffiti artist Banksy?'

'Yeah! Oh, he's the ultimate graphic designer. I've got his book, *Wall and Piece*.'

Si liked the idea and got cracking on designing us our tribal identity.

The results were brilliant. Like most things in life, if you get it right first time, don't change it. The first page Si sent through had the Tribewanted logo at the top left, exactly as it looks today, and the island image with the words 'TRIBE WANTED' rising above it into the blue sky, like the opening credits of a *Star Wars* film. It was dramatic. It was happening, and I was enjoying being part of creating something that was really exciting. Only when I saw the image for the first time did I realise the brilliance of the name, Tribewanted. As I stared at the words floating over Vorovoro on the screen in front of me I couldn't imagine a better clarion call for people who wanted an adventure. MJ had nailed it. Over the next week Andy, Si, MJ and I worked together on the images, the content, and the integrated PayPal pages (this was the only payment option open to us as a start-up). I wrote the terms and conditions and MJ built a MySpace page and continued to network the potential online leads fervently. Tribewanted.com was coming to life.

Next we started looking for a presenter for Tribewanted TV. MJ and I had talked a lot on Vorovoro about how we were going to tell the story, online, to the watching tribe in their homes and offices around the world. We knew we would be incredibly busy running both ends of the business if it took off and would therefore not have time to film, present and produce the online TV updates that we wanted. MJ had the idea that we should put an ad out to see if anyone was interested in the opportunity to live on a Pacific island and present 'Tribal TV' telling the story of the project. MJ posted the 'Tribal TV Presenter' ad on shootingpeople.com, an online job-shop for aspiring actors and actresses. Within forty-eight hours over two hundred wannabe Tribal TV presenters' CVs and pictures had flooded into our inboxes. I couldn't believe it, these people had no idea who we were, there was no website, and yet they were still prepared to send their addresses, phone numbers and pictures to us. More unbelievably still, when we picked our top twenty candidates (academic excellence and relevant work experience determining our selection criteria, I can assure you), every single one agreed to an interview the following week. This was the first real sign to me that there are quite a few crazy people on the internet.

The following Sunday MJ and I and two friends – Marco, who had been my 'phone a friend' back in Devon, and his girlfriend, Joey – held a marathon day of interviews in a cool work space we'd found called The Hub in Angel, London. I realised how surreal the situation was when our first interviewee asked MJ and I what TV projects we had previously worked on. 'Umm… well, travel and media ventures have both been an important part of our work,' I quickly bluffed. Bloody hell! Now we had to pretend we were TV producers as well as island investors. The day was as hilarious as it was frustrating. One girl, called Kiki, said in a Scandanavian accent that she worked on 'Babestation'. Mmmm.

Another girl brought a bag of things that 'represented her' and amongst them was a picture of her cat and a framed photograph of Phillip Schofield and Fern Britton, daytime TV presenters. 'They're my heroes, my inspiration.' I was sure they were but I wasn't convinced I wanted to wake up on Vorovoro next to pictures of them. Next up was not only a TV presenter, an avid conservationist (she wanted to save the wolves of the world) but also a self-proclaimed stand-up comedian. Halfway through the interview she burst into what was, apparently, a humorous routine. Stand-up is painful when it doesn't work in front of a large audience. Imagine there are just five of you, one of which is the aforementioned artiste. We all laughed but it wasn't at the jokes. Even Marco, who was filming, interrupted to say, 'Guys, I think we'd better move on.' I wished I'd been a bit more like Simon Cowell that day, so that, five seconds into an interview, I could have held up my hands and said, 'Thanks, but you're not going to Fiji, goodbye.'

By the end of the day we were worn out and, although there were some promising candidates, I wasn't convinced we'd found the right one. And I wasn't sure if we really needed to put so much time and effort into this so early on.

MJ was less doubtful. 'It's crucial that we are able to link the two worlds, the island to the online community.'

'OK,' I said. 'But by the end of this week we need to decide who is going to do the job.' There were four other candidates who couldn't make it that Sunday so I arranged to meet them in the basement of a coffee shop a couple of days later. MJ had to head back home, so I conducted the remaining interviews alone. The third girl to arrive that afternoon was the first of our potential tribal TV presenters not to wear make-up. It was a good start. Again, unlike many of the other interviewees, she seemed to get the idea, the potential, us, and within ten minutes I knew we'd found her and all I needed to do was convince MJ. Becky Hunter – blonde hair, blue eyes, trendy T, baggy jeans, skate-shoes – was well travelled and well spoken. She was exactly what we were looking for. A week later I'd convinced MJ. He trusted my judgement as I had trusted his before, and I phoned Becky.

'Do you want the good news or the bad news?'

'The bad,' she answered nervously.

'Well, you're going to have to work in an office for a few months.'

BULA OR BUST

'And the good?' she asked, sensing this was going somewhere.

'After that you're going to have to work on a Fijian island.'

I had to hold the handset away from my ear for about ten seconds as Becky screamed and shouted. After I put the phone down on our very excited new tribal TV presenter I suddenly felt the pressure. We now had our first employee, our first bit of responsibility, and there wasn't even a penny in the bank.

We settled on the target of five thousand tribe members. This business model seemed to fit best – five thousand was a capacity figure for the island over three years, and anyway we didn't expect everyone that joined to visit Vorovoro. We guesstimated that ten per cent would be content with just the online experience for their money or would not find the time to travel to Fiji. This would mean we would have an average of just under thirty on the island at any one time with room for more who wanted to stay longer than a week.

We needed the membership to be cheap enough to entice people but expensive enough to seem credible. The figure we had had in our heads from day one was £100. We didn't have any time to look into the potential costs of building a village on an island and an online community and run an international business and everything else, so we guesstimated again and forecast the budget and costs as best we could. Which wasn't much. Eventually we settled on £120 for the bottom-level membership entry – Nomad. That was cheap for a week's stay on an island in Fiji including all meals, but we were doing something new, people would be taking a bit of a punt on us when they got their credit cards out and, besides, Vorovoro was no five-star spa. But £120 was also enough, we thought, to sound convincing, it's comparable to a week's backpacking in certain parts of the world, or a ticket to Glastonbury. And if we got the numbers joining that we hoped for, the project would be financially viable. If.

As a Nomad you would be entitled to a seven-night stay on Vorovoro any time within your one-year membership. To prevent everyone coming at once we would limit island capacity to one hundred at any one time. We had decided this whilst on Vorovoro and, although it was a figure we never anticipated reaching, it gave us the flexibility from the beginning for tribe members to help shape the project. Membership would begin either when we reached five thousand (if that happened fast enough) or when the island opened its doors. We knew that if we got a start, and a few hundred members or more joined and then it slowed, we would still need to get the project moving otherwise people would want their money back. Goodwill would not last for very long we knew, even with the promise of an island adventure.

For those that wanted to stay on Vorovoro longer, we were also going to offer longer memberships. For £240, 'Hunters' would have a two-year membership entitling them to a two-week stay on Vorovoro within that time, and for £360 you would be granted 'Warrior' status, giving you a three-year membership (the length of the lease) and a three-week stay on Vorovoro. Why did we want to limit the stay of any member to three weeks? Surely people would fall in love with Vorovoro and want to stay a lot longer? My main concern was that if this project was going to work we needed a community in flux, both online and on the island – people coming and going, logging on and off, arriving and departing. If any one individual or group remained for more than a few weeks on the island I feared that cliques and hierarchies might appear and the chance for conflict would increase. If there was going to be a difficult personality to manage on Vorovoro, three weeks would be bearable, three months might not. MJ and I guessed that if this took off there would likely be comparisons with other (failed) island communities and we wanted to show that this one would have structure and that, aside from the local family and Tribewanted team, there wouldn't be any permanent residents. At least this model gave us room for movement later on in case we or the tribe members wanted longer stays.

So how were we going to get all these people that joined from around the world to discuss and vote on island issues and then put their decisions into action on Vorovoro itself, taking into consideration our budget, the island environment and the local community and culture? It's a good question and one the social experiment that Tribewanted would become would have to answer. But we needed at least some kind of framework from which to start. I had studied political systems at university, from contemporary democracies in Europe and America to the thinkers that had actually dreamed up concepts like democracy in the first place. From what little I could remember, I didn't think anyone had come up with a solution for an online democracy that impacted on a real-world community. Maybe it was hidden in the shadowy virtual reality of Plato's cave and I'd missed it. Unfortunately, there was no time to start searching for answers in philosophical caves (that could wait until we were stargazing on Vorovoro). And at the moment I was more interested in the philosophies of our postmodern age in which more people would vote for the winner of *Pop Idol* than for the Conservative Party at a general election. And why are high streets perpetually crammed full of shoppers? I guess the general feeling is that if there doesn't seem to be much choice between political parties at a general election so why should anyone bother? People go shopping instead. And because I'd learned that we humans are political animals, I knew that participation in communities whether virtual, on an island or on Mars are always going to need some kind of political system. So what kind of system would our twenty-first-century tribal community have?

In his original email to me, MJ had outlined the direct form of democracy that would link the virtual and the real. The online tribe would elect a chief each month from within the online community. The chief would then spend a month on Vorovoro working alongside us and the Fijians to build the village. Beyond that it was more of an experiment. Along with the members we would build both an on-island and online structure for the communities to coexist. Did I think this would be easy? No. But I was up for the challenge and a combination of naivety, idealism and restlessness was propelling me forward.

We were making some good progress, but we still didn't have our island deal. That didn't worry us too much in those frantic days. We were too busy and too fired with enthusiasm to consider the possibility that it might still fizzle out before we had even got it properly off the ground. But again luck or some other force was with us, and our trust in ourselves and our idea paid off. Two weeks after getting back from Fiji, MJ and I got an email from Peni Qalo at the NLTB. It was a written offer for the lease of Vorovoro. More importantly, it was an offer pretty close to the terms we had set out at the Suva office a few weeks before. OK, there were some extra fees that I hadn't been aware of before, stamp duty, administrative charges and so on, but the acreage offer of Fiji $3,000 had been accepted. Bullseye. The offer said that we had three months to accept and pay the premium on the lease of Fiji $60,000 with an additional Fiji $18,000 in assorted extra costs. Excitedly, I calculated what we would need to make Vorovoro our home for the next three years. This time in pounds sterling, which gave my reckonings a greater sense of reality. A total of £27,000 would need to be paid within three months and a further £20,000 for rent and community donations paid in instalments over the period of the lease. I thought £47,000 for an island for three years wasn't bad. But finding twenty-seven grand within three months wasn't going to be easy. It was the equivalent of a decent year's salary. Before tax. And neither MJ nor I had any salaries at all. Three months. How many tribe members would we need to recruit to secure the lease? I took an average spend of £150 – halfway between a Nomad and a Hunter membership fee – and did the simple arithmetic. After PayPal commissions, web payments and credit card bills I worked out that we would need a minimum of two hundred people to sign up if we were to make the first instalment. If Tribewanted was going to work at all I thought this was a reasonable target. MJ agreed.

'No problem. If we can sell ten places, we'll sell two hundred. It's all about the initial momentum, about how much buzz is created round the idea. And if some people do see £120 as worth a punt then I think it's just a case of getting Tribewanted in front of a lot of people fast.'

I wrote back to the NLTB and immersed myself in negotiating

some of the finer points of the agreement. We would later use a lawyer to make sure it was all above board.

I still don't know how MJ manages to get in touch with some people online, he is the best internet networker I've ever come across. Like some people possess the natural ability to locate, charm and connect with the right people when they walk into a room, so MJ has the ability in the online world. Even at this stage in our plans, prior to the launch, MJ had gathered supportive emails from all kinds of entrepreneurs and potentially useful contacts. One day he even forwarded me an email from a Sir Richard Branson. How do I know it was from Branson? Well, because I called his secretary on the number on the bottom of the email to see if we could arrange a meeting. Unfortunately, Sir Richard was out of the country, probably on his own island, otherwise she seemed sure he would have made time to meet us. 'Why don't we meet there?' I wanted to ask but didn't. I made a mental note, 'Call Sir Richard when next back from Fiji.' Part of the time the whole thing just felt like a bit of a game. I knew in reality, of course, that it was far from that. MJ also networked his way into Alex Tew, Danny Bamping's (eco-entrepreneur who had been on *Dragons' Den*) and Duncan Bannatyne's inboxes, and received responses.

We really wanted to get the site online before Easter and the start of the summer, hoping the English winter would make a stark contrast to the allure of South Pacific sunshine and inspire people into grabbing their tribal membership. A few days before our launch target date in the first week of April, I took a call from a number I didn't recognise.

'Hi Ben, I'm Andy Barr. I've been chatting to Mark about Tribewanted and I love the idea. I think I could get you some great press.'

'Sounds good Andy, tell me more.'

'OK. I run a PR and viral marketing company called 10yetis. Tribewanted has real potential to get coverage.'

This is how it kind of happened. MJ would start and build the online relationship and then pass it on to me for the phone and face-to-face stuff. It felt like MJ and I were a good team, reflecting the virtual and real worlds we were shortly going to try and connect. So we met Andy from 10yetis at Paddington Station and he said he would be happy to delay any invoicing for sixty days because he was confident that the story would get coverage. An enthusiastic and likeable guy with a classically dry sense of humour, Andy was going to be a fun and, more importantly, a cheap member of the team. The three of us wrote the press release:

5,000 people. 1 Unique Tribe. 1 Fijian Island.
A tribe is wanted.

We were almost ready to go, and I phoned Ulai. 'Bula, Boss,' I said to him. 'Have you seen the final NLTB agreement?'

'Yes, Ben. Well done. It's a good deal and Momo [the Fijian name for his uncle, Tui Mali] is happy. We're just waiting to see this project kick off now. I'm surprised how fast it's happening.'

'Me too. Listen. I'll email you when the website goes live, should be some time tomorrow. Vorovoro will be open to the world.'

'Cool. Listen there is something I should tell you.'

'OK,' I said, suddenly nervous, not knowing what weight those words carried.

'*Survivor* turned up on Vorovoro on a sea plane the other day.'

'Are you serious? You mean, *Survivor* as in the huge US reality TV show?'

'Yeah, they walked up the beach and asked Momo if they could lease the island, I think they had a blank cheque in their pocket!'

'And what did Tui Mali say?' I asked casually, trying not to sound as petrified as I felt, still fully aware that we had yet to sign or pay for our lease.

'He phoned me for advice and I asked him what he thought. He told me that we should stick to what we had agreed by leasing Vorovoro to you and besides, he likes your idea more,' Ulai replied laughing. I breathed a massive sigh of relief.

'That's good news, Ulai, please thank Tui Mali for his faith in us and honouring the agreement, we won't let him or his people down.'

'Vinaka Ben, I will. Good luck with the launch, we'll drink some kava here to send the virtual Vorovoro our best wishes.'

'Vinaka, Ulai, I'll let you know how it goes. Moce for now.' I tossed the handset onto the chair next to me and collapsed back into the cushions. I laughed out loud. *Survivor*! Tui Mali turned down *Survivor* and its dollars and its global publicity for us, for me and MJ and our dream? Maybe they didn't do their sevu-sevu properly. I smiled at the thought of a pair of TV executives jumping out of their sea plane and asking 'How much for your island, Chief?' Though not even a great believer in it at this stage I could feel the good karma washing over me like Fijian sunshine. Tui Mali was an honourable man, we had found a good Chief to lead us. We couldn't let him down.

Just after midnight on 3 April 2006, MJ pointed the domain name Tribewanted.com that we'd bought for £10.99 in January at the sparkling new, ten-page website Komodo had built us. He was on MSN messenger.

'It's live, bud. Are you ready?' he asked.

'I guess I'll have to be, no turning back now.'

I told him about the *Survivor* story. MJ sent back a 'smiley'. He sounded tired. 'OK. I'm going to get some sleep. Andy from 10yetis will send out the press release first thing in the morning.'

'Cool. Sleep well, you've done a good job.'

He had. I was proud of where we were, on the threshold of something. I wasn't quite sure what. It had only taken a push of a button to make the leap but it was still pretty terrifying, much more so than buying those tickets to Fiji. Now we were going to ask the world if they would join us on this adventure and be prepared to dig into their pockets to do so. I wasn't ready to sleep, so I opened a new Word document on my Apple Mac laptop, now the only light in the darkness of the Devon night, and typed the day's date followed by the words 'Bula or Bust'.

It was to be our first blog. Would others take the leap with us or would people laugh at our crazy plan as we retreated, red-faced, back into our daydreams? Would tomorrow be the day that took me from this cosy quiet barn to an island on the opposite side of the planet? I honestly didn't know. I hoped it would be 'Bula'. I was seriously scared it might be 'Bust'.

7
RAI VOU
REVOLUTIONARIES

I woke up early. It was 3 April 2006, a day that would tell me whether the last few weeks had been an utter waste of time or the start of something that would change the direction of my life. Nothing I could do about it now, though.

The phone started ringing at ten thirty. It was Andy, from 10yetis. 'Ben! Are you sitting down?'

'Yes. What's happening?'

'What's happening? It's all happening! You and Mark have really got something! My phones haven't stopped all morning!' Though I was trying to stay calm, Andy's excitement was contagious and I felt an adrenalin rush quivering down my spine.

'So tell me.'

'The *Daily Mail* has been on. So have the *Express* and *The Observer*. They all want more. And *Metro* wants an interview. I said you'd speak to them this morning, is that OK?'

'Of course it's OK,' I told him. 'Who's going to call, and when, and what sort of thing will they be asking?' I reached for a pen.

'A journalist called Suzy Austin. In an hour. Just tell her about the whole concept, how you and Mark got the idea, what's going to happen next, that sort of thing.'

'But I don't know what's going to happen next,' I said, trying not to panic.

'You'll be fine. Just let the story do the work. Got to go, phones are going mad again. Speak to you later, good luck.'

'That's easy for him to say,' I muttered. I had less than an hour to marshal my thoughts and try to make some kind of sense out of the apparent chaos of the last month and a half.

In the end I needn't have worried. Suzy was the personification of efficient, brisk charm and guided me through the interview without mishap. At the end, she too seemed to relax a little bit. 'Thanks Ben, that was great. I think it's a fantastic story.'

'Excellent. So what happens next?' I asked, trying to sound more composed than I actually felt.

'I'm going to take it to my editor now. I think we might get it on page three.'

'That would be great. When do you think it'll come out?'

'Tomorrow.' My self-control evaporated.

'Wow!'

The first response to the *Metro* piece came in a text from a friend at seven the next morning. 'Hey Ben. Just read about you and a tribe and an island. What's going on?'

Suzy had been as good as her word. Plastered all over page three – I got an email with the copy – was a banner headline: 'Warriors Wanted! Have you got what it takes to run an Island Paradise?' The article ran a pretty accurate description of what Tribewanted was going to do. It was like a full-page advert. I couldn't believe it. The calls, texts and emails came in solidly all morning from people I knew all over the country. The London Underground was scattered with pictures of Vorovoro beach and Tui Mali. If that wasn't going to grab people's attention on the way to work in the dark I didn't know what would. The first dozen or so tribe places were taken by friends and people I knew who had heard we were launching the previous day. And it seemed appropriate to me that my good mate Andrew Trotter, who I had spent my gap year with working and living in an Outward Bound school in Australia, and his girlfriend, were the first two people to back the project, members one and two.

But the real buzz came when the first tribe members whose names we didn't recognise started to appear in our PayPal account. Andrew McIntyre and Jonathan Dugdale's payments for membership places 15 and 16 were names I didn't recognise, but they had both just spent £120 on joining Tribewanted. I would later meet Andrew on Vorovoro and shake his hand to say thank you for backing us straight away. It was people like him and Jonathan that meant this whole thing would get off the ground.

Each time a new member joined we would receive an email from PayPal titled 'Notification of payment received', with details of who and how much. MJ would then log their details onto an online database system he had found and send them a 'welcome to the tribe' email. 'Notification of payment received' has to be one of my favourite titles in the world for an email, especially when it's addressed to you. You never tire of an inbox filling up with 'notifications'. People are backing you, your project, your dream. It's totally thrilling. Within twenty-four hours we had sold fifty memberships, about fifteen of which were people we had known before it launched. That meant we had over £5,000 in the bank. We were on the way.

Up north in the Wirral, MJ was getting keyboard cramp, managing the website and dealing with a sudden rush of email queries, most of them positive and sane. That was the way we had agreed to play it: I would handle most of the personal interviews and provide the public face of Tribewanted and MJ would keep the site and emails under control, set up a 'frequently asked questions' page and deal with the online PR and admin. It suited us both that way.

Just as well. The next few days were frantic. I gave interviews by phone to *The Observer*, the *Daily Express*, *The Times* and a few regional radio stations and newspapers, and fielded phone enquiries from all over the country. It was probably a good thing that my dad was in America on business. His absence meant that I could deal with the media storm from the barn on my own without having to provide a lot of overdue explanations. One call was from Deirdre Fernand, from the *Sunday Times*, who invited me for lunch and an interview two days later. Without hesitation I told her, 'I'd be delighted,' and noted down the details.

I took the two-hour train journey from Tiverton to Paddington and, as I was sitting at a table preparing for the big interview, I started to eavesdrop on a conversation happening behind me. I did a mental double take when I heard a guy in the group say, 'Yeah, and have you heard about this tribe that's starting on an island in Fiji?'

'No, what is it?' a girl replied.

'Don't really know. A mate told me about it yesterday. Sounds like you get to help build a village and hang out there,' he explained.

'Mad. Sounds cool,' another girl replied.

'It's called tribe wanted or something, I'm going to check it out.'

Blimey. Random strangers on a train were talking about Tribewanted and we had only started it four days before. How many more conversations were going on like this around the country? I glanced over at the group as I got off the train – students, I would have put money on it.

I was fired up as I headed to St Catherine's Docks, just past Tower Bridge, still answering phone calls and picking up messages every time I climbed the stairs from the Underground. As I sat waiting for Deirdre to arrive I wondered what the consequences of it all. I mean, suddenly it looked like we were going to be landing on people's door mats all over the country on Sunday morning. My name would be attached to this. I needed to be sure of what I was saying. What would they think about all this? I also thought about what it meant for our friends back in Fiji. The way I described this project and their home and culture would be crucial to how the reputation of their beautiful island home would be perceived from the other side of the world.

REVOLUTIONARIES

Lunch was great. Steak, wine, island talk, the psychology of social networking – Deirdre seemed to be increasingly enthused by the story. After lunch we went south to News International headquarters where I was introduced to one of the paper's editors. Paul Nuki had lived in Tonga and enjoyed hearing about our plans for Fiji as we traced the position of the islands on his world map. 'Listen, Ben,' he said to me. 'If it works, and even if it doesn't, be sure to let us know.' Then a young Aussie guy called me into a separate room and told me to stand against a blank canvas. 'The team want a shot of you for the Focus feature.' The feature! A shot of me! I had thought this was going to be just a quick filler for the travel section but we had been upgraded.

On the Sunday morning, I woke even earlier than normal and drove to the nearest petrol station that sold papers. I opened the *Sunday Times* first, trying not to tear the pages in my eagerness to find the Tribewanted article. When I saw it on page 14 I closed it again quickly. A short glimpse had shown me a half-page photograph of myself, staring straight up at the camera. My first thoughts were: 'Is my head that much bigger than my body? Do I actually look 14?' The headline read: 'Want to a join a South Sea tribe and help build a Utopia on an adventure island? If so, this man wants to hear from you today.' I grabbed it, and a couple of other papers, and drove a bit too fast back to the house.

Back in the barn I read the article as calmly as I could. The opening line shocked me: 'It's a unique social experiment and one that could revolutionise tourism.' Revolutionise tourism! That was a big call and the *Sunday Times* is hardly renowned for its sensationalist journalism. I thought Tribewanted might challenge some people in the way they think about travel and I hoped we could make a difference to the local communities in Fiji and educate ourselves about living more sustainably in the process, but start a revolution? Surely that was what revolutionaries did. And, sitting there in the barn that morning, I didn't feel like we were on the crest of a revolutionary wave. But if the *Sunday Times* thought so then why not, maybe our little project had potentially bigger implications than we first imagined.

I checked the website. There were sixty new membership bookings, and it wasn't quite eleven o'clock. Tribewanted was going to work.

I sat down and composed an email to Dad. 'Hi Dad. How's things? All OK here, though Career Break Cafe is a bit slow. You know I've been working on something with this guy Mark? Well, there's something about us in the *Sunday Times* today. If you can't get a copy over there, here's the link. Check it out, and let me know what you think. Love, Benj. PS. I probably should have mentioned it a bit sooner…'

I needn't have worried. When I got an answer, it was: 'Brilliant, Benj. Looks a fantastic project, well done. Speak soon. Dad.' That felt as good as anything.

Over the following week Tribewanted was featured in *The Observer*, Saturday's *Times*, the *Daily Express*, *Grazia* magazine and, for me most exciting of all, we made front page on the *Malvern Gazette*! Malvern-on-sea had made it to Malvern, England. I think my grandparents were a bit shocked. A few days later Dad, now home and following the project with great interest, wandered up the barn stairs to where I was busy typing and dropped a paper across the keyboard. 'I'm guessing you haven't seen this?' What lay in front of me made my heart jump. A double-page spread with a picture of a balding man blowing a conch shell on what was unmistakeably Vorovoro's beach was accompanied by the headline 'The timeshare eco-tribe.' This guy must have gone to Vorovoro to write the story and we knew nothing about it. Until now. I was petrified by what it might say. I looked up at Dad, 'Is it OK?'

'Actually, it's fine, comes across very well.' Phew. I started to read fast and ever so slowly began to relax as Richard Shears, the journalist sent to Vorovoro to get the scoop, described his happy adventure on the remote island. Tui Mali had not been there when he turned up, but Ratu Poasa, his brother, had taken good care of the uninvited journalist and his photographer and answered his probing questions thoughtfully. The result was that the piece came across very much from a Fijian perspective

REVOLUTIONARIES

and was positive. We weren't involved at all and the story read well, the only problem being that the journalist forgot to mention the website. It didn't seem to deter people though. As I later discovered, many tribe members found out about the project from this article. From the newly launched forum that MJ had put on the front of the website, I later found out how other tribe members had heard about the project. I read one post which said that a guy had been driving home when he heard me talking to John Inverdale on BBC Radio 2. He was so excited he pulled off the motorway onto the hard shoulder and called his wife so that she could get online and reserve their places. It was fantastic to hear that other people were getting as excited about Tribewanted as we were and it was also great for our immediate goal of the 200 members we needed to secure the all important island lease.

What for us felt like a media explosion over Tribewanted also led to a herd of television producers calling and emailing us daily. MJ and I counted at least fifty different production companies who had contacted us within two weeks of launching the website. We had thought Tribewanted might have the chance of being filmed as a documentary and that we would perhaps get some interest further down the line, but not like this. Not this media avalanche, we were overwhelmed. But we knew we had to act pretty quickly to get a deal so we picked our top ten production companies – by reputation and recommendation – and off we went on a TV tour of our capital city.

I didn't know much about the television industry and though always drawn to the media I was never someone that would happily watch a whole night of TV regardless of what was on. So when MJ and I started to meet these producers I didn't have a clue what half the programmes they'd made were. MJ on the other hand was an expert and was able to prep me for each new exec's office we visited. For us, it was about finding a production company who understood what we were trying to do. A company that wouldn't just see dollar signs but would recognise the opportunity to follow a potentially exciting and inspiring real-life adventure. We met some great people and we met some weird people.

It eventually came down to two companies: Lion TV and Shine TV. We'd been really impressed by the directors at Lion, they seemed down to earth and were producing the kind of programmes we liked. Shine were more last minute. On the way back from yet another meeting (by this stage I was losing track), my phone rang:

'Hi, this is Tori from Shine Television...'

'Tori, thanks for calling but we've had loads of interest and I don't have time—'

Tori was insistent. 'If you're in Notting Hill, why don't you come and have lunch?'

Did Tori *know* we were in Notting Hill at the time? Had she somehow tom-tommed my mobile? Fifteen minutes later we were eating coronation chicken sandwiches with Tori and Shine's creative director, John Silver, who had previously made *Jamie's Kitchen* and *Grand Designs*.

A couple of weeks and more meetings later and we still couldn't decide. I was edging Lion, MJ wanted Shine. We knew this was a crucial decision; we had to get it right. My mobile vibrated: 'Hello Ben, this is Elisabeth Murdoch from Shine.' Gulp.

I was back at Shine the following week for my meeting with Mrs M. Whether we worked with Shine or not, I wasn't going to pass up on the chance to meet someone of her calibre. We all have our opinions of the Murdoch empire, so I was intrigued to know how the successful daughter of the great media tycoon would react to Tribewanted. I was pleasantly surprised and very impressed. She was not only charming and down to earth, she also 'got' it. She got it more than anyone else in TV-land had so far. She told me why she loved the idea of empowering people online and why it would work. Had she read our business plan? Even with her family's far-reaching credentials I don't think she could have seen it. Within a couple of minutes, I had forgotten I was in a meeting with a Murdoch and shared a great conversation with someone who I instinctively felt was genuine in her enthusiasm for what we were trying to do. It was her work behind the scenes of Make Poverty History, Live8 and more recently RED, a diverse fundraising campaign to halt the spread of AIDS in Africa, that really impressed me – this was the kind of social entrepreneurialism we were searching for.

I phoned MJ: 'Shine it is mate.'

'I knew you'd say that,' he replied.

By that time we had over 200 tribe members, which meant we could secure the lease of Vorovoro and we had a TV deal. It was a good first month. No, it was a bloody great first month. We knew television would help Tribewanted further down the line both financially and through the exposure it would give the project when it was broadcast. The key for us was that it was to be observational television, that it wouldn't intrude, or dominate island life or the project. It needed to be small-scale in its production, and if we pulled it off it would be the best holiday film we'd ever have! What we didn't want was reality TV – Tribewanted was trying to tip that on its head.

The following week, I was heading south from Newcastle after a productive meeting with Andy at Komodo Design, when I received a text message: 'Ben. Are you free tonight? Having BBQ + there are some people I'd like you to meet.' It was from Liz Murdoch.

'Sounds great. When?'

'Eight. Bono will be there.'

BONO! What the hell, I was going for a Sunday night BBQ with Bono! I went for a pint with my brother and Mollie, his girlfriend. The whole BBQ thing at the Murdoch's with Bono was making me thirsty. My brother Dan and I had seen U2 live twice the previous summer, first at Manchester and then in the front row of Live8. I had ten U2 albums, U2 framed records, U2 T-shirts, U2 DVDs. U2 had been a soundtrack to my life more than any other band and tonight, because I'd started a website a month ago with a mate, I might be eating hotdogs and drinking G&Ts with the main man. This was mad.

I rang the door bell. An attractive young girl welcomed me,

took my jacket and directed me to a sweeping staircase before disappearing through another door. Tribal T, jeans and baseball shoes (I didn't want to look or feel anything other than myself), I headed up the magnificent staircase. Matthew, Liz's husband, greeted me at the top with a beer and started to introduce me. 'This is Ben, he's a Chief on an island.' The lady with long red wavy hair in the Chinese dress asked me what that meant. I later found out she was the editor of *The Sun* and went out with Ross Kemp from *EastEnders*. I had no idea. Next, in strode a tall man with a wedge of paper under his arm. He high-fived his media buddies and threw six (I counted) documents down on the table: 'These, my friends, are worth millions of dollars to the Global Fund even before a phone is sold.' This was Bobby Shriver, the well-known American philanthropist, and the documents were signed contracts with different mobile operators all promising to pay the Global Fund, an international AIDS charity, money when they sold and people used their RED branded phone. Tonight was a warm up for the launch of Motorola RED, Bono and Bobby's money-making scheme for the Global Fund. The nation's newspaper editors were there to chat with them. And so was I.

Later on in the evening, while enjoying a five-star kebab, I found myself sitting next to Bobby Shriver. He was captivating and as excited at what the contracts meant as a kid on Christmas Eve. Bobby leaned forward and whispered: 'Elvis is in the building.' Elvis? Now I knew that wasn't possible so I assumed he was referring to his twenty-first-century rock 'n' roll buddy, Bono. Sure enough, a few seconds later a pair of wraparound RED Armani glasses and a leather jacket strolled into the room. I found out a lot more about RED that night and I loved its simplicity – Bono, Bobby and their team had created a brand that did nothing but good. It was classic Robin Hood but without the stealing. It was a solution – it was consumerism with a conscience. Bono would later eulogise about this 'moment' and, as you would expect, he was a great speaker, brilliantly impersonating the mobile phone execs from America who didn't care that he was a rock-star. This was a passionate man and he and the others BBQ-ing that night understood the power of celebrity currency to do good.

'Have you met B yet?' Liz's voice came over my shoulder. I spun around, 'No, I haven't met, er, "B".' I mean I've gone nuts in a stadium of 90,000 people when he's belted out 'Where The Streets Have No Name', but I've never actually met or had a beer with the guy. 'B, this is Ben,' Liz said, interrupting a conversation he was having with a national newspaper editor. Bono listened intently, hands clasped, head down, as I explained what Tribewanted was.

'Sounds cool,' he said. 'Reminds me of the ONE campaign we did in America – uniting people through the internet for a purpose.' Well, yes, I guess it was kind of similar, except we didn't have more than two million sign-ups, like that anti-poverty pressure group did. I knew that in order to keep Bono's attention I needed a hook. I remembered something.

'How did your last trip to West Africa go?' Bono was off. He loved Africa, I knew that, and so did I. Ten minutes later, I was telling him about my trip to Timbuktu and he told me about visiting Togo. I wasn't trying to impress a rock star any more, I was having a beer with a traveller and a dreamer.

After the speeches, I excused myself. As I walked back to the tube I was buzzing, not just because I'd met an inspiration of mine but because I'd been inspired by what they were all achieving. That if I had somehow ended up in that room with those people, it meant that they saw something in what MJ and I had started. That gave me massive confidence. I called my mate Trots, tribe member number one. 'Hey bud, I just had a beer with Bono, how you doing?'

I was flying.

8
DOLA O MEREKE
BREAKING AMERICA FROM OUR BACK GARDEN

One thing MJ had always maintained was that for Tribewanted to work quickly we had to crack America. I thought about how the Arctic Monkeys had used MySpace to build a fan base before releasing their singles in the UK and the US. It had worked brilliantly. But how could we replicate that success?

So, after the headiness of BBQ-ing with the stars and running the London Marathon, I was by myself again, taking time to recover and prepare for the next part of the adventure. The marathon had gone well, the best time I'd run the distance in the five times that I'd had a go, but I only really felt the pain for the last couple miles so perhaps I didn't push myself hard enough. I wasn't too worried; it was no longer my main focus. I actually think the buzz I was getting from Tribewanted starting helped take a few minutes off the clock for me that day.

Afterwards I returned to Devon and got straight back on the phone. Although I was physically tired, I felt motivated. I would need to be. Membership sales for Tribewanted were still coming in, but the torrent had slowed down. We needed to kick-start the project with something that would keep the momentum going. We needed to ramp up our approach to tribal recruitment in the same way that I had tried to match or better each mile I ran around the streets of London a couple of days before. If only by a second or two each week, we constantly needed to be moving forward, and faster.

As had happened so often before, the answer came online from my business partner. I was sitting at the table in my quiet office when a forwarded message from MJ caught my eye. He had been talking to Alex Tew, the Million Dollar Homepage guy, who had been following the project with interest and giving us a lot of helpful advice.

'Hi, Mark,' he wrote. 'You were asking about getting publicity in the States. I would try a lady called Imal Wagner. She did all my stuff and she's brilliant.'

MJ was ahead of the game and had already sent off a speculative email to Imal, telling her all about Tribewanted and enclosing all the links to the publicity we had already had in the UK. He had also spoken to Imal and told me that she was going to be calling in the next day or so. 'See what you think of her,' he said.

Six hours later, my phone rang. It was eleven at night and I was just going to bed. I was still tired from the marathon and answered in a kind of haze, expecting some mate calling for a chat. 'Ben Keene?' The voice was piercing, strident, American.

'Yes, this is Ben.'

'Imal Wagner. Mark asked me to call.'

'That's great. Thanks for calling, I didn't expect to hear from you so—'

She cut me off. 'Listen, Ben. This is a fantastic project, and we're going to work together just fine.'

'Are we? Oh, great, but I need to discuss—'

Imal was off again, unstoppable. 'I've been talking to some people. Everyone in New York is very excited to be in on this. I have a lot of really great ideas, you're going to love them. You're going to need more than one island, trust me!'

'Oh, really? I mean that's great, but—'

'But? But! Listen Ben, and don't be with too many buts. Got a pen?'

'Yep.'

'Write this down.' She fired off a long telephone number, then another one. 'The first is my mobile. The second is my other mobile. You can get me any time, I mean it, twenty-four hours a day. I'm waiting for your call. I'm there for you and MJ, I want you to know that.'

'Thanks, Imal, and I'm really grateful, but I have to talk to MJ a bit more, and—'

'MJ? Ben, MJ already loves this. I've already chatted with him at length. Listen. I have one word for you. NBC.' I felt an electric surge shock me out of my weariness.

'NBC? The TV station?'

'The TV station, he says. Listen to him. I love you, Ben, you crack me up, you really do. The TV station. Yes, Ben, the TV station. The National American TV station.'

'Cool!'

'That's more like it. Now get this. I've been talking to a contact I have there, and *The Today Show* want to pick it up, make a feature on you and the whole Tribewanted shebang!'

'*The Today Show*?' I tried to sound a bit more alert and intelligent. 'That's a New York programme?'

'You kill me, Ben. I mean that. You British. *The Today Show*, Ben, is national TV. It runs coast to coast. In a few days I'm going to have Tribewanted all over America!' For a moment, I couldn't speak.

'That's awesome! Fantastic!' I gathered my wits. 'When? And where? Will I need to come over?'

'Uh uh. No way. *Today* want to film you in little old England. Now, what day is it?' She answered her own question. 'It's Tuesday, right? So the crew will be over in three days.' I could hear another phone ringing in the background. Imal had stopped speaking to me for a moment and was shouting at someone, telling them the best way to avoid the traffic. Her voice came on again. 'That OK, Ben?' Again, she left me no time to answer. 'Great. Look, I've got to go. I'll call you tomorrow.' I could hear her voice answering her other phone as she turned her attention from me. 'Imal Wagner. Tammy? Hi, honey. Yes, it's all fine. Don't worry. They love it—'

Her phone cut off. I looked at the receiver of my own mobile for a while and then disconnected and put it down on the desk as calmly as I could. Though it was late, I knew MJ would still be up. I told him my thoughts on Imal and her big plans. 'So you think we should go for it?' I asked him.

'Definitely! Look, I want to be in on this interview. OK if I come down to Devon and we do it there?'

'Should be fine, need to check a couple of things. I'll let you know as soon as.'

I closed my Mac down and slid back into the old film director-style chair that Dad had brought back for me once from one of his big conferences. I looked up at the map of the world on the sloping wall above my desk. But for once I wasn't gazing at the South Pacific. This time, I was looking at America.

The next few days passed in a whirlwind created by Imal Wagner. We sorted out a proper contract. I told Dad, got his go-ahead and, more importantly perhaps, the approval of Frances, my stepmother, for an American film crew to descend on their quiet haven in the Devon countryside.

Frances is a great woman. Unflappable and thoughtful, she took the news with easy good nature, merely enquiring what sort of arrangements she ought to make, and how many people we might expect. I had found out from Imal, in between her shouting at whoever her poor driver was and taking calls on her other phone that we should expect an NBC producer called Tammy Filler, accompanied by a sound engineer and a cameraman. They would arrive early in the morning of Friday 6 May and would leave that night. Imal had also informed me that NBC was aiming to get about three to four minutes of film from the day, and that the whole expedition was costing them $24,000. A sobering thought.

MJ came down to Devon the day before shooting. Though he had met Frances on his last visit, this was his first meeting with Dad. It would be interesting. We all had dinner together and, over a long, delicious meal with good wine, MJ was confident, assured and even slightly cocky. We had something to celebrate, apart from the prospect of our obvious imminent elevation to the status of American superstars. Five weeks in, we had hit another target: 300 memberships. We had enough now to consolidate the project, pay the guys at Komodo and 10yetis, ask a lawyer to look at our island lease and TV contracts and think about expanding the team. It was all getting a bit much for two guys to handle. Though I thought that he was in awe of my dad, a successful businessman with a lot of experience, tonight MJ was almost playing him at his own game, smoothly countering his challenges to the Tribewanted business plan.

'So,' Dad asked MJ, testing him, 'Tribewanted is doing pretty well. You've got money in the bank, you've paid your suppliers. Time for you guys to take on some staff and sit back and enjoy the ride?'

MJ suddenly got serious. 'No way. Things are going well, sure. Better than we could have hoped at this stage, to be honest. But Ben and I will never sit back. We may have the immediate financial concerns taken care of, but there is still such a long way to go. And before we commit to any major overheads, we have to make sure that the project is secure in the long term, and that the people who have signed up get what they paid for.' He took a sip of wine. 'Remember, this isn't our money.'

My dad, with a raise of the eyebrows and a nod, topped up all our glasses. I could see that he was impressed, and to be honest, so was I. This was a side of MJ that was new to me. All I had seen of him so far was the dreamy traveller, the internet wizard with a creative overdrive for far-fetched ideas. I'd never seen the tabletop entrepreneur before, the side that was aware of the scale of what we were attempting and the responsibility that was on our shoulders.

Later, as I helped Frances clean up the kitchen, she turned to me. 'Blimey,' she said. 'He's a lot more confident than last time!' It was true. The project was having that effect on both of us. What had started off almost as a daydream was turning into a serious proposition, and it was changing us both.

Tammy Filler arrived at seven o'clock the next morning. It was a horrible day, wet and windy. The NBC crew arrived in an estate car hired at Heathrow and, though they cannot have had much sleep, they seemed full of energy and enthusiasm. Real professionals. I went out to the front door to greet them. First came Tammy, tottering towards me as fast as she could on high-heeled city shoes, a raincoat thrown over her head to protect her hair. She made it into the kitchen with only the briefest of hellos and stood looking about her, smiling and brushing herself down. She handed me the raincoat and introduced herself. 'Hi! Tammy, NBC. Are you Ben?'

'Yes. Hi Tammy, welcome to sunny Devon. This is my dad, and Frances, and this is Mark – MJ – the guy who dreamt this whole thing up.' Frances was looking at her with some consternation, and took over from my rather inept attempt at welcome and introductions.

'What *are* you wearing?' she exclaimed, incredulous. Tammy, it is true, was not dressed for a cold, wet day in the South West. She was wearing clothes more suitable, in fact, for a mild day in Manhattan. Tammy looked ruefully down at her light summer clothes and shivered slightly. 'I didn't know it was going to be this cold, it's my first visit to England.'

'You need a hot drink,' continued Frances, taking motherly command of the situation. 'What can I get you?'

'Coffee! Black. Not decaf, no sugar.' There was a slight pause. 'Please,' she added, suddenly aware she was not in Starbucks.

Frances bustled about while MJ and I went outside to help the crew, two pleasant, easy-going Australians who were unloading a pile of silver cases from the back of the car. By the time we had sorted everyone one out with hot drinks and towels, the weather was improving. The wind had blown away most of the clouds and the rain had stopped. The sun was even coming out and it looked like soon we would be able to get the interviews under way. Tammy was insistent that these took place in the garden with the rolling hills and ploughed fields in the background. 'It's got to look really English,' she had told us. Tammy was in a hurry. She and the crew would only be in the country for one day and for all the dollars being spent it was important that everything worked on schedule and according to plan.

Even so, it took two hours to set up the cameras. Tammy fussed about arranging chairs in exactly the right positions and when she was satisfied she produced a clipboard and went through the questions she was going to ask. She had certainly done her homework. Of course, I had sent Imal all the information about what Tribewanted was going to be and MJ's and my backgrounds but I hadn't expected that Tammy would be so well prepared.

I went first. It took an hour and a half. I wasn't nervous, Tammy's professionalism was reassuring and she'd allowed me time beforehand to think about the questions and the answers I was going to give. We covered the whole thing, from MJ's initial idea to flying out to Fiji on a whim and doing a deal with a tribal chief. We talked about online communities, the power of the internet and the importance of doing everything in an ecological, sustainable way. Though pretty relaxed, it was still fairly tiring, and I was glad when it was MJ's turn to sit in front of the cameras and do his stuff. I went back to my office in the barn where I could check for messages while still keeping an eye on the proceedings in the garden below me. All I could hear for most of the time was laughter, and Tammy's occasional shrieks of 'Stop! You're killing me! God, I can't work with this guy!'

I listened a bit harder. 'So, MJ,' Tammy was asking. 'Why Fiji?'

'You don't need to ask me that,' came MJ's response. 'Ben's already covered it.'

'Will Tribewanted be a huge success?'

'What do you think?' My friend was utterly unfazed by the cameras, the sound guy and the businesslike interviewer interrogating him for American network television. My immediate reaction to MJ's interviewing technique was fear – how did he know Tammy wasn't laughing this all off only later to edit his question buffering into what looked like a pair of guys who didn't have a clue what they were getting themselves into?

I later asked Tammy how it had gone with MJ. 'Great, you guys are so different, it really works well.'

The interviews concluded to Tammy's satisfaction, and at two o'clock we broke for lunch. Frances and Dad, unobtrusive but the perfect hosts, had laid on a full lunch. Relaxed now that she had the main body of work in the can, Tammy was very entertaining about some of the stories she had covered and the places she had been. The crew, pretty relaxed anyway, opened up a bit more and we all laughed a lot at the absurdity of an American and two Australians filming an interview with a couple of Englishmen about a community which would exist half in virtual space and half on a tiny island in the middle of the Pacific Ocean. But the buzz of having NBC in the back garden was definitely tempered by the reminder that we were responsible for delivering on promises we had now announced to breakfast America.

In the afternoon they wanted some shots of me and MJ walking, deep in conversation, in a 'typical old rustic garden'. We were finished by about six o'clock and were all breathing sighs of relief when Tammy announced that she absolutely must have some shots of MJ and me talking together in a typical old-world English Inn. Slightly alarmed, I telephoned the landlord, an old Devonian with fairly firm views on what he considered suitable behaviour on his premises. 'An American film crew,' he repeated doubtfully.

'Yeah, but they'll be fine,' I promised, hoping that Tammy in particular would not be too loud.

'No problem, bring 'em all down then,' he said, in a thick Devonshire drawl.

It was a beautiful evening. All the morning's bad weather had disappeared and in the late sunlight the thick hedgerows glowed with early summer vigour. Situated on the banks of the canal where I ran every morning, the scene was redolent of everything that Tammy wanted out of an 'Olde Englishe Inne'. The landlord was friendly and the crew set up their kit and bright lights with a minimum of disruption.

I ordered five pints of Otter ale, which the Aussies grasped gratefully, and Tammy looked at with frank amazement. 'This is beer?' she asked, perhaps just a teeny bit too loudly. 'Real English beer?' She took a sip and put her glass down in a corner. 'I'm not sure I drink beer.' She beamed at the landlord, showing a lot of immaculate American teeth and hurriedly started arranging me and MJ at the bar.

It didn't take long to get what she wanted. I ordered another four pints and a dry white wine for Tammy, which I could see didn't taste to her exactly as she expected it to.. It was soon time for them to leave. Tammy insisted on paying. 'Will the guy bring the tab over here?' she asked.

'No, you pay at the bar,' I told her. She tottered over on her heels and smiled warmly at the landlord.

'So what's the damage? And thank you so much for your hospitality. I just love your cute little inn.'

'That'll be £19.50, miss, please.' Tammy nodded and reached into her bag for her wallet. I still hadn't fully relaxed and was keeping a close eye on the situation, expecting some sort of last-minute surprise, so it didn't come as too much of a shock when I saw Tammy slide a jet black Morgan Stanley credit card across the bar towards the bemused landlord. It wasn't one he'd seen before. I was on my feet in a flash. Oh well. We were going to be beamed across the USA thanks to this woman and her network, so £19.50 was a small price to pay to help us break America.

9

SOTA NA LEWE NI YAVUSA
TRIBAL GATHERING

We may have been on our way to breaking America, but there was still a lot to do in the UK. The day after Tammy Filler and her crew left, MJ and I took the train to London to finalise the TV deal with Shine. I was thinking about all that needed to be done: the increasing workload seemed daunting. As memberships increased, so did the level of administration required.

But MJ, as usual, had his mind on the bigger picture. 'Ben,' he nudged me to take my attention away from the rows of figures I was poring over on the little table folded down from the back of the seat in front of me. 'I've had a thought.'

I looked up, experience having taught me that it was always worthwhile to listen to MJ when inspiration struck him. 'Go for it, mate.'

'We've got three hundred members, right?'

'Yeah, probably a few more than that, by now.'

'I think it's time we met some of them.' I looked at him, not, at that point, really taking in what he meant. He went on. 'It's the whole point of this thing, right? Or half the point, anyway. Bringing the members all together to give them a sense that Tribewanted isn't just virtual, that it exists in the real world as well; and that their fellow members are real people too. Maybe like themselves, maybe not. But united by the same island dream.'

I thought about this for a moment, as the train clicked through the neat fields and rolling hills of Southern England. As usual, MJ's idea made a lot of sense. It was what Tribewanted was all about. Just because I had always envisaged the actual community meeting on Vorovoro rather than anywhere else didn't mean that we couldn't bring the tribe together in advance of the island adventure. I thought about it more, and the more I thought, the more I liked it. And my business sense liked it too. Local Tribewanted get-togethers could generate a load more publicity for us and create a word-of-mouth vibe that might increase membership sales. It would certainly be interesting to see what kind of people were joining. 'OK, let's do it!' I told him. 'You got a plan?'

MJ smiled. 'Sure have. We'll post a time and place on the forum for a central London social and see who turns up.'

So, in London, while I signed the contracts which the lawyers had drawn up for the TV deal, MJ set to work on his laptop in the office which Shine had already allocated for our use when we were in town. I went through to see how he was getting on. 'Hey, mate. Contracts are all done. We're going to be on television!'

The deal with Shine basically meant that we would be available for filming at any time over the next eighteen months. They were aiming for five one-hour programmes, to be broadcast on the BBC. That meant a lot of footage and, though we had agreed that they could show what they liked, there was also a firm understanding that if any tribe member did not want to appear in anything more than the background of a shot, they didn't have to. We trusted Shine. We knew that they were not out to make some cheap reality TV show but rather a fly-on-the-wall examination of what would happen when we and the tribe members that were joining us would attempt to turn this ambitious idea into a working reality. If anyone was going to look foolish it was going to be us. MJ leaned back and looked at me, slightly distracted. 'That's great, Ben. Well done. But come and look, I've set up the meeting. It's out there. Now we just have to see if anyone turns up.'

'Brilliant! When's it going to be? Next week?'

'Tomorrow.'

While I had been in the meeting, he had booked the upstairs at Mook Bar, near Notting Hill Gate. MJ had scheduled it for 7.30pm, and had posted the details on the community page of the Tribewanted website under the banner: 'If you want to come and meet us, come to the first Tribal Gathering. The Tribe heads to Notting Hill.'

The next day we turned up at Mook's with no idea what to expect. Dozens of people, or none? Loonies, misfits, loners? Or people like us who shared the dream? We needn't have worried. Even at less than twenty-four hours' notice, more than forty eventually turned up. The first person I saw as I went in, to my relief, was Jo Tuomoto from the Fijian Visitors Bureau, another of Ulai's cousins I had recently met at a Fijian promotional event that I had spoken at in London. He smiled at me in recognition and beckoned me over. Jo was talking to a guy with longish hair in his early forties who turned out to have come all the way from Cardiff especially for the gathering. As I joined them, I could see MJ make his way over to a group of young guys in a corner and introduce himself.

I greeted Jo with a big handshake. 'Great to see you, I'm so glad you could make it tonight, thanks for coming.'

'No problem, Ben. I'm glad to be here. This whole project is very exciting for Fiji. It's such a great idea. I was just saying to David here how much Tribewanted could potentially mean to us.'

I looked at the guy Jo had been chatting to, and introduced myself. This was the first of the tribe that I had met in the flesh. This was my first 'met you online' experience. This was a real person standing in front of me, not an email address or community profile. Someone who had bought into MJ's and my vision. It was an important moment. 'Hi,' I said. 'Ben. Great to meet you.' We shook hands. 'So,' I went on. 'Why did you join the tribe?'

'I just love the idea of building a community,' David told me. 'I'm a consultant, working in IT. Don't get me wrong,' he laughed. 'I'm not some sort of saddo nutter. I have plenty of friends and a normal life. But to be in at the start of something like this is an incredible opportunity. I spend a lot of time online, and the thought of having that sort of fellowship on a real island, building something from scratch, that's fantastic!'

I saw Alex Tew come through the door, and, leaving David with Jo, I went over to greet him. 'Hey Alex, how's it going?'

'I hear you got on fine with Imal,' he said to me, amused.

'Yeah, thanks for the introduction. She's nuts. In three days she had a film crew from NBC filming me and MJ in my dad's back garden!'

'I thought she'd help. She likes the project. She'll be a big asset.'

'What's she like in real life?'

He laughed out loud at that question. 'Wait and see.'

I didn't have time to ponder that one. The evening was getting more surreal and I hadn't even had time to get a drink in. Identical twins came over, dressed in identical bright-red polka dot summer dresses. Suzy and Alison Robinson were striking. Immaculately made up, they looked like models or TV presenters, but it turned out they were anthropology graduates from Oxford University. 'Are you Ben?' one asked me. 'Ben?' echoed the other. I admitted it, and was instantly smothered in hugs and kisses and expressions of delight. 'Oh my God, we're so excited about this.' And so was I. 'Where's Mark?' I pointed him out to them and they tottered off on high heels to offer their congratulations.

I made my way over to the bar, suddenly aware that I needed a cold beer. 'Here, let me get that.' I looked round, and set eyes for the first time on a guy that was going to make a big impact on me and on Tribewanted. I had exchanged emails a few times with Warren Wright, and though I had never seen him before I knew at once that it was him. He was a tall guy, getting close to fifty, I guess, with a slightly receding hairline and a gruff Cockney accent. He was wearing an extremely brightly patterned Hawaiian shirt and was calmly rolling a cigarette from a battered old tobacco tin. 'Warren?'

'That's me. Good to meet you at last, Ben. This is going to be a hell of a ride.' Not completely sure what he meant by that, we took our drinks over to a quiet table and sat down. Warren was a fascinating man. He'd trained as a carpenter, but now he made a good living playing poker on the internet. 'The thing is,' he told me, 'you've got to understand who you're playing against, and stay disciplined. If you just roll home from the pub, looking for a game and feeling confident, you will lose. But if you are the sober one, you can take most of the pots, if you're careful. You've also got to be aware what time it is where your opponents are. So I regularly stay up until it's two or three in the morning just to catch the boozers in other parts of the world.' I could see that Warren, with practical skills as well as a cunning grasp of human psychology, would be a passionate addition to the tribe. 'I like what you and Mark have started,' he went on. 'At least, the sound of it. I need a change from London. I need some fresh air. And getting out to the South Pacific and getting my hands dirty will do me good after too long alone on the net taking money from fools that I'll never meet.' He looked at me shrewdly for a moment. 'That's not what you're doing, by any chance?'

I laughed, but it was a moment that would come back to haunt me. The dark side of the internet had shown its face, if only for a brief instant.

'The island's real, Warren,' I said, looking him in the eye. 'And I've shaken hands with the Chief. It's going to happen. We're not in this to rip anybody off. If I wanted to make a quick buck online I'd probably ask you teach me how to play poker.'

'Good enough for me, Ben mate, good enough for me,' said Warren, taking a deep pull at his beer. 'Anyway, I like a punt. And I want to believe in this, whether it's real or not. I'm sick of just taking stuff. I want to put something back. The planet's going to the dogs, and with Tribewanted, in a small way, I can do a bit to help. And I'll tell you this as well.' Warren lit another cigarette. I looked at him, expectantly, not sure what this rather strange, rather brilliant, cocky gambling eco-carpenter was going to say next. 'I'll tell you this, my son. I'm going to be your first Chief.'

I met a lot of people that night. I made sure I met all of them. Most were quite young, but then, I thought, with twenty-four hours' notice it was only the young and the occasional maverick like Warren who were going to be able to make it. They were all keen, all enthusiastic and, in the quiet moments when I had a chance to reflect on what I was picking up from all these people, I began to realise a little more about what it was that we had started. I started to realise what the alienation of modern life actually meant to so many people. How they longed to be part of a community, and that, even though many of them were already part of virtual communities online, they still yearned to focus that sense of belonging, to ground it in real life, to interact with real people. Tribewanted, I realised, was going to be bigger than the sum of its parts. It could be the catalyst for a disenfranchised body of people from around the world, uniting them with one purpose but attempting to give them democratic freedom to make real decisions in real time about a real place. They would each play their part, but they would choose the parts that they wanted to play; no one would impose their will on anyone else.

It was humbling. It didn't feel like I was the originator any more, one of the bosses of the company. It felt like MJ and I were the facilitators of people's dreams. I looked over at the bar to where Warren, leaning at a seriously casual angle, was chuckling with the anthropology twins. Everyone was laughing and talking, excited, full of plans and hopes and possibilities. I suddenly felt like the noise and the people and the room were starting to move around me. I couldn't be drunk on one beer, but I felt pretty spaced. The numerous possibilities as well as the increasing anxiety over the responsibility of what we had started was to blame. For some reason my mind briefly shot back to the summit of Kilimanjaro, to the triumphant icy dizziness of the roof of Africa. I felt triumphant and dizzy at that moment too. There was electricity between people in the room that night but I also felt the fear that things could easily spin out of control very quickly if we didn't stay absolutely focused. And, just like Kilimanjaro, I knew I needed to get off the summit fast to survive.

The evening had been a success. This was confirmed to us the next morning when we checked the Tribewanted message boards. They were busy and there were requests for more, as well as people suggesting their own tribal gatherings. I even saw a discussion about a gathering in America. I left MJ responding to them all and went off, elated but still worried about the workload that was building up. Last night's first face-to-face meeting with the tribe had made a lot of things clearer to me. For one, we really needed to start thinking seriously about what sort of things people would do on Vorovoro besides helping to build the village. That raised questions about safety, cost and cultural interaction. In addition it was becoming more obvious each day that the administrative burden was becoming too much for the two of us. While I was out of the office I took a call on my mobile which brought these problems even more sharply into focus.

It was Imal. 'Ben! How are you, honey? Good? Everything going well?'

'Hi Imal, yes, everything's fine. I was just—'

As usual, Imal was on a mission. 'That's just great, Ben, just great. Now listen. Here's what I want you to do. NBC are very pleased with the footage they got with you last week, and they're going to run the show in a couple of weeks, the beginning of June.'

'Wow! Awesome, that's—'

'So here's what I want you to do. I need you and Mark to be in New York for the launch.'

'Er, I'll need to—'

'Great, Ben. Fantastic. I'll set everything up this end. Don't worry about a thing. We're going to get some great coverage out of this. I'll call you.' And she had gone.

Stunned, I finished my coffee and went back to the office. MJ was in a buoyant mood. 'Hey, Ben! The response to the gathering has been brilliant. They're already talking about setting up others, all over the country, and a whole lot more people want to get involved.'

'Great. But listen.' I told him about Imal's call.

MJ's response was instant, and matter of fact. 'Well, we can't both go.'

'Then who?'

This time, Mark thought for a moment. 'You, for sure. You're the better front man of the two of us, and I've got too much to do here, running the online stuff.'

'Just me?'

'No. Someone should go with you. Why not take Becky? She's our Tribal TV girl after all, she can help with the publicity. It'll be good experience for her and, besides, I expect you're going to be pretty busy.' He was smiling at me and I could see that he was teasing, but he had a point. It would be good for Becky, and it would be good for the project. So that was settled. But I still had things on my mind.

'MJ, I've been thinking. We need to take on more people. I've been worrying about admin, managing members' emails, organising and ordering the tribe packs, the PR, the website, finance, partnerships; there's getting to be way too much to cope with. We've got 350 members, and they need looking after. Then there's what's going to happen on Vorovoro when we get there. We need to start planning for that now, we can't just leave it till the last minute.'

'You're right.' MJ got analytical. 'So we need to take on two more people. An office manager who can probably move to Fiji when we start, and someone to set up and coordinate what tribe members do on the island?'

'That's about it.' My thoughts turned glumly to the whole advertising and interview process that lay ahead.

'And the next questions are: how do we find people who can

start next week, who can do the job, and who won't need paying, at least immediately?' I shrugged. 'It's easy. Nepotism.' He leaned back in his chair looking pleased with himself. 'One: my sister. Sara Jane's got a degree in psychology, and she's been working as a mortgage broker for the last two years. She'd make the ideal office and tribe manager. Two: your brother Dan has a BA in Outdoor Education. He'd be perfect for setting up the island with you. There you are, sorted.'

I looked at him in wonder. I never knew for sure with MJ whether he'd been thinking about stuff for ages or whether he just managed to come up with these kind of solutions out of nowhere. But I still had some objections.

'OK. Maybe. But I've never met Sara Jane, and Dan's got a job. A good one. And a girlfriend. I don't think he'd drop everything and go to Fiji just like that.'

'You can meet Sara Jane any time you like. But she's my sister, and I trust her. She won't let us down. And as for Dan, well, look at this.' He showed me a printout of a list of suggested activities he and some of the tribe members had been putting together. There were camping weekends in the New Forest, and survival weekends in the Brecon Beacons. At the bottom of the list was a suggestion from a few of our members in the South West. They were keen to hold a beach event in Devon in less than a week, at Woolacombe, somewhere MJ knew my brother and I had visited many times together. 'There you go. Invite Dan down for that, and talk to him properly when you see him. I don't need to meet him, he's your brother.'

Five days later, my brother and I had just left the sea and were walking across the flat sands of Woolacombe Bay. Our surfboards were under our arms and our hair was full of the raw freshness of the Atlantic in late spring. There was no sun that afternoon, but the brightly painted doors of the beach huts ahead of us provided a colourful horizontal rainbow against a backdrop of dunes and a leaden grey sky. It was a good moment, one that we had repeated many times over the last few years since we had left school in Malvern. At moments like this, I had always felt closest to Dan, but I didn't want to take advantage of the general mood of weekend wellbeing. We had discussed the prospect of his joining Tribewanted already, but I hadn't had a solid answer either way. A few hundred yards away I could see the banner that Becky had made: 'Join Our Tribe!' and already a few people were milling around underneath it.

'So,' I asked him. 'What do you think? You want to join?'

He looked at me. 'I'd love to. But you know I'm going to have to talk to Mollie before I can commit.' Relief. We put our arms around each other's shoulders and carried on walking up the beach with our boards. I said nothing, but Dan hadn't finished. 'And I have to give two months' notice to my current employers. I'm not just going to walk out on them.'

'I understand. That's fine. It should fit perfectly.' I looked at him smirking. 'But there's nothing to stop you doing a bit of prep work, is there, providing it doesn't interfere?'

He laughed, and punched me on the shoulder. 'Cheeky sod. No worries.'

One final point was niggling at me. 'Have you talked to Dad about it, about giving everything up and joining Tribewanted?'

'Yes. He said it was a no-brainer.' That was what I wanted to hear, the final link in the chain. Dad's words to Dan meant that he fully supported the idea. After all, he might have been able to accept one son going halfway round the world on some madcap scheme, but if he was happy for both of his boys to go it meant he really believed in it.

We reached the banner, where Becky was talking to about twelve young people, most of whom had just come out of the surf as well. We were joined by a couple, Jim and Amanda, who were on their way round the world. They would be leaving England the next week, heading to a new life in Australia where, before settling down, they were going to try and cycle the circumference of that huge country. The next time we met would be in Vorovoro. With every moment that passed, the project was becoming more real.

The mention of Australia immediately reminded me of MJ. We

had agreed that, aside from the USA, Australia was going to be a key region to try and recruit tribe members from. So before I was due to head off to the USA, Mark had travelled to Australia to try and generate some interest in Tribewanted, stopping in Fiji on the way home to give the news and updates to the family on Vorovoro. It was surreal thinking about the fact that here was I with tribe members on a beach in England while MJ was on the opposite side of the world heading to the beach on Vorovoro. The bigger picture of what we were trying to do sometimes took my breath away, with excitement and fear.

I was brought down to earth again after my reveries about paths crossing in weird places round the world when my phone rang – I was glad that at least in the sea I got some peace – and a strange, Mr Bean-like voice said: 'John Wright here. I've come for the Tribewanted meeting, but I don't know where to go.'

'Hi, John. This is Ben. Where are you?'

There was a pause. 'I appear to be in a car park.'

I looked over to where he ought to be, it was visible from where I was standing. 'Well, if you get out of your car and wave, I should be able to see you.'

'Very well.' The door of a Volvo estate swung slowly open and a rather extraordinary figure got out and waved a tentative hand in the air.

'I see you!' I waved back. 'Over here! We're the group with the surfboards and banner, on the beach!'

'Ah. There you are. Jolly good, I'll come over.' As he got closer and I was able to see more of him, I grew a little concerned. The guys already in the group were all about my age and surfers. The man who was stomping towards us did not look, at first glance, as if he would easily fit in. For a start, he looked like an enormous hobbit. He had hair like Bill Bailey, long and straggly, but a bit bald on top. He had enormous sideburns and glasses. He was wearing black denim shorts cut off at the knee, and huge lace up walking boots. A 'No Fear' T-shirt completed his outfit, and when he turned round to make sure that his car was still there I saw the words 'Second Place Means First Loser' emblazoned on the back. I decided he must be very cool, or very mad. I was to find out he was a bit of both.

'John, hi. Ben. Great to meet you.' We shook hands, and John's face broke into a massive and rather inane grin revealing irregular and stained teeth.

'John Wright, p-p-p-pleased to meet you.' A stammer, as well. Once he got talking, though, it was hard to stop him. It turned out that he was an engineer – useful, I thought, beginning to warm to the guy – and had worked thirty-seven years for the same firm. He lived alone in London and, after he saw the publicity for Tribewanted, he knew instantly that he wanted to be involved. He was 57 years old, and it was time he did something amazing with his life.

'So, what is it that you are particularly interested in doing on Vorovoro?' I asked him, once we had moved to the pub. Those around fell silent, keen to hear what this bizarre-looking addition to our group was going to offer.

John looked round at the expectant faces and gave his unique, brown, gap-toothed grin. 'Ammm, I'm particularly interested,' he told us, in his reedy voice, 'in the sanitation aspects of island life.'

It was a great afternoon. Despite my initial misgivings, John got on with everyone. He had a natural, boyish enthusiasm and a great sense of humour. Once I got to know him better, I wondered if he played up his strange appearance for comic effect, either to put people at their ease or to see whether he was judged for it. He certainly fitted into the group.

Looking about me, I could see why. We all believed in the same thing. Though most of us were young and many had done a fair bit of travelling, the discussions were not the standard backpackers' tales. No, we talked of practicalities: water supplies, food production, fuel, raw materials for building, and, of course, sanitation. It turned out that John was interested in the construction of compost toilets. I would never have believed that one day I'd sit in a Devon pub by the sea, surrounded by friends and a small dog, listening with rapt attention as a man more than twice my age described the processes whereby human waste could be easily converted into useable compost.

I felt good. And it wasn't just the beer and the company. We had got a team together, one we could trust – having my brother on board meant more to me than I can say – and soon a lot of the vital day to day work could be offloaded without worry or excessive expense. And the tribe was taking shape in my mind as well. These people were committed. All sorts of people, one goal. It had to work. Although I knew that in a few days I would be flying to New York to meet Imal and deal with all the franticness that was PR American-style, I was sure of one thing. In John Wright's capable, no-nonsense hands, the toilets were sorted.

10
MUA NA YAVUSA KI NIU YOKA
TAKING THE TRIBE TO NEW YORK

A week later, I was sitting on a plane bound for New York, Becky beside me. We were both excited. While Becky chattered on about everything that she wanted to see and do while we were in Manhattan, I let my mind go back over the events of the last few days. MJ and I had had to make some tough decisions; at least, some of them were tough for me. While we were in the air, MJ was in Newcastle. Not only had we agreed how we were going to form the team that would be the nucleus of Tribewanted, bringing in Sara Jane and Dan to support us and Becky, we had also agreed a new split in responsibilities between ourselves. It had become clear to both of us that we had to devote more time, cash and effort to the development of the online community.

It was also clear that this was MJ's domain. So he was in Newcastle talking to Komodo and I was on my way across the Atlantic to follow up the NBC broadcast with TV and press interviews. It felt strange. It wasn't that I was a control freak, but I still felt weird giving up part of the management of the business. But I knew it had to be done and I trusted MJ. A simple idea had become very complex so it was right that I was going to deal with the real world and MJ was going to handle the virtual.

We wanted to make the site a reflection of what we planned for Vorovoro itself. A village, online, where members could wander around and check out the things that interested them, interact with each other, debate the issues, explore. And I knew that I couldn't do that but MJ and the Komodo team could. Yes, I consoled myself, as we swept over Greenland, we were on the right track.

Cruising at 27,000 feet, I looked at my watch and realised that in about two minutes Tribewanted would be broadcast on *The Today Show*. I looked over at Becky, fast asleep next to me, and hoped the rest of America wasn't doing the same thing.

As soon as we entered the arrivals terminal, I checked my mobile. There was a text message from Tammy, the *Today Show* producer who had visited us that rainy day in Devon: 'Show didn't air. Hopefully tomorrow. Katie Couric, the lead anchor, is leaving the network this week, it's going to screw up the schedule. Hang in there, Tammy.' So we spent every morning for the next three days glued to the TV set in our hotel room, which we were sharing for the sake of economy, waiting for our few minutes of fame off the back of which Imal had planned our Big Apple media work-out.

When we weren't working online, we took time to wander about the famous concrete island, getting sore necks from staring up at the giant man-made canopy. I loved the architecture and brightness of the city but hated the smells that rose up with the steam from street vents. Sitting on a triangular pedestrian island in the centre of Times Square with the blur of downtown traffic and giant pixelated billboards surrounding me, while Becky chatted to Japanese tourists about an island on the other side of the world, I started to think more about Vorovoro. I felt like a stranger from a different time. I imagined the contrast with the island in the sun. No traffic, no concrete towers, no cars, no adverts, and a lot less people. I smiled. I loved the buzz of NYC but I couldn't wait to get to Vorovoro and start building this thing for real. I suddenly felt like we should be getting on with it sooner rather than later.

Simon, the series producer for the Tribewanted documentary from Shine Television, had now arrived in New York, to follow us on our American adventure. We took Tribewanted postcards to STA Travel branches and chatted to the sales consultants. Simon got shots of us in yellow cabs, in Central Park, in Times Square. There was no word from Imal.

Finally, on the fourth day after our arrival, I heard the magic words: 'And coming up after this message, we'll be talking to two young guys over in England who have rented their own tropical island to start a tribe. Stay with us.' I looked over at Becky. This was it. The worst thing about seeing yourself on television is hearing the way you sound. It's never like you hear yourself in your own head. So there I was, in a hotel bedroom in New York City watching myself in my dad's back garden, and trying not to flinch.

The piece lasted three and a half minutes. It was a slick production all about Tribewanted with some great shots of the island that we had taken on our first visit, although it obsessed with the fact that there were no toilets.

The second it had finished my phone rang. It was Imal.

'That was great, Ben. Just great. Now this is what we're going to do. You're going to do an interview on camera for Reuters in thirty minutes. I'll pick you up in twenty, OK? OK.' She rang off. I looked up to where Simon was still filming me. 'What are you thinking?' he asked. I tried to gather my wits.

'I think it's time to take this town. I'd better get ready.' I told him. I was still in bed. 'Somehow I don't think I'm dressed for the biggest news agency in the world.'

Twenty minutes later, we were all standing outside on the pavement. There was no sign of Imal. Though not normally too bothered about what I wear, I had made a bit of an effort for Reuters. Wanting to give a serious impression, I had put on a linen Paul Smith jacket and the smartest pair of jeans in my backpack. A Tribewanted T-shirt completed my TV outfit.

I don't know how I was expecting Imal to arrive or what she would look like. I certainly didn't expect to see the huge people carrier that screeched to a stop beside us a few minutes later. A tousled head appeared out of the passenger window. 'Get in! We're late, c'mon guys, gotta go!' There were two rows of seats behind the driver and his companion and Becky and I climbed into the middle row with Simon struggling to fit his camera through the door and keep filming us at the same time. Imal kept up a constant flow of conversation. 'Hello. So pleased to meet you all at last, what a great show that was. This is my husband Marcus, he does my driving.' She tapped him on the knee with one of her mobile phones. 'Not this way honey, make a left.' Marcus smiled at us and said nothing.

When Imal's phone rang I had a brief moment to study her. Her hair was wild and big, coiling about her head like it had a life of its own. She was wearing a large denim dress with pink trainers. While she yelled encouragement and abuse down the phone she continued to tap away at the laptop on her knees, barking the occasional instruction at her husband. The Reuters office was on Times Square, just round the corner from our hotel. As we got out, Imal looked me up and down, 'OK, fine. Here's your phone.' She handed me a brand new mobile.

'But I have a phone.'

'This is better. You can get me on this any time. My number's programmed already, you just hit any key. Now, c'mon, Ben, we're late. I'll tell you what you're going to do on the way up.' She set off at a brisk walk, her dress and her hair billowing behind her. 'We're going to do TV with these guys and, hopefully, also a print interview. Reuters syndicate all over the world, the TV will go to maybe two hundred different countries, the print all across America, at least.' I nodded, hurrying to keep up. Simon and his camera were stopped at the big glass doors by a security guard and a Rotweiler. An amiable and amusing guy who was going to become a good friend over the next year, Simon knew he wasn't going to be able to talk his way past the news agency's security guard. So we left him filming us as Becky and I followed Imal inside. Apart from us, everything was calm, quiet, and air-conditioned. 'I want to make sure you tell the story properly. Make out that Fiji is some kind of Paradise.'

'But it is!'

'Yeah, but with snakes though, right?'

'Maybe a few, but they're not very dangerous. I mean, well they are dangerous . . . '

'Don't mention snakes.' She stopped for a moment and looked back at me sternly. 'This is middle America you're talking to, they don't like snakes. You've gotta make out that this island is some kind of special resort. Tell them about the facilities, the bedrooms. About everything you've got going there, why it's better than Hawaii.'

'But, Imal, there's nothing like that there at all, it's just a tropical island! We haven't started building anything yet! And anyway it's not going to be a resort.'

'OK, honey. I know.' We had reached a door and she paused. 'Just sell it, OK? Be yourself. Now, let's go!' She opened the door and we entered a small studio. Soon, from the studio chair with bright lights shining in my eyes, I could see the rest of my little posse squeezed up against a far wall with Imal standing slightly in front, giving me a thumbs up sign. In every interview I had done so far I was given time to get to know the interviewer, get settled. Not so with Reuters. Just as the camera started rolling the door opened again and a woman with a notepad came in and sat down beside the TV interviewer. 'Hi,' she said in a mild Scottish accent. 'I'm Claudia, and I'll be taking notes for the print article. I may ask some questions too. OK?' She didn't wait for any response from me but turned to her colleague and said 'OK, thanks Jerry.'

'Ben Keene and Mark James, two 26-year-olds from England, have leased a tropical Paradise in Fiji in the South Pacific, and they're going to turn the travel industry on its head. Ben, tell us about this new enterprise.'

So I told them. How the idea of Tribewanted began and that it was all about making communities, on the internet and in real life. How people would vote on decisions and how every member would get a chance to be elected Chief for a month. How ecology was high on the agenda. How we had the support of the local people and would be working with them to create jobs and hopefully help with education. Occasionally I noticed Imal waving frantically at me from the back of the room, which was really distracting. I was thinking hard, concentrating on getting the truth of the story across and how it was going to be fun as well as worthy. And that people could still join and influence it. Today!

I don't know how long I was on that chair, but it felt like seconds. When Claudia signalled that they had finished, I checked my watch. Thirty-five minutes! But everyone was all smiles. Claudia seemed really intrigued by it all. 'That was great!' she told me. 'I'll write it up now and we'll get it online right away. Should be about an hour.' Imal, never far away, butted in at once.

'Now, wait a minute. Hold on there. Would it be at all possible for the print to go out at the same time as the TV, we get more impact for the story that way.'

Claudia was adamant. 'Sorry, Imal, no can do. The footage is going to need a lot of work before it's ready. I want to put this out right away. I need to do it before anyone else gets the story. It's big. I think they'll have their 5,000 by tomorrow.'

Imal turned to Jerry, who was removing the tape from the camera. 'C'mon, Jerry, I need your help here. How fast can you work? How long's it going to take you?'

Jerry shrugged. 'The rest of the day, minimum.'

'That's it?'

'That's it. Can't rush it. Got to get it right.'

Imal sensed that she was not going to get her own way. 'Well, that was great. Thank you Claudia, thanks Jerry. I think you've got a great story here. Do the best you can with it, OK?'

We all turned for the door. At the lift, the Reuters people shook hands with us amid expressions of mutual admiration.

Claudia even said she would come along to our tribal gathering the following night. As soon as the lift doors closed, Imal started fuming. 'That woman! What does she know about getting a story out?'

By the time we reached the street, Marcus and the people carrier were there. Before we piled in again, Simon wanted a reaction shot from me so, surrounded by the rush of New Yorkers and tourists, I faced yet another camera. 'We've just done an interview for the biggest news agency in the world and in about three hours it's going to be sent out to over 200 countries. So it's been a good start to the day,' I said, smiling, as I climbed into the back of Imal's media wagon.

Imal had decided that what we needed was a lunch to celebrate, and not just any old lunch. She took us to one of the most famous Italian restaurants in New York. A well-fed head waiter greeted Imal like a long-lost daughter and led us to a table. Black-and-white photographs of actors and boxers lined the walls, many signed. The producer of the *Jaws* movies was sitting opposite us. Imal recommended the lasagne and ordered for all of us before we could argue. The lasagne was a good choice, it really was the best I had ever tasted. So there we were, in a restaurant where Robert De Niro and Martin Scorsese were regular diners, eating the best pasta in the world and washing it down with Coca Cola. It was another surreal moment in a most unusual day.

About halfway through, when the rest of the party were being shown the photographs on the walls by the famous chef, Imal leaned over to me. 'So what is this, this *thing* I'm getting from you, Ben?'

'Er, I'm sorry?'

'You know. You're young, you've got this great business idea. You guys are all set to take over the world.' She checked her watch. 'In fact, in about one hour you probably will be all over the world. So I can tell you're excited about all of this. In fact, when I was listening to you give the interview this morning, you nearly had *me* convinced too.'

'What do you mean?' I asked her, a bit confused.

'Come on, honey. I heard you. And it was a really good pitch, all that stuff about communities, and sustainability. It's a great line, but what are you going to do with all the money? Cars? Boats?' She looked a little coy for a moment. 'Girls?'

I laughed. 'Imal, I haven't even thought about it. I mean, MJ and I, we're not interested in that. We have to bring in money, certainly, but to make sure Tribewanted succeeds not for us. Or not until this thing really works.'

'So you really believe all that stuff?'

'Sure. Why would we be trying to do it otherwise? It's a seriously massive challenge. Not a way to a quick buck,' I said, obviously a little too determinedly. She suddenly shrieked, nearly causing an old Mafioso at the next table to spill his glass of carefully poured Barolo. 'He's a true believer! Oh my God, Ben. With that sort of passion you're definitely going to need two islands!'

Later, back at the hotel and alone at last after another round of phone interviews, including one with *USA Today*, I plugged in my laptop and checked in with the website to see how the memberships had been affected by all the coverage. Yesterday we'd been hovering about the 350 mark. Now we were well over 450.

There was something else, a message in my inbox that stood out: 'Hey, guys. Love the idea, and I'm keen to get involved. Let me know if I can help in any way.' The writer had included a phone number. It was from Corbin Bernsen, the star of *LA Law* and the baseball classic, *Major League*. After the sort of day I'd had, nothing much seemed strange anymore. When I called him, Corbin was friendly and enthusiastic. He said he would be happy to help with some publicity and then invited me to visit 'the next time you're in LA'. 'Sure, Corbin,' I'd said. 'I'll call you. The next time I'm in LA.'

That night, I sat up late with my laptop and phone to follow things online. Off the back of the Reuters print release we were being picked up all over the place. Digg.com, a chart-ranking user-generated site, was particularly good at spreading the tribal word. As bloggers 'dug' us, we flew up their hugely popular pages. Memberships were flooding into PayPal, and by 11pm we were past the 500 mark. I had a quick chat on the phone with MJ. He seemed pleased without being overawed by the membership sales, he knew this was our only chance of selling really fast. It was all about reaching that 'tipping point' where people would be convinced it was going to sell out and rush to grab their memberships. It was a risky but exciting marketing technique that so far, without any prior research, was working fairly well. I told him to relax and just to make sure all those who had signed up got their welcome email. I eventually dozed off, laptop and phone at my side.

Before I knew it I was awake again with daylight drawing a bright frame around the thick heavy curtains. I flipped my Mac open again and reconnected to the hotel network to find out if we had sold out. We hadn't. I wasn't surprised but I was still a bit disappointed after all the hype. The reality that a new day always brings told me that Imal's prediction that we would need 'more islands' would not come true. To be honest I was relieved, building a community on one island was going to be hard enough.

But the good news was that in less than twenty-four hours we had crossed the 500 marker. It was an achievement. And, with the Reuters TV piece and *USA Today* article to come, I was confident we would have a lot more members over the next week. I checked our web stats, we were averaging 7,000 unique visits to Tribewanted.com a day! That was massive. A hard-nosed salesman might say our conversion rate to paying members should have been a lot higher. But to me, it didn't matter as long as people kept joining. It was a good day's work and although MJ's emails were concerned that it wasn't enough, my attitude was that a couple more days like yesterday and the magic tipping point could be reached. The number I had in my mind was 1,000. Perhaps it was easier for me out on the road, living the real-life adventure. MJ's focus was that it really needed to happen now but I sensed that he might be finding it a bit hard, stuck at home with his laptop. Who wouldn't? We both needed to keep our motivation levels high if we were going to find the energy to make this whole thing work, and this was only the very start of the project after all.

That morning, our last day in New York, Becky and I went to Central Park, followed of course by Simon and his camera. We'd had a banner made up in London, and some flyers, and we decided to do some face-to-face marketing to see if anyone had been watching breakfast TV the day before. It was a hot, sunny day. The park was full of sunbathers, roller-bladers, young people throwing frisbees and American footballs around. Becky and I walked around Sheep's Meadow with our banner and handed out about a hundred flyers.

Becky was great, walking straight up to people with no fear and asking: 'Did you see the tribe on *The Today Show* yesterday?' Her outgoing and flirtatious personality won over almost everyone. And out of the hundred or so people we flyered, at least ten had actually seen the Tribewanted clip the previous morning. A lot of people now knew about Tribewanted. It was a mad thought. Virtually everyone we spoke to, whether they had seen it or not, was genuinely interested and enthusiastic about Tribewanted.

At the airport the next morning, I picked up a copy of *USA Today*. On the inside section of the travel section was the headline 'Tribe Wanted on Fijian Isle', with a large photograph of the two small Bures in a clearing that Tui Mali and his gang had built a few years ago, before they had run out of money. It was a great article, clearly explaining what Tribewanted was all about. We stretched out in our seats, as far as you can in economy. I was knackered, we all were. As the plane banked into the East I closed my eyes. There was still a lot to do, a hell of a lot to do. But I felt that at last we were really on the way. After all, that week, in our own little way, we had broken America.

11
TAU NA LEWA
DECISION TIME

'You know that we're not going to make our target, don't you?' It was the second week of June. I was back in Devon and MJ was in the Wirral, worrying.

We had stated, possibly a little rashly, when the Tribewanted website had first gone online that Vorovoro would open when, and not before, membership sales reached 5,000. In the business plan we said that if it looked like we were not going to hit that within six months of launching (our estimated goodwill period) but had enough cash to secure the lease, build an online community and cover other start-up costs, then we should open the doors of Vorovoro. What we had to remember was that once the lease was paid for we would start to eat into that 'rented time' which we should be using, and more crucially we wouldn't be able to give people their money back if we decided it wasn't going to work. You have to love taking risks at times. The line you tread is so very fine, as we were both about to find out. So, if it looked like 5,000 wasn't going to happen, we would have to work out how and when we were going to open the island. If we got to that point we knew it would be a huge call.

'What are we going to do, Ben?'

'Calm down. What are the latest membership figures?'

'Just over 700 – 702, to be precise. Nowhere near enough, and at this rate it doesn't look like we're going to hit 5,000 by October. We've got to do something.' There was an air of panic in his voice.

'But we've doubled the size of the tribe in a week, we've got a lot of people in America following this and our 700th member is from Finland! I think things are going well. OK, I know you're worried, I know 5,000 is still a long way off. I'll have a think. You too. Let's speak again in a couple of hours.' I put the phone down, then decided to go for a run.

Though it was June, at ten in the morning it was still quite cool, and I started to feel better as I pounded along by the side of the canal, ducking the bridges and swerving to avoid the willows and elders which overhung the banks, much more lush now. So much had happened. Was MJ right that the whole project looked like stalling after we had achieved so much?

As I got into my stride, my thoughts calmed and I stopped thinking about the problems of the company and just concentrated on breathing, regulating my air flow, letting the natural rhythm of the exercise soothe and relax me. There was no one around, quite a contrast from the excitement, glare and noise of New York. As I paused for breath at the halfway stage I considered the success of the recent PR trips – mine to America and MJ's to Australia, which didn't seemed to have made any real impact. I certainly wasn't blaming him. We had no Imal in Australia and it was planned in a bit of a rush, but it was frustrating as, apart from the visit to Vorovoro, it had seemed like a bit of a wasted and expensive journey. There had been a tremendous leap from where we had been before *The Today Show* aired, but the rate of sales had now slowed again and my friend was probably right to be worried. Though there was a lot of coverage still to come from the Reuters interviews, it was clear that it was going to take us a long time to hit our target figure. Soon people who had already signed up were going to be wondering what had happened to their money and when they could start getting involved with their island. I turned for home. I was eager to get back too. As I knew it would, a plan had come to me as I ran. I increased my pace, a more confident smile now taking the place of the tensions of before. I knew what we had to do.

I didn't even wait to have a shower when I got back to my office, I was straight on the phone to MJ. 'Hey, mate. Just been for a run. Feel a lot better.'

'Oh, that's good. Fantastic. Big help.' MJ sounded a little sarcastic.

'No, it's OK. I know what we have to do.'

'What?'

'We announce the island launch. Tribewanted will go live on Vorovoro on 1 September.' There was a long pause.

'But that's less than three months!'

'I know. But it's the right thing to do. The momentum is there, we know we have a success on our hands. If we wait to hit the magic number of 5,000 we're going to alienate the existing members and we'll lose a lot of goodwill as well as the media interest. Five thousand is just a number. We have the cash to get going and as long as people keep joining we'll be OK. We can scale back some of the budgets, but we need to turn this into something real and credible fast, before the doubters set in.'

'There's a shedload we'll have to do.' I could hear that my partner was already on board with the idea. 'I'll need to put it out online. The tribe are going to go crazy. We'll have to start online discussions about what's going to happen. The community is going to have to get organised.'

'So what do you think? Because if you agree there's a hell of a lot we've got to discuss. Can you get down to London in the next few days?'

'I'm on my way.'

So began the next frantic phase of the project. We had an island

and we had a fledgling tribe. We just needed to organise ourselves so that one would be ready for the other in under eleven weeks. It was a tall order, but at least we had a firm date in mind and it helped to clarify our thinking. I liked that. MJ came down with his sister Sara Jane the next day and we talked all day in our corner of the Shine office. We worded the announcement of Tribewanted going live and then posted it on the website.

The response was almost instant and came from members all around the world. Mostly there were questions, though there was also a huge buzz of excitement. But it became obvious that this was going to take a lot of co-ordination. The other issue, of course, was Vorovoro itself. The first chunk of the rent had been paid and the place was ours but we had made no arrangements to accommodate the 'first footers', the initial influx from the eager online group. Where would they sleep? Where would they go to the bathroom? What about water, food and transport? There were as many questions surrounding the practical set-up of the project in real life as there were about the virtual community.

And, as usual, there was no argument between me and MJ about who was going to be the best at dealing with which area. It was clear to both of us where our responsibilities lay. I would go out to Fiji as soon as possible and stay there for the foreseeable future getting ready for the launch date while MJ would stay in the UK and manage the website, the development of the online community and the forum. Dan, as soon as he was free of his other work commitments, Sara Jane and Becky would join me once they had sent out the first load of tribe packs. MJ would manage everything else online, including the logistics of taking the first bookings and advising on travel arrangements and all the million and one other things to do with making sure everyone knew what they were doing and where they were going

I first met Sara Jane at a tribal gathering that night in London and she immediately struck me as a down-to-earth, friendly girl. A bit calmer than her brother, and less dreamy, she still had a thoughtful quality and a maturity that made her seem older than twenty-three.

I also met another important player in the development of the tribe that night. A woman introduced herself to me halfway through the evening saying she headed up a Masters course in Environmental Engineering at University College London and was interested in her students doing a module on Tribewanted, perhaps helping us develop a sustainability plan.

The words sounded like manna from heaven. I made sure to keep the appointment to meet Dr Sarah Bell the following week at UCL to discuss how it would work. It was agreed that the students would look at every aspect of life on Vorovoro and how we could develop our community in the most sustainable way possible. It was like being handed a team of free consultants and I knew it would bring much-needed kudos to our sustainability aims. After all, even with an enthusiastic tribe and a determination to do the right thing, none of us were experts. The only down side of the UCL support was that it wouldn't begin until January 2007. This meant that for the first few months at least, the tribe would have to manage on its own.

At the same time we formed a partnership with Climate Care, who were going to manage the offsetting of all our team flights and island carbon generation (taxis and boats). I met Michael Buick from Climate Care, who was excited about the project and especially the potential proliferation of the green message online. I believed putting money into renewable energy projects to offset our travel emissions was the right thing to do, so we did it.

At the same time, a chap called Jodi Willis called me from a company called MTT Sustain. He told me he loved the idea and would like to help the tribe with its sustainability plans and development. Could he come to Fiji for a couple of weeks near the start of the project to help assess the challenges? I asked how much it was going to cost. His answer was 'nothing.' 'Then, yes,' I said, probably a bit too loudly. 'Book your flight to Fiji, Jodi, it will be awesome to have you there.'

The final green card fell into place with someone I knew through a social entrepreneurs network called Striding Out, people who want to have a positive impact on society as well as make a profit. Helen Lang got in touch to ask if she could help us with the community partnership. Helen was starting up a fair-trade tourism consultancy called Global Sense and wanted to use Tribewanted as a case study for how you can build the right kind of relationship with a local community from scratch. Within a couple of weeks she had delivered a fifty-page 'strategy' to me outlining who the different stakeholders were (Tribewanted, Tui Mali's community, tribe members) and what their roles were. It was pretty full-on and theoretical, but it would be a useful guide and reference for me to get things right in Fiji with the local people from day one. We paid Helen for her work. We weren't always going to get free consultants and besides, she was starting up her own venture so it felt good to help someone else in a small way get their idea off the ground.

Plans for Fiji and the real-world part of the project were starting to fall into place. We were quickly building a committed and talented team to work with the tribe online and on Vorovoro itself. I was feeling really good about the decision that MJ and I had made to set 1 September as the start date. It was well received online by the tribe members and in Fiji, where Ulai said he would start preparations even though we hadn't yet given him a date for the team's arrival. The anticipation was palpable and it felt like we had timed it right. I knew the memberships had to consistently increase and that the business itself was still a fledgling but now there was no turning back. I knew at last that I would be moving to Fiji to build a village on Vorovoro with a tribe.

12
VEIBETAKI NI ILE LASULASU
SCAM ARTISTS

The next week our big plans for Fiji and the island paradise began to fall out of place. Badly out of place. It was 19 June, and I was in the office early checking the Tribewanted forums when I noticed that one of the members had posted a link to something called the 'Jem Report'. All the message said was, 'Check this out.' I clicked on the link and there it was.

I read it with mounting disbelief and anger. The report, written by Jem Matzen, a self-styled 'tech journalist and hardware enthusiast' from the USA, was over 4,500 words long and gave the impression of being a serious piece of journalism. To anyone who didn't know us or what we had achieved, it would have looked well researched and thoughtfully reasoned. And it was cleverly done too. It didn't accuse me or MJ of anything, but he raised a series of red flags that would cause alarm among our members and potential members who did not know us or Tui Mali personally, or about the deal we had signed with the Government of Fiji. The criticisms were pretty simple, but none the less devastating for that. Jem suggested – and he was very cunning in that his words were only suggestions – that the whole thing was a scam.

The report was even entitled 'Is Tribewanted.com a scam?' It insinuated that Tribewanted was just a huge internet hoax to fleece the gullible out of $220 or more. He implied that MJ and I had set the whole thing up to make money and never intended to build a village on an island. After all, he wrote, who in their right minds would part with their money without some firm guarantee? He asked what was being done with the subscriptions we had received so far. Were the Tribewanted owners funding the development of the project with membership money, and if so how could it be returned if we didn't sell enough places? His biggest criticism centred on the target of 5,000. He implied that unless we got our 5,000 members by 1 September, when the island project would begin, then the whole thing had failed and we would run off with the money! He didn't seem to want to consider the possibility that we were going ahead because we had enough cash to do so. But he stopped short of saying Tribewanted was a scam, pointing out explicitly:

> I'm not accusing Tribewanted Ltd or any of its officers of fraud; I'm merely saying that they have created a scenario in which a scam could be easily executed…

Easily executed! I thought of all the work, the effort, the promises. All our supporters, from the tribe members themselves to UCL, STA Travel, Climate Care, and so on. We'd gone pretty public, after all. I thought of Shine TV and wondered how many con artists signed up with a major TV production company. Jem's argument was laughable and it made my blood boil that he hadn't bothered to email or call either Mark or me directly with his questions. Our numbers and emails were on the website, his 'investigation' could easily have discovered that. Why didn't he call us? I also noticed that Jem concluded his report with a list of suggestions for alternative adventure holidays some of which he had 'used himself', encouraging those who felt Tribewanted was a risk to look elsewhere. The last alternative recommendation read as follows:

> If you prefer to plan your own adventure, National Geographic Society magazines like 'National Geographic Traveller' and 'National Geographic Adventure' specialize in finding and documenting interesting travel/vacation/adventure ideas.

Knowing that we had just secured an exclusive for *National Geographic Adventure* to come to Vorovoro to write a feature on Tribewanted, I smiled at the irony that the magazine that he was recommending would be running a story on the people he was doubting.

I had, rather abruptly, discovered the flip side of the internet. The wonderful tool that allowed us to get our message across the world instantly could also and with the same speed transmit doubt, suspicion and fear. Feverishly I started typing notes, answers to all the accusations and suggestions that had been so subtly inferred. I thought of all the ways that we could disprove Jem's claims, but I didn't post them, not yet. I needed to talk to MJ first, at whom Jem appeared to be pointing his 'scam-o-meter' particularly. MJ would know what to do. I called him. He didn't sound good. 'You've seen it then?' I asked him.

'I don't know what to do, Ben. I'm sorry. This isn't good at all. I think we're finished.'

'Finished?' I was incredulous. 'What do you mean? This is all rubbish, we can fight it! I've written most of the answers to this crap already. We'll just post them on the website and that'll be that. Every one will know that this isn't a scam, that we are honest, our intentions are sound and that Tribewanted is a credible operation.'

'It's not as simple as that. You don't understand. This is how the internet works. In a few hours, everyone who Googles Tribewanted or goes onto our forum will read this, anyone who sees any of our publicity online will read this and have serious doubts. No new members will sign up. It's over.'

'Bollocks!' I was losing my temper now, as much with the disintegration of my partner as with the spurious report that had done the damage. 'We'll fight this. It's just words on a blog, it's not exactly printed in a national broadsheet. If a bad message can get round the planet in a flash, so can a good one, and what we're trying to do is right. This guy, whoever he is, is not going to finish us. What he is suggesting is not true!'

'Truth isn't the point, Ben. You're being naive. The internet doesn't work on simple things like truth or falsehood. It works on belief. It's like a bubble. While it exists, it's beautiful. But if somebody sticks a pin in it, it's gone.'

I thought of our island in the South Pacific, of Ulai and his uncle, Tui Mali. I thought of the kava that I had presented to Tui Mali with our word that, if he would allow us, we would bring jobs to his people and the world to his island. This same Chief had turned down other potential investors because he had already given his word to us. I wasn't going to let him, his people or our tribe members down or roll over and let some online blog undo all our good work and dreams. 'OK. I'm going to call Imal.' Concerned as I was about the mental state of my partner, whose instant capitulation I found disturbing, I wasn't going to let this lie. I needed the advice of our hard-hitting PR person in New York and, besides, Jem had mentioned at the beginning of his piece that his curiosity had first been whetted by Imal's refusal to grant him an interview.

It was 7am her time, but I guessed correctly that she would be awake in the city that never sleeps. I explained the situation to her, trying to stay calm.

'Don't worry about it honey, this is bullshit.'

'We have to do something, Imal. People are going to read it and take it seriously. I've written out all the answers, we can publish them on our website and then everyone will know that we're not a scam.'

Imal suddenly sounded quite sharp. 'No. Don't do that, Ben. You'll just get everyone talking more. There's nothing these people like more than getting attention. It'd be like pouring gasoline on a fire. You'll turn it into a major incident.'

I wasn't sure if she was right, but I was prepared to take her advice, at least for a while. 'OK. But why didn't you pass this guy on to me when he got in touch? I would have spoken to him. He could have raised his concerns directly and I would have answered them. Maybe this would never have happened.'

'Listen to me, Ben, and listen good.' She sounded angry. 'Pass what guy on to you? I get an email from some guy called Jem. He doesn't work for any of the news outlets on my list, and believe me my list has every media player in the US. Do you know how many calls I get every day from cranks? Would I be doing my job if I passed on every schmuck who wants to talk to you just because he's seen you on the breakfast show? He doesn't exist. He ain't on the radar. And besides, I was kind of busy getting an exclusive for you with *National Geographic* at the time!' Her tone softened a bit and I was talking again to the old familiar Imal, reassuring and motherly. 'Look, he would have written it anyway. These guys write what they like. There's no control and they don't answer to anyone. Trust me, this is gonna blow over.' I put the phone down still not totally convinced. But for the time being at least I agreed to do nothing.

For the next few days MJ and I anxiously monitored our own website and any others that we thought might have followed up the Jem Report. The report was copied onto numerous blogs and forums and was being dissected and discussed 24-7. People love a conspiracy, they love to see failure as much as success, and this report had created a ripple through the web, that Tribewanted was a scam, that we were crooks. Bloggers were feasting on it. This was not a good time for either of us, but MJ in particular seemed to get very depressed. It was almost as if he took it personally, but I put that down to his being on the receiving end of most of the personal criticism. One site in particular made for grim reading. Digg.com, as a user-generated content site, had been full of favourable comment about us after we had appeared in *USA Today*, but now every posting was full of bile and ill will.

Our magic island was suddenly under serious threat. The only good thing about that time was that it brought MJ and me closer together. There was a vulnerability to him that my own strength responded to and he calmed my anger and my frustration at being unable to fight back. I desperately wanted to pick up the phone and say, 'Hey Jem mate, just thought I could answer some of those pretty big scam-like suggestions you've published on the web.' But I listened to MJ and Imal and tried to focus my anger into working even harder on the project, determined now to prove at least one person very wrong. We worked together answering direct questions from our own members, all of whom were incredibly supportive. Our message was that we were not going to dignify Jem's accusations with a response, and we discouraged tribe members from entering the debate on our behalf. MJ had explained the viral nature of the internet to me a bit more and now we tried to communicate it to our supporters. If the debate was to widen it would generate more hits on more sites, and so the disease would spread. Imal had been right, it would have been like pouring oil onto naked flame. Though it was a hard time, we were encouraged by the confidence shown in us by the tribe, and we gained strength from each other. It was also good to have both our families so closely involved with the project; without Dan and Sara Jane life would have been a lot harder for both of us.

In the office a few days later, MJ was a little more like his normal self again, which was just as well considering the next bombshell that was going to hit us.

My phone rang. I looked at the screen and recognised the number. I nudged MJ. 'Hey, mate, It's Imal! Now what?' MJ stopped what he was doing and listened as I pressed answer, putting the phone on loudspeaker. 'Imal, good to hear from you. What—'

As usual, she cut me off. 'Oh. My. God. Ben, you are not going to believe this.' Imal sounded even more excited than usual, and she was not a calm person.

'What?'

'*Good Morning America*! Only the biggest breakfast show in the States! They want you, they love this. I need you here now.'

'Now?' Somehow, I always sounded sort of dim when Imal charged into my life with one of her outrageous demands.

'Sure now. What, you have a better show you wanna do?'

'No, of course not. This is great. Do you have a date? I'll sort things out here and let you know as soon as possible when I can come.'

She rang off without waiting for the normal familiarities and I looked at MJ. 'Looks like I'm off to New York again.'

It was just what we needed to lift our mood. Since Jem, we had mostly been firefighting. Though we had been busy enough making plans, me to leave the UK for goodness knows how long and MJ for the construction of discussion groups, we still needed some outstanding jolt to get us really buzzing again and, as usual, Imal had done the trick.

I was about to get on the phone to Becky, to tell her to pack her bags again for another trip across the Atlantic when MJ stopped me. He suggested that I take Sara Jane instead. I wasn't at all sure about this, Becky was our TV girl after all, but he was adamant. He felt that his sister, working most of the time from her shared house in Chester, was not getting enough of a handle on the project. A trip with me to New York to take part in a live TV show would really give her a chance to see what Tribewanted was all about, to pick up on some of the excitement. He also suggested that we contact some of the members who had signed up from that part of the world as well and invite them along too. At that point, I didn't want to argue with him. He had a point, after all. Becky had done the previous trip and it was a good way of getting key players more involved. And the idea of getting some real live enthusiastic Tribe members on to American TV would go a long way to dispelling the ugly rumours started by Jem.

In a more buoyant mood than I had been for days, I made my arrangements for a trip that was going to take me away from England for months. I had no real idea of when I would be back, because after we had finished with ABC in New York I would keep going westwards to LA, en route for Fiji. To be honest, it felt really good to be doing something positive again, to have a firm goal ahead of me. There was a lot to be done but I didn't need a lot of clothes for Fiji anyway so packing at least was not a problem. And how much stuff do you need on a tropical island?

I went down to Devon for one night to get my things and say goodbye to Dad and Frances. My mind was clear and I knew what I was doing. The fact that I didn't know exactly how I was going to do it didn't bother me too much. I'd travelled enough and been involved with sufficient DIY projects in strange places to know that sometimes it pays not to make too many detailed plans. And the thought of appearing live on TV in front of an audience of millions was as good a motivation as any.

I looked out over the soft rolling hills of Devon in the midsummer evening light and tried to imagine the contrast with the blues of the ocean and the sharper hills of where I was heading, Vorovoro, half the world away.

Two days later I was back in New York, this time with Sara Jane. In fact, the time we spent together before we went on live TV was really useful and we formed a strong bond that would see us through difficult times in the future. The interview on *Good Morning America*, audience six million, flew by.

'Tribewanted is a unique global project ... the adventure of a lifetime ... MySpace with real space ...' My enthusiasm took over as it always did, and I ceased to be aware of the cameras and the lights and the crowded studio and just talked about everything we had achieved so far and everything we wanted to do in the future in as tight a series of sound bites as I could summon up.

Imal was delighted and rushed off full of congratulations to find her car and the long-suffering Marcus. At nine in the morning it was way too early for champagne but some sort of celebration was absolutely necessary so I took everybody to a diner and bought us all a full American breakfast.

I was just questioning the others about why it is that Yanks feel the need to put syrup on their bacon when I took a call from MJ.

I was still full of adrenalin and delighted to hear from him. 'Hey! How's it going?' There was a long silence, which I was too excited to see as ominous.

'It's not good.'

'What do you mean it's not good? It was awesome!'

'Not *Good Morning America*, Ben. It's Jem. He's written an update, and it's not good. Not good at all.'

I tried to console him, saying it couldn't be that bad and besides we had just been given four minutes live prime-time exposure on one of America's largest TV networks. It didn't seem to help. Before hanging up he told me to get online and read it as soon as possible. He didn't sound good. Sara Jane looked over at me by the bar, aware that something was wrong and sensing her brother might be involved. I didn't have time to talk to her then. I simply sucked it in and walked back to the table to carry on the celebration as if nothing had happened. We spent the next three or four hours in Central Park hanging out with the tribe members and their friends, filming their thoughts with the Shine video diary camera I had been given to take to Fiji. They were a great crowd and for a while I forgot about the problems online and enjoyed the company and sunshine. Mid afternoon it was time to say goodbye. 'See you on Vorovoro, guys!' I said, thanking them for taking the time to come and do the show with us. As soon as Sara Jane and I were alone walking back to the hotel, I told her about the phone call from her brother. Her mood changed, worried about what it meant. I was still hopeful that the TV show would mean plenty of new tribe members, which would bring confidence as well as more funds to the project and blow away whatever online clouds were gathering.

'Update on Tribewanted' was the simple title on the Jem Report homepage. But, as I sat on the bed in the hotel and started to read, I quickly realised why MJ had sounded so depressed on the phone. The opening paragraph read:

Since my first investigative report on Tribewanted Ltd., I have discovered more information that warrants a new article on the subject. This time I'm going to show you some of the history of the Tribewanted founders, Ben Keene and Mark James – who many may know as Mark Bowness – most of which they probably don't want you to find out.

The report then went into an all-out attack on Mark, his work history and the signs that suggested he must be a scam artist. Jem had found an anonymous post on a website forum that didn't suggest but rather stated outright that Mark was a conman who 'has scammed a number of people out of money and services'. And that, because of this, 'Tribewanted should be avoided at all costs or you will end up losing your money through them. Do not pass on your money or trust them at all!' Jem was careful not to agree with the mystery accuser but to simply 'investigate various claims'.

The big concern was over MJ's name. Was he Mark James or was he Mark Bowness? Well, I knew the answer to that conundrum. His name was Mark James Bowness, which is the name that appeared on the records when we registered Tribewanted as a limited company. The reason he was only using two out of his three names for Tribewanted was because he was concerned that his previous involvement in Christian ministries would potentially cause some journalists to report that Tribewanted was a Christian-based project and therefore bring a whole new set of prejudices. MJ had told me all this the day I met him in the pub in Manchester Piccadilly along with everything else about his past, including his recent divorce. At the time I remember wondering whether he would be in a strong enough state emotionally, so close to such a traumatic event, to take on an ambitious project, but MJ had reassured me that it would be good for him to focus on something. MJ was trying to use what had happened in his past as a motivation to do something positive in his life and in the lives of others. I liked that attitude and that's why I backed him. The choice of using one name over the other was neither here nor there for me, it was a personal decision. I never anticipated it would lead to accusations of scam artistry!

Our great internet detective then went into a detailed investigation of all of MJ's working history. I was already aware of it, having gone through it all that same day in Manchester. He had worked for one non-profit organisation which was involved in magazines, books and volunteer programmes. All the other websites Jem was referring to were spin-offs from this one organisation. As a foundation for what MJ wanted to do next in his career it was very clear to me, and it made sense. I had done my own 'investigations' at the time and, although I found MJ's past to be pretty different from mine, I was never concerned that my potential new business partner was a criminal. To be honest I wasn't particularly interested. All I had thought at the time was 'good bloke, great idea, let's go'.

Whichever way you read the report, Jem had it in for MJ, claiming that his past ventures pointed to a pattern that appeared to keep repeating itself. The 'modus operandi', as Jem described it, would start when MJ had a great idea that would 'make him rich and famous while having lots of fun and avoiding actual work'. He would then go on to create a website that would be promoted before asking supporters to donate money. Then, when not enough money materialised the website would disappear off the face of the Earth or internet or wherever. Tribewanted, according to Jem, was 'following this pattern perfectly so far, and currently waits September to determine what will happen. If tradition holds true, tribewanted.com will disappear and members might get some or all of their money back – and they might not.' Still somehow convinced that we needed our 5,000 before 1 September, Jem argued that we would need to sign up a further 4,100 members in forty-nine days.

What he wrote next infuriated me the most. After all his extensive research, Jem wrote of MJ that he had actually come 'to greatly pity him. I have no doubt that Mr James is not a scammer.' Hold on a second, Sherlock! You've just spent the previous dozen or so paragraphs and the first lengthy 'report' outlining all the reasons that point towards Tribewanted being a scam, before quietly slipping in near the bottom of report number two that actually, you have NO doubt that Mark James is not a scammer. What the hell was this guy up to? I even wondered about the timing of this second report, published online the same day we were on *Good Morning America*.

Perhaps I was getting angry because up to this point I hadn't even had a look-in, MJ was getting all the attention! Well, the next paragraph changed that. 'What about Ben Keene?' I couldn't wait to hear what he was going to say about me, this would be brilliant. Jem hyper-linked my site Career Break Café, which was very considerate of him, describing it as a 'partially completed' site with an 'abysmal traffic history'. That hurt. OK, I had been pretty busy, but Career Break Café had no commitments to anybody. It was a website with information and I would come back to it when my tribe-finding and island-building days were over. That was about all he could 'dig up' on me, but he hadn't finished with MJ:

> Perhaps you can find some satisfaction in knowing that I'm convinced that Mark James is more careless and immature than he is malicious and greedy. You might well lose money through Tribewanted, but I doubt that it will be because Mark James (or Ben Keene) plotted to steal it from you.

Sara Jane had been sitting next to me as I'd been laughing and swearing while I read the webpage. She got up and walked quietly over to her bed. She was obviously upset. I looked across at her with real sympathy. 'Hey, what this guy has said is really not nice, especially about your brother, but he's going to desperately need your support right now. You're going home tomorrow and then you should be with him, it's going to be really important. But we can all get through this.'

'I know, it just hurts reading all that crap about my brother, he doesn't deserve that.' Sara's mobile rang. It was her mum, who was obviously very upset too. The tears began to flow on both sides of the Atlantic.

A minute later my mobile rang: MJ. 'I just don't know what to do, Ben. I feel like everything is falling down around me and I really don't want to bring down Tribewanted.'

'You aren't. You won't.' I was less convinced this time round, but there was not much more I could say.

MJ continued: 'There have been hardly any new members signing up since the show this morning and you know why?' He didn't wait for me, 'It's because the Jem Report is right near the top of Google when you search for Tribewanted, just beneath our site. The word "scam" is all over the net, no one is going to join any more. Especially as these anonymous posts keep appearing.'

'Yeah, who is writing them? They're nasty.'

'I have a pretty strong idea that it is someone connected to my ex-wife, which is a real shame, but that's personal, and nothing to do with Tribewanted. But it's bringing Tribewanted down, it's destroying everything.' MJ was obviously extremely upset and confused. I was worried. This online bullying was clearly consuming my business partner and for the first time I was seriously concerned about his strength to get through it. After all, this was going to be a big challenge with potentially quite a bit of confrontation. I was worried that he wasn't up to it. I hoped Sara would get him back to a point where he would be firing on all cylinders again. As for membership sales and PR, I was already forming a plan. I wasn't going to go after Jem. No. The best way to prove the doubters wrong was simply to go and do what they were suggesting we wouldn't.

The next morning we woke early to get to the airport in time for our flights. I gave Sara a reassuring hug after she checked in and told her to stay strong for her brother and for Tribewanted. I was sure she would. Then I turned and left. I took the next flight to LA. I arrived at about 10pm, local time. I had no idea by then what time my own body clock thought it was.

I got in a cab, totally knackered, and gave the driver an address in Hermosa Beach where some friends of my brother's lived. I was hoping for a quiet place to crash and catch up on as much sleep as possible before an interview the next day with a webcaster from Microsoft, but I was not in luck. When I got there there was a full-scale house party going on. Beautiful young Americans, a crammed roof-topped terrace and sound-system, kegs of beer, drinking games, and some nakedness. Normally I would have jumped at the opportunity for a party. That night it was all I could do to grab a cold beer and make polite conversation with whoever was around. 'So what are you doing here, dude?' one laid-back young guy asked me.

'Well, tomorrow I'm spending the afternoon with a guy called Corbin Bernsen. We're doing some interviews together about this island project I'm involved in down in Fiji.' Suddenly the guy seemed to wake up.

'No Way! Corbin from *Major League*, he's a legend. An island in Fiji!' He called over some of his buddies and I was soon surrounded as I explained again what Tribewanted was all about. They loved it! My weariness fell away for a moment and I felt myself getting back some of the energy that the events of the last couple of days, with all the travel and emotional strain, had stripped from me. One guy was so enthused as well as drunk that he opened his laptop, logged onto the network and joined up on the spot. 'This is crazy shit man! I'm doing this! And Corbs, that dude rules.' It was the perfect antidote to the doubt and uncertainty brought on by Jem and his weasel writings. But I felt, when the cops arrived to tell the guys to 'turn the music off or we'll arrest you jerks', that it was time to find a sofa and crash.

The next morning, feeling kind of refreshed, I did the webcast with Microsoft on Hermosa Beach, before heading to Corbin Bernsen's place in Beverley Hills to work through a busy schedule of radio and press interviews which Imal had arranged from New York. Corbin was relaxed, friendly and extremely eloquent. We did about ten interviews together from Corbin's studio, sitting side by side on an enormous leather sofa, and the thing I noticed was that when the interviewer, naturally enough, tried to focus on the star and his roles, Corbin would always deflect them, gently but firmly, back to Tribewanted. Afterwards we had lunch in a diner and then we went back to Corbin's house to do more phone interviews until it was time for me to go to the airport.

As the sunset over Beverly Hills, Corbin cooked steaks on a barbeque while I made a succession of calls, which I had missed through the day. Some of them weren't easy. I had to tell Imal that we just didn't have the money to keep her on for another month. She had done so much for us and I knew we still needed her but she wasn't cheap and bookings had slowed up massively since the Jem Reports. We needed to be a lot more cautious over our spending.

Another was from Becky, who was very worried about all the negative publicity. She didn't even know if she wanted to come to Fiji any more; she had her future career to consider and didn't want to be associated with anything dodgy. Such is the power of the internet. I spent twenty minutes on the phone to her, calling in all my personal store of credibility to convince her that the project was real and it was too soon to give up.

In between calls I looked around me at the idyllic setting of a Hollywood star's private house, and felt guilty that all my friends and colleagues were going through so much grief back in the UK. I felt I was the only one holding it all together, and being in such a beautiful spot didn't help. Despite the warm companionship of Corbin Bernsen and his family I felt very much alone.

Later Corbin drove me to airport, despite my protestations. He was still brimming with enthusiasm and his early training as a carpenter was showing. 'Shelter! Human beings need shelter, Ben! That's the priority for the tribe.' When we got to the airport, he got out of the car and came round and shook my hand and gave me a Hollywood hug. 'Good luck, buddy,' he told me. 'I believe in you.' As he drove away I looked after him, feeling suddenly stronger. Corbin's confidence had helped mine, it had restored some of my own reserves which had been drained over the last few days.

I walked towards the check-in and another journey. I did a video diary at the boarding gate, trying to sum up everything that I was going through; the anger, the fear, the excitement and the determination. When I finally took my seat on the plane, I was feeling a bit more relaxed. Sure, there were troubles ahead but I had something to do, something positive. No matter what the doubters might say, no matter what lies were circulating online, I was going to Vorovoro and, with the help of the tribe, I was going to turn the virtual into real.

II
TARA O PARATAISI
BUILDING PARADISE

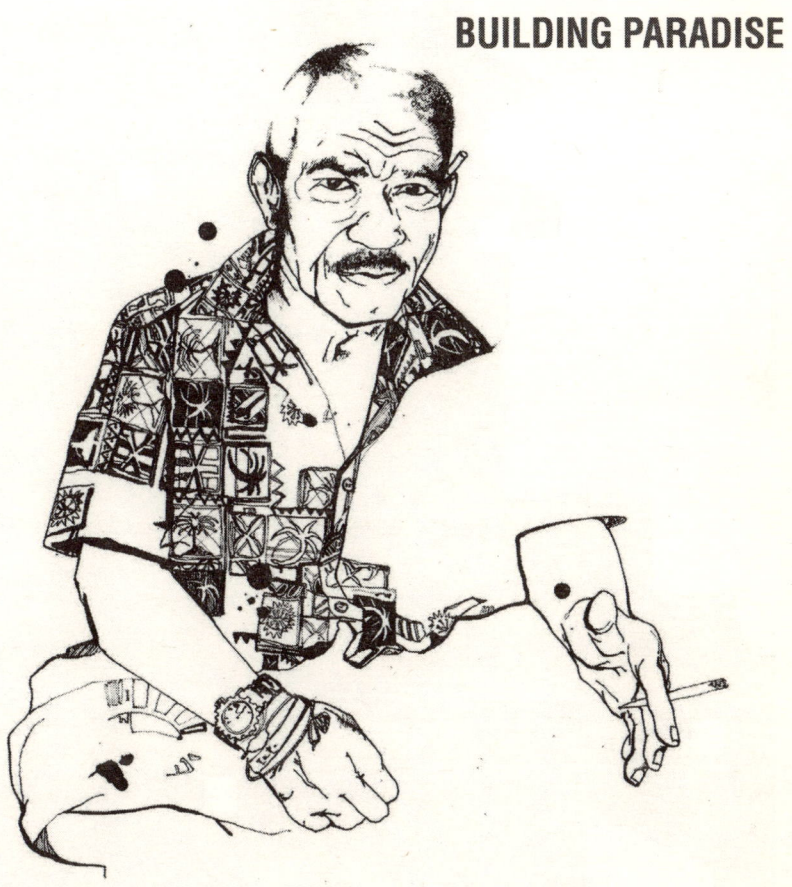

13

SAGAI ME KILAI NA BULA E VITI
FIGURING OUT FIJI TIME

So there I was, six months on and back in Fiji, and this time with a much bigger challenge than simply chatting up a Chief and negotiating a lease on an island. Now, somehow, I had to turn this whole venture from an online debate and the chatter of tribal gatherings into a real-time, working island community in a developing country. I had to do so with a budget that seemed to be shrinking by the day while an increasing number of online sceptics were salivating at thought of Tribewanted failing and saying 'I told you so'. I knew I would need plenty of energy and a lot of focus. I didn't know at this stage just how deep I was going to have to dig. If I had, I might well have got on the next plane home.

But for now I was happy, enjoying the adventure in a country I had been telling the world about for the past few months. And it lived up to its promise – the tropical air, the green mountains, the turquoise sea, the friendly locals. On the surface at least, Fiji really is the Pacific paradise it sells itself as.

I headed to the now familiar Skylodge five minutes from Nadi Airport, checked into a $24 dorm and crashed out for a few hours. I woke at 9am and showered, mentally and physically trying to switch myself quickly to my new time zone. I knew a day couldn't be wasted on something as trivial as jet lag. At 10am, Ulai walked into the lobby where I was sitting with my diary, bang on time. We embraced like old-school mates and within minutes I felt a surge of confidence about what we had to do. Being so focused on the business before I left the UK, then on the PR in New York and Los Angeles and the subsequent scam accusations, I hadn't had the time or energy to consider how we would go about preparing for the arrival of the first footers, which was now less than six weeks away. But with Ulai at my side I felt we would soon have everything planned and then it was just a question of doing it. Simple.

'So Ben, I think we need to move pretty quickly, I know how long things can take in Fiji. We've got just over one month to do what I estimate would normally take six.'

'Really? What do you think is going to take so long? Have you started to list everything?'

'Some of it, but most is just in my head.' Ulai, I would quickly learn, was a bit like me when it came to planning. He would think a lot about it, write some of it down, and then get distracted by something more important. So yes, things would happen but sometimes things got missed. But for the next few weeks it was down to both of us to get things moving. So we did. We got moving.

'OK, here's some coffee,' I said. And without any more small talk I went straight for the jugular: 'What do you think our priorities are and how should we go about getting them sorted?'

'Well, first of all we need to make sure we are a recognised legal entity in this country. The bureaucrats here really can stop you dead in your tracks unless you've dealt with the red tape, and here, Ben, there is enough red tape to decorate a small town for Christmas.

'So we need to register Tribewanted as a company here in Fiji;

we need to get a trade and investment certificate and we need to get the plans for all the building work to the health department for approval before we begin construction. Here are the forms for company registration and trade and investment – start filling them in. I need to confirm our meeting.' And before I could ask him what the meeting was about and who it was with he had walked outside and was on his mobile speaking Fijian.

I filled the forms out and stopped halfway through, thinking about the final part of what Ulai had said, 'health department approval for our building plans'. Building plans! Health department approval! Before we begin construction! Those three phrases scared me. They seemed so foreign, so not me. We were just a bunch of connected travellers who were going to camp out on an island for a bit, weren't we? Surely we didn't need to involve the health department in our architectural musings. What if the tribe decided we weren't going to build anything, that actually camping would be the way forward? Would the health department approve a mini-Glastonbury on Vorovoro? I doubted it.

Ulai returned and sank the rest of his coffee. 'OK Ben, you finished those forms? We're running late.'

'Yeah,' I said, snapping out of my tribal-village visions. 'Let's go.'

In the taxi, Ulai told me we were off to Air Fiji to see if they could offer us a deal for Tribe members, all of whom would need to take the domestic flight from Nadi to Labasa. He reminded me that I had asked him to set up this meeting and one with Sun Air, the other local carrier that ran the route. In the pre-Fiji whirlwind, I had forgotten. At least Ulai hadn't.

Air Fiji's office was upstairs in the main airport terminal and consisted of three or four desks separated by dividers. I wondered if they had more planes than office stations. We met the manager, whose desk had so much paper strewn on it that it looked like it had been snowing A4.

Ulai introduced us: 'Good morning, sir. I am Ulai Baya, representing Tui Mali and Vorovoro, and this is Ben Keene,

Director of Tribewanted. We have come to discuss an airfare deal with you for the soon-to-be visiting tribe members.'

The manager smiled, shook hands limply and started shuffling paper on his desk as though he was looking for something. He soon decided he wasn't and asked about Tribewanted. I explained what we were doing and that there would soon be a lot of members wanting to fly between Nadi and Labasa. The manager said he would write up an offer and email it to us that day. Great. We left and headed round the corner to see if Sun Air could top that. They could. They had an offer on the table of a set price of Fiji $299 return for anyone travelling with Tribewanted. 'I thought you said this country was slow?' I said to Ulai.

'No, it's a good start, Ben. I'm surprised. I think the publicity here has helped.'

'Publicity in Fiji? I haven't seen any.'

'Yes, we were in the *Fiji Times* last month – pretty much everyone in this country reads the *Fiji Times* – so people know already who you are and what Tribewanted is going to do on Vorovoro.' Blimey.

Back at the Skylodge I met the manager of the hostel who agreed to offer Tribe members a free airport pick-up and cheap rates on the dorm rooms - and even a free drink. I hooked up my trusty laptop onto the network in the hostel's far-too-air-conditioned internet room to write my first Fiji blog to the tribe. I had only been in the country twelve hours but already I could tell our eager members about the air and hostel deals and the publicity about Tribewanted in Fiji. I also discovered a distinct advantage to being in Fiji other than the climate. By being a full twelve hours ahead of the UK, and even more ahead of the USA, I would be given a half-day head start on the rest of the world for getting news out. I hoped this would show that even in Fiji things were moving pretty quickly. I wanted to get tribe members excited about what was going to happen on Vorovoro, and if our first day was anything to go by, it would be a cake walk. Oh, the joys of having a good start.

FIGURING OUT FIJI TIME

Ulai and I flew to Labasa the next day and travelled straight to Vorovoro. Our next focus was to look at the leased land in more detail and discuss with Tui Mali and the family what needed to be done before the first tribe members arrived. My mental list had the following on it: water, food, toilets, kitchen, shelter, transport. Of course the list would be a lot longer but we needed to start with the absolute basics.

Tui Mali greeted us at the Malau wharf, just as he had done six months ago, with a big smile. 'Now you have come home for good,' he beamed. And I did feel like we were going home, even if I didn't know for how long yet.

But the minute I was on the water with our Chief and Ulai, the sunshine spreading across the blue ocean like soft butter, I started to slow down. My mental checklisting reined back, my flickering fear of what the next online battle might bring melted into the middle distance and my lungs filled with sea air and warmth. An island home! This time the villagers really were welcoming our little vessel back after a long journey, a six-month rollercoaster around the planet and along the axis and spokes of the world-wide web. I breathed out the intensity and sucked in the adventure.

The best thing about landing on a tropical island, even this one, was that I couldn't actually do that much. I couldn't get on the phones, online, on with it. I had to sit, contemplate, slow down. Every minute seems to last longer, the clock ticks more slowly on Vorovoro. So slowly sometimes that you often don't even notice it. Time disappears as the tide quietly slides down the beach, taking with it any understanding that the world lives by numerical time. Here, within moments of arriving, you forget that kind of time and you discover island time. The sun, the moon and the tides, that's what you plan your life around. The thought of 'doing diaries', as Dad would say, seemed absurd on Vorovoro.

Raijeli and Mila, Tui Mali's nieces and Poasa's daughters, were hanging clothes on the washing line between two coconut trees. They rushed over to say hello, giggling. 'Where's Marika?' Raijeli asked, referring to MJ's Fijian name.

'At home. He is busy looking after the tribe before they come.'

'And when are the tribes coming?' Mila asked.

'In September. Soon', I said. The girls burst into big gasps of laughter, showing off their immaculate teeth and beautiful smiles. 'You see, I told you we would come back, didn't you believe me?'

'Yes, we knew you would come.' Raijeli replied, looking straight at me. For a moment I thought she was going to cry. The thought of the world coming to her quiet little home was close to being overwhelming.

The first thing I did after greeting the family was to string up a brightly coloured hammock I'd bought in Peru six years ago on the veranda in the third house in the village, which was earmarked for the team living on Vorovoro. Two small bedrooms, an open front room and this veranda were to be our home. I swung gently in the breeze.

And that is how it began, my life in paradise. Perfect except for one thing. I couldn't lie in that hammock for long. I couldn't have this all to myself for ever, I had to share it. For a moment, I wished I didn't have to. But just as Tui Mali had promised to share it with MJ and I, so we had promised to share Vorovoro with many more people. People from all over the world were waiting to visit soon. Very soon.

That evening I presented a new sevu-sevu for Tui Mali, thanking him for welcoming me back to Vorovoro and signalling the beginning of the preparations for the arrival of the tribe. We sat together quietly in the dusk as I answered his questions about what had happened since Vorovoro went out to the world. I told him about the television, the newspapers, the magazines, about the questions about his island, about the people that were coming. I told him how his home had created a story that was being told across continents and oceans. His face, lit from below by the dull yellow light of the hurricane lamp, accentuated his wise-Chief lines as they rose and fell and creased and straightened at the thought of his island becoming a global story.

FIGURING OUT FIJI TIME

If you ever have the pleasure of drinking kava with Tui Mali, you will often hear him ask, after the formalities of the sevu-sevu and the greetings are completed and the circle look to their leader for what's next, for a story. No natural development of a conversation as the shells are sunk, not with Tui. He'll simply turn to his audience and, more out of actual nerves of what to say to his new guests than anything else, ask for a story. And of course most people don't have 'a story' to tell a Chief and a circle of new faces. Most people aren't that spontaneous or prepared. I always laugh at those moments as I watch perplexed faces instantly concerned about what would happen if the Chief didn't get his story? A fast expulsion from Vorovoro, or maybe worse? Luckily for the tribe, Tui Mali wasn't like some of his ancestors. Anyway, tonight I was lucky, I was the storyteller and, for this Chief, boy did I have one tale to tell. As the *tanoa*, the large bowl that the kava is served from reached low tide, Tui Mali turned to me after a couple of minutes silence and said, 'So what next?' It was a good question, and one that Ulai, laughing loudly in the kitchen with the women, wasn't there to answer.

'Now we have to start on Vorovoro. We have to work together with the people that come here and the people who live here already and build a new home.' Tui Mali nodded, so I continued. 'Do you agree that the most important thing is water? Because I know, apart from your tank, that there isn't any here?'

'Yes, you will need water. Even though you are surrounded by it, on Vorovoro it is the hardest thing to find.'

Tui was a straight-talking man, spelling things out exactly how they were. I looked up at the clouds gathering in the sky. I turned to the wise one and wondered if he could help.

'Will it rain tonight?' I asked, hoping for some great explanation about island weather patterns and maybe even a hint of prophecy.

'Well, it depends,' he said leaning back and peering into the moonlit heavens. I thought I was going to get the prophecy. 'If the rain is there it will rain, if it is not there it will not rain.' Now, if most people gave that as their answer, it would sound ridiculous, meaningless pap. But when Tui Mali said it, with his masterly intonation and completely unintended contempt for my banal question, it sounded like fruit from the tree of knowledge. I nodded slowly like I had just grasped a complex philosophical concept, and the funny thing was I felt I actually had. Another shell of kava was passed. I clapped, stopped thinking about tribal rain dances and sank the increasingly tasty muddy nectar.

The kava rituals continued the next day as Tui Mali and I took the short journey to Nakawaga village (pronounced 'Nakawanga'), opposite the eastern end of Vorovoro. We were there to meet the Tikina council, the body that represented the whole of Mali, of which Tui Mali was the head. It was a coincidence that they were having one of their sporadic meetings that day. The elders from the four different villages in Mali who held posts on the council were making their way by boat and foot to the village. Tui Mali and I sat on the mat in his house (he has one in each of the four villages) and waited for the tardy councillors to arrive. Two men in sulus walked in one of the doors and sat cross-legged a good twenty feet away from Tui Mali. After a minute, one of the men pulled out some kava roots, placed them in front of him and began talking, his hand resting on the bundle as he did so. A much older man, sitting to Tui Mali's right, opposite me, took the kava, knelt up and began chanting quietly. At one point, all four men joined in an almost song-like call before clapping out a short rhythm. The kava received, it was placed on the mat beside Tui Mali. Silence ensued. I had no idea what was going on but I was ready. I had my notepad, to-do list and, dare I say it, a diary.

After a good minute's silence Tui Mali turned to me and said, 'This kava comes with a message. A different message to the one you brought last night. One of our clan has passed away and they have brought it to me so that I can tell everybody. It means some of the council members will be late.' I nodded and thought about saying something but decided it would be inappropriate.

So I remained quiet as Tui Mali began addressing the growing number of council members that had drifted into the house, a tanoa now at the far end with a younger group forming around it sitting on three sides and behind each other.

An hour and a half later, still cross-legged on the same spot and after another kava presentation and drinking all round, Tui Mali again turned to me and said, 'OK, everyone is here. Now we can begin.' We had arrived just before ten in the morning. It was now after midday, and we were just beginning. For the next ninety minutes – I kept checking my watch as my stomach gurgled – there was a conversation between Tui Mali and four or five key councillors. Occasionally I heard Vorovoro mentioned in the local Mali dialect, this tribe's island-evolved version of the national language. There was no arguing, no talking over each other, everyone who had something to say could do so, and in their own time. It was refreshingly different.

Shortly after 2pm, Tui Mali turned once more to me, smiled wearily and said, 'OK, Ben, it's your turn now.' Four hours earlier, I had been ready with my inspirational 'thank you and pleased to meet you' speech. Now I was shocked out of still-seated and kava induced numbness. My mind had spent most of the last few hours wandering. I think it's the longest I've sat in one place, just thinking. I had to recover quickly.

I knew the council were aware of what was going to happen on Vorovoro, but I sensed that they hadn't, understandably, completely grasped the Tribewanted idea. I wondered how I could communicate it simply and swiftly. I looked up and spotted an A3 poster taped to the wooden wall. I asked Tui Mali if I could use it. One of the boys carefully took the poster from the wall, revealing a much darker rectangle of wood beneath. I looked at Tui Mali, and pointed to the centre of the room, asking if I could move forward. He eagerly beckoned me. So I crawled as close to the centre of the wide circle as possible and signalled for people to move closer so they could see what I was drawing. I flipped the poster over and on the back drew two overlapping circles. In one circle I wrote 'Mali yasuva' and in the other circle I wrote 'internet tribe'. I briefly explained the differences and then I asked the council if anyone knew what was in the middle, where the circles overlapped – what similarity did the two tribes share? Quizzical faces looked down on me, the circle was crowded now. No one knew the answer, or if they did they didn't say it. As I asked the question for the third time I pointed out of the window towards the sea. They followed my arm, and then looked back at the diagram. 'Vorovoro?' one of the boys whispered. 'Vorovoro,' another said. 'Vorovoro,' a third nodded, slapping his neighbouring councillor on the back. I retreated to my place, leaving the tribal Venn diagram on the centre of the mat, not quite sure if it had been the best explanation of what was about to happen on the island next door. But as we all sat and soaked up this idea of a meeting of two very different types of communities on little Vorovoro, they started to laugh and smile and clap. Their English was sketchy but, wise and free-thinking, without ever having been 'online', they got it. They understood and they were excited.

Cross-legged on the floor, we ate a lunch of fish, yams, cassava, taro leaves and *mitti*, the delicious coconut sauce that is poured generously over everything. One of the elders sitting next to me started talking in between finger-fed mouthfuls of fish head. 'If you are going to build a village, first you build a bure. A big one, for everyone.'

'Yes, a great bure in the centre of the village, for the community to meet in,' those listening to him agreed. 'It's good, Ben, a bure is good.'

Finally Tui Mali said, 'So what do you think. Should we build a bure in Vorovoro?' I paused. Rather suddenly the council were proposing the first structure for the tribal village and although I thought there might be more important priorities than a meeting hall, this was obviously a serious proposal. I looked up. Everyone was listening.

'Yes, it's a good idea. If you can provide me with a drawing of what it will look like, I will show the tribe. If they agree, we will build a bure. A big bure.' And that was it. The Tikina council had decided how we should start our village, I hoped the internet tribe would agree. Outside, I took photographs of the assembled council and shook hands with the delegates as if it was the end of some kind of global summit on the lawns outside a historic building. It was.

The next day, Ulai and I did a quick plan of where the tribal settlement might be situated. Beyond the toilets and kitchen, the tribe would work out with us how the village shape would develop. I looked across the long grasses, at the two tired-looking bures that the family had built a few years ago after Tevita had told them they must prepare. But money and support had run out, until now. As the ants climbed up my legs, I wondered if the people who would come here in just over a month would really like this place, would be able to live here. It was, after all, just a clearing in the jungle.

On a small table and bench that had been built under a tree right on the edge of the beach, Ulai and I sat down with our notepads. We were both having a serious sweat, brought about by the heat of the day and the prospects of what lay ahead. We were starting to go round in circles about what we needed to tackle first, our project management skills already being tested. We had to go to Suva to nail the business set-up but, at the same time, to get water, toilets and some kind of shelter organised here we needed to decide what and how. I also knew I wanted to involve the online tribe in as much of the decision-making process as was possible within the short time we had. I pulled out a clean sheet of plain paper and in the middle wrote 1 September 2006. Five weeks.

Ten minutes later the word map we had scribbled onto the blank page looked a total mess. We were in spider-diagram hell. Deciding that that was enough for the afternoon, Ulai rested while I jumped on a boat with Marau, a local fishermen who was visiting Tui Mali and had offered to take me to Lingaulevu, the next village on Mali, to meet with the headmaster of the island's only school. Marau's boat had a forty-horsepower engine, and he showed off all its grunt as we bounced at full speed across the sharp crests around the top of Mali. Being on the water in the sunshine was, I decided, the best way to travel.

The entrance to Lingaulevu – the green land – is between the curving arms of mangroves that open up into a bay, at the far end of which is a stone wall that's the edge of the village. Unlike Nakawaga, the protruding village on the point of Mali, you can't see Lingaulevu until the mangroves allow you. Once you've walked up the stony beach you reach the most vast and ancient of trees that I've ever seen, a giant, knobbly warrior of growth. After greeting the Chief of the village, an elderly and disabled woman with a big, mainly toothless smile and a never-let-go handshake, we walked slowly past the small church, over the stream and up an avenue of coconut palms. It was a spectacular parade that guided you inland, past the small raised wooden bungalows with their corrugated roofs and smoking chimneys, towards the school. At the entrance of the school was a signboard raised across the path that read, 'Welcome to Mali District Primary School' and on the list of 'What to bring to school' I read, amongst other things, 'your toothbrush'. I smiled and walked under the board and along the side of a perfectly green and manicured playing field where I envisioned tribe members coaching and playing all kinds of sports with kids. The school buildings, three of them, were situated at the end of the pitch, beyond the bell and the multicoloured plastic bottles that created a fence between small wooden pillars topped with conch shells. Reusing plastic bottles: sustainability had reached Mali. I wondered if it was for environmental or economic reasons.

Unfortunately, the school had already closed for the day, so I'd missed most of the kids, but a few were still there and I soon found myself kicking an old football around the pitch with a dozen boys and girls. Like children I'd met in the villages in East and West Africa, they were so open and friendly; happy to meet you, happy to play, happy to be alive. It was the first of many happy days that I and lots of tribe members would spend at Mali School.

After the game, I walked back into the village with a couple of the kids clinging to me like they weren't going to let me go. Just like their elderly Chief, I thought. After wandering around the village, greeting everyone I met with a handshake and a 'Bula Sia', I sat down with some of the men and the headmaster of the school. We drunk kava – surprise surprise – and talked about the village and what was going to happen on Vorovoro. I told the headmaster that we, the tribe, would like to help the school in any way we could, with teaching, maybe with books, and possibly with bigger developments. He was very grateful at the prospect and simply said, 'When the tribe come, you make sure you bring them to school.'

'I will,' I promised.

Before I realised it, it was dark, six-thirty, and inside the community hall where we were sitting on the floor drinking, a large crowd was gathering. I was going nowhere. I looked across the room at Marau, my taxi service for the night, and he smiled, waved his hand and said three great words: 'Sega na leqa'. Pronounced 'senga', with a soft 'g', and 'lenqa', again with a soft 'g' even though it's a 'q', it means 'no worries'. No worries, I thought, about time too.

I sank into the kava session. I got the grog on as they say, and forgot that time and the rest of the world existed. Later, I've no idea when, Marau looked at me and flicked his eyes to the right. I nodded and tried to stand up. The combination of the kava and sitting in the same position meant I really did struggle to my feet. I said my goodbyes, big handshakes and 'moces' (mothee), and wandered back down the beach to the boat. The stars were stunning. I lay on my back on the plywood deck as Marau skimmed across the black ocean. It was spectacular. What a way to come home from the pub, in your own private boat with a view of the universe. I was happy, high and heading home, my new Fijian life had truly begun.

14
WILI SIGA KI NA DOLADOLAVI
COUNTDOWN

I took a taxi to Nadi airport just after 4am. I had spent the previous few days with Ulai in Suva registering Tribewanted as a legal operation in Fiji, meeting various useful island-building contacts and enjoying an extremely successful push to get the story in the local media. We even made the front page of the *Fiji Sun* and Vorovoro became a featured slot on Fiji TV news. I was now back at the other end of the main island, Viti Levu, about to welcome my brother Dan and our Tribal TV girl Becky who had flown from London together followed all the way by Shine. This was it then. From the moment they walked through the arrival doors, the camera was watching us and how we reacted to the daily challenges, examining minutely what questions we could answer. I made a conscious decision then and there that I would do my best to ignore the camera and just carry on with the job. I guessed this wouldn't be easy to start with, until we became used to being filmed, but I knew that, whatever this documentary would become, I wanted us to be ourselves, even if it meant looking half asleep in an airport arrivals hall.

Sitting quietly on the vast leather sofas as the soft dawn began to take over from the airport's strip lighting, I also knew that whatever was going to happen from now on, it wasn't just going to be Ulai and me trying to manage things in Fiji. I would have my brother, Becky and soon Sara Jane for support.

I thought back over the last couple of weeks, remembering with a wry smile what had just happened with the voting for the first Chief and the never-ending emails that I kept finding piled up in my inbox every time I logged in at frustratingly slow Fijian internet cafés.

Voting on the online community had only just begun but there was already controversy. Four men had put themselves forward for the position of Chief on Vorovoro in September, each submitting a manifesto and a one-minute Chief-cast, a video about why the tribe should vote for them.

Warren Wright, the man who had foretold that he would be the tribe's first Chief over a pint of lager in Notting Hill in April, lounged in a garden chair as he informed the tribe that he would bring a career of construction skills to Vorovoro as well as a lot of love and harmony. Another idealistic carpenter like Corbin Bernsen – how many of these guys were there?

Doug Holt began his with a running charge at the camera across what looked like a stretch of sand. He welcomed us to his home, a self-built bunker-type house submerged in the sand dunes of the Arizona desert. He showed off his crop of giant watermelons before appearing in black tie (his formal side) only to rip it off to show his Tribewanted T-shirt and a pair of boxer shorts (his tribal side). This was entertaining stuff!

Next up Justin Martindale appeared on the screen in front of a lake wearing a shirt with such an intense combination of bright colours and patterns that, if you stared at it long enough, you would go cross-eyed and see a 3D images. Close your eyes and you could have easily mistaken Justin's Alabama drawl for Tom Hanks's Forrest Gump. 'Well hey there, tribe, I just wanna tell y'all why I'd like to be your Chief on Voooorovoooro.' I wasn't sure Justin was as convincing a leader as the first two applicants, but I looked forward to meeting him on Voooorovoooro.

The fourth and final wannabe first Chief was a chap called Paul Handley. I couldn't find out much about him and guessed that he wouldn't, therefore, be getting many votes.

The Chief-casts submitted, the tribe members went to the polls. It would be an important decision. The result was a convincing victory for our carpenter, Mr Wright (61 per cent). MJ and I had seen his daily involvement in online discussions and apparently he had been to every tribal gathering so far. He had made a lot of friends in a short period of time. Warren's campaign, if that's what it was, was flawless. Apart from his big grin and croaky promises to lead the tribe in the building of a life in paradise, he had managed the campaign single-handedly. His budget? A few pints at tribal gatherings for him and his new friends and the cost of an internet connection. Maybe politicians could learn something from Warren; dedicate time to chatting to your electorate online before going down the pub and buying everyone a beer.

So the tribe had voted in their first Chief. In September, Warren would lead them. This democracy malarkey was easy. Or so I thought.

Shortly after the vote closed, MJ and I received an email from Warren, who was now calling himself by his tribal name 'Poques', after his burgeoning career in online gambling.

Dear Founding Chiefs,

I have spoken to Doug who came second in the September Chief vote and we have agreed how to play this. I am still able to stand for Chief in October whereas Doug can only be Chief in September, he can only be in Fiji for that particular month.

So, with your permission, I would like to stand down as Chief for September and allow Doug to be Chief. I will then put myself forward for Chief in October and the tribe will hopefully re-elect me. Is this OK with you guys? I think it's best for the project and gives Doug, who obviously has a lot to offer the tribe, a chance to lead us.

Looking forward to hearing from you, Poques

I opened MSN messenger on my laptop hoping MJ would be awake. He was.

'What do you think?' I asked. 'This is our first vote and we don't want it becoming controversial. I mean, there's no tribal constitution to decide what we do in these situations.'

'Yep, it's a difficult one. But I think we need to go with Warren, it's up to him really. This is about the tribe working this out as we go along, remember.'

'OK. Well, why don't you have a chat with Warren and ask him to write a news piece to the tribe and I'll give Doug a call.'

Doug and Warren thought it was a good plan and so 'Poques' announced to the people that had just voted him in that he would be standing down as Chief so that Doug, who had come second with 38 per cent of the vote, could be Chief in September. He would then stand again in October. We didn't really know what kind of reaction to expect but it definitely wasn't the tidal wave of anger and complaints that crashed down on our inboxes, the forums and over the phone throughout the next week:

Warren, you can't stand down, we voted you in!

This is outrageous and a breach of the democratic process that we're trying to build, I'm disgusted.

Disgusted! That was pretty heavy. We knew people were really getting into this project, but being disgusted by the outcome of a vote as to who would be our first Chief revealed a collective sense of ownership over the project, at least from a core group of members, that none of us had anticipated. This was only the third vote and the first real opportunity the tribe had had to have their say. They had voted for one thing and the outcome was going to be different. They, or at least some of them, felt betrayed. MJ, Poques, and the team had to do some quick repair work, otherwise we might have had a rebellion on our hands before the first footers even stepped onto the Vorovoro beach! Poques, after some dramas, accepted what the tribe deemed unacceptable and told members he would be their first Chief. Poor Doug in Arizona didn't quite know what was going on. He had come a respectable second and was then elevated to first before being kicked back off the gold medal spot by the man that pulled him up there.

Of course there was nothing malicious in any of this, no discovery of Chief-enhancing drugs or embezzled funds in the pint buying, no sir. It was simply that Poques had misjudged the reaction of the tribe, as had we. While I was a safe distance from the reaction, MJ, Sara Jane, Becky and Dan, along with the Chiefs themselves, were stuck in the middle of dealing with the controversy. It was taking its toll on them, sapping valuable time and energy. MJ, especially, took it personally that people were unhappy. I tried to give him a sense of perspective in that we should expect this from time to time. We were, after all, attempting something fairly different. Like me, he was just determined to make it work.

I spoke with Doug after Poques had been reinstated and suggested the tribe's idea that, as a compromise (Doug had already booked his flights to Fiji by this stage), he be Poques' deputy in September and, like Poques, he would have a free month on Vorovoro in return for helping to lead the tribe. It would, we all knew, be a busy time and the extra support and leadership would be useful. Doug, Poques and, with no resistance this time, the tribe, agreed this was a good solution. Our inboxes all breathed a collective sigh of relief. We had a Chief and a deputy for September at last. I hoped the next vote, about what kind of sanitation system we would have on Vorovoro, wouldn't be quite as controversial, otherwise the pressure on our evolving political system might quickly become too much to bear.

Dan and Becky walked through the automatic doors and into Fiji.

I gave them both a big hug. It was really good to see them and, even after a long flight, they were pretty excited. I thought Becky might actually pass out through a combination of too much adrenalin and not enough sleep. We headed to the Skylodge where I cracked open a couple of beers I had kept on ice in a bowl under the bar for the occasion. 'Welcome to Fiji, Dan, Becks, I hope you're ready for island life,' I said as we clinked bottles.

'We'll do our best, Ben, although I think I'm really going to miss getting on the tube every morning.' He smiled. I think it was a bit of a mad moment for all of us, pausing briefly just like MJ and I had done a few months before in the same place, to realise where we were and what we were about to try and do.

After a day and a night's rest we headed back to the airport to catch our domestic flight to Labasa. At the Sun Air check-in we were told that, apart from my ticket, no one else had reservations. Dan and Becky, and Simon and Nics from Shine, apparently didn't have any seats on the morning flight. I knew how tight time was, that we couldn't afford to miss a day hanging around in an airport, so Simon and I leaned over the check-in counter with the kind of determination you might show on the front row of a rugby scrum before you engage with the opposition. Luckily, that morning Sun Air came up with a solution. In fact, they did better than that: they found a plane, just for us. The eight-seater air taxi was easily the most exclusive mode of transport I had ever taken. We walked out onto the tarmac not quite believing that suddenly we had our own private carrier, and at a fraction of the amount it would usually cost. The pilots were casually looking at a map on the nose of the plane, a bit like people do on the bonnet of their car on the side of a dual carriageway. I shook their hands and looked at the flight path laid out in front of them. Spotting Mali island and then Vorovoro I could see the arc of the flight drop a few kilometres south of our home. I placed my finger on Vorovoro. 'That's where we're going,' I said.

'Vorovoro Island?' one of the pilots replied.

'Io' ['yes' in Fijian, pronounced 'Eeyore', like the donkey from Winnie the Pooh]', I replied. 'Would it be possible to fly over?'

'No, I don't think so. Our path follows this line, you see.'

I smiled politely and squeezed into the back of the cabin. Dan and Becky sat in the row in front, whilst Nics and Simon sat just behind the pilots. These guys are going to get some great shots, I thought. A shame we can't fly over Vorovoro though.

But what a flight it was. The width of the cabin was less than the span of my arms. Outstretched, I could put a hand flat on each side of the plane. You could feel every bump and change in air pressure and the view of the mountains, reefs and islands was spectacular. As we tracked the marked path along the north coast of Vanua Levu, I leaned forward and pointed out Vorovoro on the horizon. I knew any moment we would turn inland to Labasa and Simon would get his best chance of a shot of the island. But we didn't turn, or at least not at the same point as we had the last time. Within a few more seconds, the small craft started to turn, not inland towards Labasa and the airstrip but north-east out towards the sea. They *were* going to fly us over Vorovoro! A nervous anticipation built inside me as I realised that I was now going to get to see the island properly for the first time from the air. I checked the battery on my camera. Full. I was ready to photograph paradise.

The plane headed straight for Vorovoro before arcing to the east and dipping its wings so that it curved around north of the isle, the headland, and completed the 180-degree loop. I started clicking. Click, click, click as this island turned below us like a piece of emerald driftwood in a bright blue lake. Vorovoro was magnificent. Her shape from the air suggested to me that the island was in flight, like a leaping dolphin, or a bird of prey, or even a dragon. Vorovoro definitely had a character that other islands we had flown over hadn't. As we crossed through the direct line of the sun, the island began to reveal its majestic colours. The reef in front of the main beach was much more defined and tempting than I had realised from the land. The beach, at high tide, looked like the perfect break between the turquoise blue of the ocean, the green of the palms and the golden browns and slate-greys of the dry grass and cliffs. It was easy to see the small settlement and where we were shortly planning to build our tribal village. The headland was even more striking from the air, pointing out to the horizon with the same sense of confidence and pride as a sentry defending a remote outpost. I think at one stage I let out a massive 'wooo-yeah' at what we were flying over, realising how incredibly lucky we were to be living on this earthly jewel. It was an emotional moment, and the pilots got a big handshake as we disembarked in Labasa. I knew that it wasn't just an experience for us in that plane, because the forty or so pictures I had taken in perfect weather conditions during a full tide would allow the tribe members online to get even more excited about their home on the other side of the world. I also hoped that the 360-degree full view of the island would add some reality to the online project and show that we hadn't just grabbed a few tropical beach shots and slapped them on a webpage. I hoped it would counter the doubters who didn't think it existed, who thought that we were lying.

As soon as we got to Labasa I made sure we all got online at the town's only internet café. Govinda's, with its Hari Krishna soundtrack, dial-up connection and the best vegetarian Indian food I'd ever tasted, was to become our temporary office over the coming weeks. I posted the island pictures as Becky shared her excitement online:

> It's a cliché of course, but the only way I can describe the last few days is that I feel like I'm in a dream. No doubt it's largely down to jetlag, but there's something about this place which is so enchanting. The people so far have been wonderful to us and so many are aware of what we're doing and in full support of it. No doubt the coolest thing so far was flying in a private plane over Vorovoro and finally seeing it for real. We flew across the country and got to see Vorovoro sprawled out below us in the azure ocean. It was just beautiful. Today I woke up with a funny feeling in my tummy, knowing that at last we would be off to the island that's to be our home from now on. From spectacular

sunrises to private planes, my experiences of Fiji so far are hard to compare. Luckily, I keep getting bitten by mozzies which is reminding me that this is in no way a dream, but truly real!

Sara Jane arrived a week later and, unfortunately for her, didn't get the private jet treatment, but at least she was here and now we could all crack on. We now had three and a half weeks until the first footers arrived and a lot to do. The girls prepared a basic kit for the kitchen and went shopping with Raijeli and Mila and other helpful friends and family who wanted to join in. Sara Jane then worked on menus as well as answering all the emails from members about what they should bring and what it was going to be like.

Becky ran around with a camera documenting the developments for tribal TV and helped with whatever tasks I threw at her.

Dan organised a first aider from the St John's Ambulance to visit Vorovoro and started to write all the risk assessments he had been trained to do for each part of the project. He looked at how safety would work on the boats (which we didn't have yet), in the village (which wasn't built yet), and walking around the island. One night in Govinda's I asked him how it was going.

'To be honest, Ben, it's a bit of a nightmare. There are so many uncertainties. I mean, I've now walked around most of the island and it's a pretty wild place. The rocks are crumbly and slippery, there are a lot of blind spots at the edge of big drops and plenty of holes and caves that, if you're not being careful, you could stumble into. And then there's the beach, the chances of people cutting themselves on the sharp stones and coral as they get on and off boats is high, everyone will definitely need to wear reef shoes. The biggest risk though is probably the falling coconuts. I know that sounds crazy when you've got sharks and deadly sea snakes in the water, but these things are dropping all the time and if you get hit on the head from that height you're pretty much a goner.'

'Any good news, Dan?' I asked, hoping we hadn't taken so

many risks that something was bound to go badly wrong as soon as people started turning up.

'We don't need to worry about people hurting themselves with tools yet, because there aren't any on the island,' he said with guarded optimism.

'Actually, Dan, that might not quite be the case.' I pointed to a large box on the table across the room that Dan had been too busy to notice me bring in.

'Um, that's a chainsaw, ten machetes and two chisel sets,' I admitted cautiously. Dan looked worried. He was so used to the safety-conscious world of outdoor education centres in the UK and Australia that the combination of three weeks, a tight budget and a hazardous island was making him very nervous. The last thing he wanted to hear was that his brother had gone and bought a bloody chainsaw for the tribe to play with. I got him a Coke, gave him a 'good stuff, Dan, keep going' and left him to it.

By now the tribe had voted for their sanitation system. After a great debate on the forums about how best we should manage our own waste on Vorovoro, it had been agreed by 83 per cent of the voting members that a composting toilet system would be the best solution. I remembered what John Wright, our sanitation enthusiast, had read to me from his favourite manual, *Lifting the Lid*, back at the tribal gathering in Woolacombe. 'Aah', he had said, in his stuttering and charming Mr Bean-style, 'in my humble opinion a composting system would be beneficial for numerous reasons for this tribe, and to said island community. One, all solid waste and waste water will not be left in a hole in the ground to pollute. Rather the compost will disappear into the earth for time immemorial. It is vital for our sustainability on Vorovoro that we compost our, how should I say, umm, our crap. Two, we will not need any water for flushing, which is of significant benefit on an island where H_2O is hard to source. Three, it won't take long to build.'

The tribe had followed John Wright, or J-dub, as he had affectionately become known online. They had voted for composting over and above a septic tank system (13 per cent) and simply crapping in the woods (4 per cent), until we came up with a better idea, and 107 members had voted. Now the vote had been passed, I had to make sure we built the damn thing before J-dub, Poques and their tribal mates arrived in twenty-two days. So I was pleased to recall that it wouldn't take long to build. Becky had been doing some great research on composting toilet systems, but it became obvious to me that we wouldn't have the time to source the materials, get them to Vorovoro and find someone who would know how to put it all together in the short time available. So I asked if anyone had built a compost toilet locally.

Tui Mali came up with an answer, as he usually does. He told me to call Chuck. So I called Chuck and asked him if he could help us. Chuck, a Zimbabwean-Australian, had found himself in Fiji building Christian training schools. I went to visit this local legend at the school in the hills where he showed me his work. It was seriously impressive. Aside from the grass-roofed dormitories, coconut oil production plant and vegetable gardens, there were compost toilets. The 'dunnies' were a seated drop onto a 45-degree ramp with a vent at the bottom and a pipe at the back that led to the ceiling. The air would enter via the vent, travel through the chamber up the pipe and out into the sky, drying the waste as it did so. Chuck added sawdust and fire ash to speed up the process and it worked 'pretty good actually'. They also didn't smell all that bad. It was simple and it worked. I paid Chuck for the plans and for a week of his time to come and oversee the building, and off we went to buy the concrete blocks, cement, timber and corrugated sheets we would need to construct our bogs.

For water, Ulai had suggested we buy a large plastic tank and, once it was on the island, fill it from the barge. This would set us up for the first couple of months at least. He introduced me to Henry, a local engineer and friend of Tui Mali's, who was I discovered over some grog the cousin of Justin Marshall, the All Black's scrum half. Anyone who had an All Black in their family must be a good asset to the village build. Ulai and I also visited a local Indian man called Khalid who owned lots of boats. We gave him two weeks to fix and paint up one of his old fishing boats, meaning that if it all went to plan the boat would arrive on Vorovoro three days before the first footers did. We would aim to rent a second boat from one of the Mali villages. He told Ulai and me that the captain came with the boat and that his name was Api. I asked Ulai if this would be OK with Tui Mali as Api was from Kia island and not Mali. Ulai checked. It was fine.

Next on the list was the kitchen. As decisions on kitchen design might take more than a couple of weeks online, we had to go ahead and design our own. I would have preferred every new construction on Vorovoro to have gone through the online community but at this stage it just wasn't feasible. Henry found a 'local boy who can draw', and a day later I was handed a design for a simple box-shaped kitchen.

We went to the hardware store and ordered the materials, bartering more and more as we began to buy in bulk before sending the design along with the compost toilet drawings to the health department for an approval which we really didn't have time to wait for. Finally there was the Great Bure. The online tribe had listened to the local community's proposal and seen the drawings and had, I was relieved to see, voted for it to be built. We had marked out the area on the island, although measurements didn't seem too important. From this stick to that tree stump to that patch of taller grass seemed to be the plan. I didn't have time to question the rustic dimensions. We then listed all the materials we would need and ordered them from the local timber mill and hardware stores. Mangrove wood was cut by Tui Mali's recommended chainsaw specialist, Epeli, who also owned the land where the wood was harvested. We took kava and a payment to Epeli and asked him if he could do the job for us. The old man, who looked as strong as an ox, agreed with the strongest handshake I've ever received and a wide, partially toothless grin. I warmed to him immediately. He was to become a great friend of the tribe. Epeli was very careful as to which mangroves he cut, making sure he wouldn't do any long-term damage to the ecosystem that provided him, and now his Chief's island, with shelter. The bamboo and reeds would be cut and transported at a later date.

Now we just had to work out how to get all the materials we had ordered from Labasa to Vorovoro in time for us to build the kitchen and toilets before 1 September. It was mid August. Ulai and I estimated that the build could be done in two weeks with the team of rugby players he had organised from Mali. That meant we needed to shift the materials on Saturday. The barge would leave Labasa at sunrise, head up the river and out to sea where it would turn east towards Malau and meet us, the materials and twenty boys from Mali. Barge, materials, and boys at the same time in the same place; it was going to be an interesting day.

By 11am, we had the boys and even most of the materials on the end of the jetty, but no sign of the barge. Ulai took the twenty-minute journey into town and an hour later the barge crept round the mangrove lines where the muddy Labasa river meets the Pacific. Four hours later, we had loaded all the blocks, cores (wooden posts), cement, plywood, mangroves, corrugated sheets and our 10,000-litre water tank onto the barge. It took the barge almost three hours to get to Vorovoro. Some of the boys sat on top of the materials while the rest of us travelled ahead in the small fibre punts. Watching the fleet chug across the ocean in the afternoon sunshine, I was relieved to know that on the back of that barge was the beginnings of a village; a village that would become the focal point of the island and the global community following it.

The barge arrived on Vorovoro as the sun dropped into the ocean, and manoeuvred as close as it could to the island without damaging the coral. The boys began unloading all the materials into the water and floating them to the beach.

Soon it got dark, so the older men, Henry and Epeli, lit coconut fronds to act as floodlights, as the rest of us dragged the heavy timber onto the beach. By 9pm, the final blocks were being passed down the human chain at either end of the barge. It had become a race. One group versus the other to see who could pass the concrete blocks from one end of the line to the other, from the barge deck to the beach in the occasionally flame-lit night. I stood there in awe of these men as they chucked concrete blocks to each other shrieking and yelling with delight like they really were just seeing how quickly they could pass the ball to their winger. The barge unloaded at last, we all bathed in the sea before settling down round the kava bowl for the grog and cigarettes I had bought them. As tired as I was, I sat up with the gang and enjoyed the wind-down. It had been an amazing day.

In the few days leading up to the arrival of the first footers, the toilets and kitchen began to take shape. Before any clearing of the land or building took place, however, Tui Mali had ordered that we should bless the land to warn it and Vorovoro's ancestors about the forthcoming noise. Dan recorded the day in his blog:

> The day began at sunrise when we headed to Malau to catch a boat to Vorovoro. Joining us for the journey was our dinner, a healthy plump pig and some locally grown veg. Once we arrived on the island it was clear that there were many people involved in preparing for the festivities, everyone had their job to do and got on with it. Some of the 30+ family members were scraping out fresh coconut flesh, making parcels of vegetables wrapped in leaves, and building the *lovo*. As I was to learn, the lovo ceremony is a traditional part of the Fijian culture and takes place on special occasions. Lovo literally means 'earth oven' and involves a pit being dug and a fire built inside it. Rocks are then heated up in the pit until red hot and then the food added. They cover the pit with leaves and earth and leave it for about 1–2 hours, depending on the size of the feast. It felt really good to show respect to the mountains and trees that are soon to be the tribal village and hopefully this lovo will bring us good luck in the work we're going to do.

I knew getting the toilet and kitchen finished in time was going to be tight but the boys were busting a gut, and that's all we could do. Dan and the lady from the St John's Ambulance ran the first aid course in the village for the team, some of the family and a couple of others that wanted to learn. The Fijian response to how to deal with an unconscious patient was an interesting one. 'Throw them in the sea' was the best answer I heard. But by the end of the course the mixture of traditional first aid and Fijian (non-CPR) style treatments for cuts and stings and illnesses had made for brilliant training. Everyone passed the exam, and it seemed as though the family members – especially Poasa, Raijeli and Mila – had really learnt a lot.

On the final day of the course, we were running through some bandaging exercises when a shout came up from the beach. 'Shark!' We all ran down to the shoreline. Caught in a pool between the coral and the beach at low tide were two white-tipped sharks thrashing around a few feet away from us. I watched the Fijian response as well as the sharks. This was supper as good as on a plate. But no, they just watched as the tide slowly came in and allowed the sharks to swim away. I'd seen them cook shark before on the island but this was obviously not the right way, in their view, to catch the fish. The sighting also reminded me of the very real dangers that faced us on this island: there were sharks in the water just off the beach. And OK, these were only four or five feet long, but I certainly wasn't keen on bumping into them while I was having my morning bath, especially if they were trapped by the coral. Not much we can do about the sharks though, I thought, and anyway the only Fijian I'd met so far who had been 'bitten', had had fish tied around his waist at the time. He'd lost his leg. I'd made a mental note. 'Don't swim in sea with dead fish tied to oneself.'

I was exhausted, but I couldn't sleep. It was 3am on the night of 30 August 2006, and in two days – no, less than that now – the first members of our online tribe were arriving and the experiment would begin. I rolled off my mattress and walked barefoot down to the beach, a few seconds away from the house. I didn't need a torch; the moon was halfway to full and gave easily enough light

TRIBE LIFE

It begins: "First footers" link arms with Mali yavusa 1/1/06.   Credit: Meola Bullard

First sight: the online dream comes to life as Vorovoro slides into view. Credit: Ben Keene

Hidden Dragon: I can't quite believe this 200 acre masterpiece is our new home. Credit: Ben Keene

Life in a lagoon: where we slept, drank, ate, planted, fished, danced and lived.   Credit: Adam Carter

Fijian vision: Epeli and Tui Mali present me with their architectural designs for the Great Bure.   Credit: Ben Keene

Build it and they shall come: The Great Bure rises from the earth, creating jobs for 60 men over 6 weeks. Credit: Ben Keene

Our home: The natural air conditioning of this stunning building keeps you warm at night and cool during the day. Credit: Ben Keene

Meke! James Strawbridge and I perform one of the many mekes Tevita has taught us. Credit: Stuart Kimberley

The Backyard: The Cakalevu reef is the third largest in the world, and only 3 miles north of the beach. Visiting tribe members can do as much or as little as they like on Vorovoro. Credit: Dan Keene

Lovo: A pig is roasted underground with hot rocks in its belly for a chief handover ceremony. Credit: Dan Keene

Back to School: Every tribe member visits Mali Primary and donates a book to the library. The Tribewanted Dream Foundation has already raised funds to provide wiring for the school. Credit: Ben Keene

In the family: Sara Jane sits with villagers at a soli, a local fundraising day. It is impossible not to feel totally welcome by the Mali community.   Credit: Craig Enderby

Raiceli & Kesa: Providing possibly the most infectious laughter you'll ever hear, and on a hourly basis.   Credit: Dan Keene

Kava: This bundle of roots is the enduring currency of these magical islands.   Credit: Ben Keene

Living Legend: Pupu Epeli is a man who brings new meaning to the phrase 'work hard, play hard'. You feel very lucky in life when you meet someone as charasmatic as our pupu.   Credit: James Vlahos

Storm clouds ahead: My fated meeting with the vice president weeks before the coup ousted him from office. Credit: Claire Sweeney

ARMY DEMANDS SHUT DOWN MEDIA FIRMS

FijiSun

Meet the President

Commander takes executive power, appoints PM

Coup! Bainamarama, or Bananaman as the tribe called him, whose coup almost finished us off. Credit: *Fiji Sun*

Tribe Guide: Tevita, the man who foretold the world would come to Vorovoro. *Credit: Poppy Dixon*

Cyclone: The storm took us by complete surprise, and in one violent Sunday afternoon we almost lost everything. *Credit: Ben Keene*

Tanoa Park: A couple of days with a machete, an old fishing net, some driftwood and another boy's dream comes to life as a footy pitch emerges amongst the palms. Credit: Stuart Kimberley

Podcasts from Paradise: Becky interviews Taniela about progress in the village to keep the online tribe up to date with island life. Credit: Ben Keene

Dinner or Endangered species? One of the many areas where we have had to learn about the difference in our cultures. This turtle, you'll be pleased to hear, was safe.   Credit: Dan Keene

"Born in the sea" Captain Api, as good a man as you'll ever meet, and not a bad boat captain either.   Credit: Ben Keene

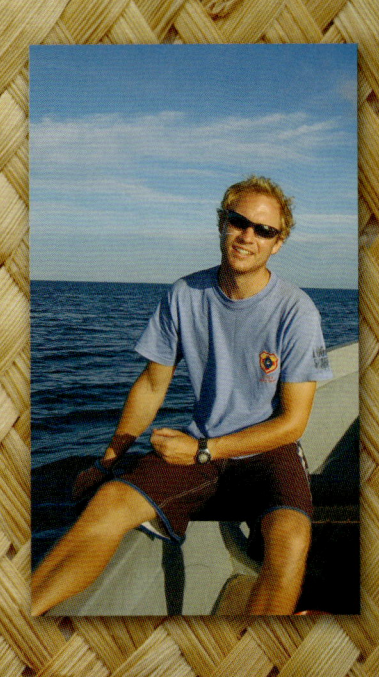

Brother Dan
Credit: Stuart Kimberley

Teach a man to fish: Ryan Garcia, our July chief, is a fine spear fisherman, and together with Marau and Api, dramatically improved our evening meals. Credit: Ben Keene

Trash trap: James leads the sorting of the week's rubbish as we aim to cut our landfill waste dramatically. There's nowhere better to realise the impact your lifestyle has on the world than on an island. Credit: Aaron Wheeler

The Coconut Evolution: With thanks to Ecotricity, Vorovoro leapfrogged the industrial revolution with the installation of a wind turbine and solar panels.

Credit: Nicola Bullard

Tourism, just not as you know it: Kimbo serves Tui Mali on the tribe's first year anniversary. The celebration of Fijian culture by the *kai palagi* 'white people' left visiting Fijians lost for words.

Credit: Anna Kemp

Isa Lei Raina: The inevitable tears that come with every goodbye from Vorovoro. Its one of the hardest places you'll ever have to leave.   Credit: Ben Keene

The backroom boys: MJ and Ulai on our first visit to Vorovoro, March 2006.   Credit: Ben Keene

7/7/07: Doug & Mary Lou tie the knot on the beach wearing traditional Fijian tapa. Four couples have already become engaged through *Tribewanted*.   Credit: Aaron Wheeler

Kavatised: High, happy and home ... despite the struggles, can there be anything better than a life like this? I doubt it.   Credit: Poppy Dixon

to see by. The tide was going out. There was no distant sound of the surf breaking over the outer reef tonight, but the water made gentle popping noises as it forced its way through the intricacies of the coral. Crabs skittered across the sand and I could hear the shrill shrieking of dozens of fruit bats as they swooped between the coconut trees in the hot, still night.

I had a lot on my mind, and I wanted to collect my thoughts. I stared up at the huge dusty arc of the Milky Way above me and imagined it connecting two worlds, light years apart. It seemed to be showing me a way, giving me directions in my own quest to link two different worlds, seemingly separate entities that had never been brought together in this way before. And, in a few hours, the two ends of the arc would meet. Would I, would the island, be ready?

Vorovoro means 'Land of Many Pieces'. A ship once crashed into its rocky headland and splintered. Not a bad place to be shipwrecked I thought. But it certainly felt, that night, that the whole Tribewanted jigsaw puzzle had been tipped out of its box and it was up to me, MJ back in the UK and the rest of the team to put it back together before anyone noticed.

I reviewed the most immediate problems as I strolled down to the headland, kicking through the warm dry sand with my bare feet. Fifteen people would land in Labasa in about thirty-six hours. Two, worryingly, were journalists, one from *USA Today* and the other from *National Geographic*. Heavy hitters, their reactions were vital for the ongoing success of the whole project. Would they like it? Would they be disappointed? What if they or the other 'first footers' got drunk, were cynical, complained, ran around naked? Would the local people like them? Crucially, would Tui Mali, the Chief of the indigenous tribe of the island, my Fijian mentor, like them or would he regret inviting such an influx of Westerners to his unspoiled piece of paradise? Could this be the beginning, as the *Sunday Times* had suggested, of 'a revolution in tourism'? It didn't feel like it to me, not then, alone on the sand. The toilets weren't even finished. Where would people go? I laughed, but quickly stopped myself. It wasn't that funny.

But would they come? Sure, fifteen people would land on the island for the first time on 1 September, and more would follow. But would there be enough? In the first three months of launching Tribewanted.com we had signed up 600 members. In the next two months we'd got 300 more but, since then, with the mystique of the project waning and the online rumour mill proliferating, the rush had slowed dramatically. With just over 900 and the income generated from their membership subscriptions, we had enough to make the first lease payment to the NLTB, build the online community, and begin work on the basic physical and human infrastructure that we would need for the arrival of the first members.

But, as we had invested heavily in all three, money was getting tight. We badly needed the impetus that a successful first week would bring; reassurance to me, to Tui Mali and his people, to the other members of the online tribe and, crucially, to the rest of the watching world. Though this whole project might have seemed like a well-meaning dream to some, to me it was much more than an idealistic adventure. Firstly, it had to bring in enough money to sustain its existence as a business. Secondly, it was mine and MJ's business and we would be held responsible if it didn't succeed. We had things to prove, to ourselves and to others. And if this was to work, there was so much more to be done. I felt like I was back on the icy ridge of Kilimanjaro, my body and mind stretched to its limits. I just needed to take small steps, focus on the next few metres and minutes and we would get there.

As I walked back up the beach in the moonlight, still scuffing at the sand and listening to the crabs scuttling over the rocks, I took a deep breath of the warm tropical night air. How naive were we to think we could just start something like this and expect it to succeed? Had it been wrong of us to stop daydreaming for a moment and try to make it work in both virtual and Pacific island reality? Shouldn't we have done more planning before risking everything and renting an island on the other side of the world? Yes, probably.

But we hadn't, and now the story was about to begin for real; a real-life adventure story, one I found myself at the centre of that night. And now, as much as I craved a few quiet days on Vorovoro to escape the pressure I felt, the real-world part was about to begin. The tribe was coming, and the toilets weren't finished. I needed to sleep.

15
I MATAI NI BUTU VANUA
FIRST FEET 1/9/06

The alarm on my phone snapped me out of sleep. I looked at the clock: 6am. I let my head crash back against the mattress. Was it really time to get up already? We had all been up until the early hours packing our first aid kits and running through the crisis management and emergency evacuation plans that Dan had put together. It would be essential that we all knew what to do should there be an emergency. I looked outside, dark clouds hung ominously overhead. Please don't rain, I thought. The forecast didn't look good. If it was too windy we wouldn't be able to travel to the island, and 1 September 2006, the D-day for the tribe, would have to be postponed and none of us wanted that. I called Tui Mali at home.

'Yadre sia,' I said. 'How is the weather looking with you?'

'I've been up for two hours praying for the sunshine to come to Vorovoro today. I think the weather will be fine.'

'Vinaka. Hopefully we will see you on Vorovoro around midday then.'

I suddenly realised how important this day was for Tui Mali

as well as for Tribewanted. For the first time in the history of his yasuva, he was inviting people from outside his community to come and live on his island. He had taken a different kind of risk to MJ and me, a much bigger one. He would have to answer to his people if it didn't work. His reputation as a Chief in the area and across Fiji depended on the success of this project. The fact that he was up at 4am praying for good weather was a strong signal that he was as keen as I was that it went well.

I sent a text to MJ, 'Tui Mali has brought the sunshine to the *babasiga*, we're off to pick up the tribe, wish us luck.' *Babasiga*, pronounced 'bamba singa', literally means the 'sunny side', and Ulai had told me that the north coast of Vanua Levu was called the babasiga, the sunny side of Fiji. Today I hoped that Tui Mali's prayers would mean that the area lived up to its reputation.

Ajay, a 24-year-old taxi company owner, picked Dan, Becky, Sara and me up and took us to the airport. Ajay had been the most helpful of all the taxi services in Labasa so I had agreed that he would provide the tribe's transport services between the airport, Labasa and Malau where the boats would leave from for Vorovoro. We arrived at Labasa airport, the shed in the field, where the Shine team were already setting up. A handful of the first footers including Warren and Doug, our first Chiefs, had already arrived in Labasa over the previous couple of days and Warren met us that morning to welcome the new arrivals. Sara Jane and Becky were dressed in matching pink and flower-patterned sulu chaba's ('chumbas'); they looked bright, pretty and welcoming. They had organised matching blue sulus for Dan and me with the same flower design as the girls, which we wore with Tribewanted T-shirts. I was kind of getting used to wearing a sulu, even one that had flowers on. The fact that I was being filmed and photographed didn't bother me. I had bigger issues to worry about than whether I looked good in a flowery skirt.

Shortly after 9am, the Sun Air flight appeared on the horizon and descended towards the tarmac. It landed smoothly with a puff of smoke and I watched from the grass verge as it turned at the end of the runway and trundled back to the parking spot in front of the shed. This was it then, I thought, here come the tribe.

We watched from inside the shed as the first footers climbed out of the tiny twenty-seater plane and made their way into the building. The first person I noticed walking across towards us that morning was tall, blonde, buxom and wearing a bright red dress and high heels. I looked at the list of names on the sheet Sara Jane had prepared. It must be Suzy Scarborough, I thought. Suzy, whose tribe name was 'walks with two spirits', was an engineer and a transsexual from the USA. She crossed the room and smothered me in a big cuddle. Suzy was tall and I found myself pretty much in amongst body parts that a few years earlier hadn't existed.

Next, in strode J-dub, our very own compost king, dressed just like he was that day on the beach in Devon – tight cut-off denims, walking boots, T-shirt – only this time he had a wide-brimmed hat. He had a big kiddie smile on his face. 'Bula sia John, great to see you again,' I said. 'How was the flight?'

'Really t-t-t-totally fantastic,' he began. 'The pilot flew us right over Vorovoro itself.'

'Fantastic!' I had called Sun Air the day before to see if this might be possible. I didn't think it would happen but it had, and I knew what it felt like to have seen Vorovoro from the air. No wonder everyone was smiling.

A tribal mêlée formed in the centre of the shed as we greeted our first footers. There was a good mix of young and old in the group. Aside from Warren, Doug, Suzy and J-dub, there was Dixie, a reflexologist; Justin, our friend from Alabama and fellow 'Burning Man' festival-goer with Suzy; Kim, a recruitment consultant from Tyne and Wear; Paul, a marine engineer from Hampshire; Steve, another consultant from London; Becca, a medical student from Nottingham; Travis, a scaffolder from New Zealand; Ryan, a Tool and Dye-maker from California; Raina, a journalism graduate from Maine. Zosia from Jersey, who at 17 was our youngest first footer, completed what I think you can only describe as an eclectic mix.

I didn't have time to really think about how they all might get on with each other; instead, we bundled everyone into the fleet of taxis outside and headed for town. For some reason Ajay's drivers believed it to be a race and, as we sped through the sugar cane fields, I was horrified to see that they were all trying to keep up with each other. At one stage, I watched in disbelief as the car in front of us attempted to overtake a large truck on a bend, its two outside wheels bouncing through the stony dust beyond the road as it did so. My heart was in my mouth. I don't know if it was the cameras or the significance of the occasion that triggered the speeding but I made a point to all the drivers when we got to the hotel in Labasa that we should not be taking risks.

The Grand Eastern Hotel is a symbol of Fiji's colonial past. Sitting on the banks of the muddy river that runs through the centre of town, it has twenty rooms ranging from standard to the presidential suite. For Fiji $120, less than £40, you can pretend to be the president.

The Grand Eastern would be our Labasa oasis, our watering hole, and a meeting point for arriving tribe members. It was safe, clean and quiet, the best place in town to relax between long journeys. That morning, the first footers piled their rucksacks up in the hotel's foyer and quickly settled down to tea and coffee. I grabbed Sara Jane, 'We got everyone?' I asked.

'Yes, everyone is now here, including James from *National Geographic* and the journalist and the videographer from *USA Today*. So far so good.'

I smiled. 'Good stuff. OK, ten minutes,' I called out to Dan. We all sat down in a circle on the grass by the pool and, with the Shine and *USA Today* cameras circling, began our welcome meeting.

'Welcome to Labasa, to Fiji.' I said. 'Today is a big day for Tribewanted as you know, the day Tui Mali opens Vorovoro to the world. Thank you all for making the big trip to get here and supporting the project, we're pretty excited about what lies ahead over the rest of the days, weeks and years. Today is the starting point for something new and, as I know we all hope, something special. There are just a few things we would like to run through before we take you to your new island home.'

I introduced the team, Sara Jane, Dan, Becky and Ulai, who all spoke confidently about who they were and what their role was on the island. Ulai then did a quick cultural introduction on how we should behave on Vorovoro.

'Do take your hat and sunglasses off when you meet somebody. Don't touch people on the head, we believe the head is a sacred part of the body. Do feel free to walk around the village and meet people, but if you go into someone's house please take your shoes off. Don't cross the circle during the kava ceremony. Enjoy the day!'

I was impressed by Ulai's sensitivity to people's tiredness, the hot sun, and how much information they could take on board in one go. He was a great link between the global village and his culture. People enjoyed his company and he quickly latched on to the *USA Today* journalist, who was obviously charmed by this eloquent Fijian.

Meeting over, we piled back into the taxis and headed for Malau, arriving safely at a more sedate pace about twenty minutes later. The only shop in Malau had been decorated with coconut palms and a painted banner which read, 'Welcome Vorovoro Tribe'. After a quick photo call, we all climbed down the low sea wall and onto the boats. The thirteen first footers and Dan would go on the freshly painted and newly delivered fisherman's boat captained by Api. Their rucksacks and Shine would go on a second boat, and the rest of us, including the journalists, piled on the third boat.

The sea was relatively calm, but I could feel a breeze picking up and the tide was turning. We were on time but we needed to get a move on. As the boat carrying the tribe members pulled slowly away from the shore, I was concerned that we had overloaded it. The hull was sitting very low in the water and as the waves began to break against it, I wondered how easy it would be for Api to steer her in the strong current. As the small fleet passed through the gap between Mali and Vorovoro, I could see the small outboard engine fighting the current, surfing forward on the growing swell. 'Come on,' I said to myself quietly, 'stay calm. Keep her steady, Api.' For a few minutes I was pretty scared she might capsize and, the immediate safety of the tribe members aside (at least we had life jackets on the boats), I shuddered at the thought of the event being filmed for the BBC and by *USA Today*. It was completely nerve-wracking. I hoped not all the taxi and boat journeys would be like this – I wouldn't survive. To pass the time, I chatted to the journalists about what was going to happen once we got to the island.

After what seemed like hours, though it had only been forty-five minutes, the first footer's boat crept around Vorovoro's headland and Api could see the finish line. Knowing we'd made it, we sped ahead on our boat to the beach so the cameras could film the landing.

And land they did. Jumping from the side of the boat onto the beach, onto Vorovoro. The first feet from the first tribe members on the first day had made it. I breathed a big sigh of relief. They walked across the sand and greeted Tui Mali, taking their hats off as they did so, under the shade of the trees. It was a great moment and Tui Mali was full of smiles and warmth for each person he met.

Becky and Sara Jane offered sliced watermelon to the new arrivals and we all walked slowly under the trees and into the clearing that was to become this tribe's new home. In the centre of which there was what can only be described as an open shed, erected over night by the local boys. A few posts roofed with corrugated sheeting were beautifully decorated with coconut palms and flowers. At the far end hung a traditional Fijian tapa, a painted cloth, forming a backdrop to the ceremony that would soon take place. On the floor lay several woven mats, with three laid out at the same end as the tapa. To the left of the ceremonial shed was our newly completed kitchen. The boys had finished the job two days previously. Under the expert guidance of Epeli, they had knocked it up quicker than it would take most of us to put together a chest of drawers from Ikea.

On the other side of the open shed, and sitting between the two small old bures that had been built a few years ago when the yasuva had dreamt of a day like this, sat a second shed, this one with raised ply-board flooring. This was where tribe members who hadn't brought tents could hang their hammocks and mosquito nets and bunk down. Since I was last on the island, the boys had even woven a coconut-palm wall around half the shed to provide some privacy. I marvelled at their ability to make something from nothing. The visiting tribe would learn a lot from these people.

The emerging village picture was complete beyond the kitchen where Vorovoro's first skyscraper, as Ulai called it, had been built. The compost toilets were a double storey of concrete blocks and corrugated iron with a steep wooden staircase and hand rail. It won points for functionality if not for aesthetics, although I was sure we could decorate it in time. Above the toilets on the hill you could see the 10,000-litre green water tank which had been filled the previous week by a barge-load of water from Labasa. It hadn't been cheap, costing us about £1,000 to fill the tank (and that was after persuading the government department to knock the tax off), but it was, until the rainy season at least, absolutely necessary. Henry, the local engineer, had fixed piping from the tank down to the back of the kitchen. It was pretty basic but it was all we needed to start and, as I looked around at the first footer's reactions, I think they were pleasantly surprised and relieved at what was already there. So was I.

Ulai came rushing over. 'Ben, we need to start now, the pig is out of the lovo, the boys are ready and so is Tui Mali.' Ulai was obviously agitated, keen to make sure things ran smoothly.

'OK,' I reassured him, 'we'll do the toilet opening quickly and then we can begin the main ceremony.'

I beckoned everyone over to the foot of the toilet staircase and gestured to Poques to take the lead and open the new dunnies. Just as I did so, three Fijian men in yellow hard hats walked down the stairs with hammers and saws in their hands. It was the first time I had seen any of the local guys wear the headgear we had bought for their safety. They were still nailing the seats on as we had arrived on the beach, and had been up most of the night to get the job done. I felt like I was on *Challenge Anneka*, when it looks like the challenge will never be completed on time but then with seconds to spare the building project is somehow miraculously finished and everyone is amazed. I *was* amazed; the boys had done themselves proud. I had no idea what we would have done if they hadn't finished it by this precise moment.

Poques climbed the stairs and declared 'Vorovoro's first, but not last, composting toilets officially open', cutting the toilet paper ribbon as he did so. He invited any willing volunteers to test out the system and so we all watched as Becky and Dixie climbed the stairs, disappeared into the cubicles and a few seconds later reappeared smiling. It was a surreal start to the tribe's island adventure but, it seemed to me, a fitting one. I saw Ulai waving at me. OK, I thought, let's get this ceremony going.

The funny thing about Fijians when it comes to ceremonies is where they all decide to sit. In this instance there must have been well over fifty or sixty people from Mali scattered around the clearing, plus all of the new arrivals. I guessed there were probably a hundred in total now on the island. Ulai gave the signal for people to take their places and the Fijians picked their spots.

But aside from Tui Mali, Poques and I, no one actually sat inside the shed. The first footers sat along one side just under the shade of the roof whilst the rest spread out from the shed's edge all the way back into the trees and down the beach. A group of men dressed in grass skirts, green leaves tied around their arms and feet, coconut oil smeared on their chests and charcoal on their faces and stomachs, sat in a rugby scrum-style formation around the kava bowl, ready to perform. Tui Mali, dressed simply and smartly in a white shirt and formal grey pocketed sulu, sat cross-legged on the centre mat in front of the tapa. To his right on a second mat sat Poques and I. We had each been given a *salusalu* to wear, a loop of straw tassels with brightly coloured woven stitching. We were told to wear it around our shoulders.

The traditional *yaqona* ceremony began with the mixing of the kava. Two boys stood at the back of the seated rugby scrum, each resting a bamboo pole on a shoulder. One now walked slowly forward and knelt some distance from the kava bowl resting the tip of the bamboo on its edge. The man sitting directing behind the bowl removed the grass that decorated it before the carrier then gently tipped the shaft of the pole so that it now pointed slightly downwards. Out of the open hole water trickled over the pounded kava and into the tanoa. The grog mixed, the first bowl was carried the thirty or so feet from where the boys were sitting, to Tui Mali. The man knelt and poured the brown liquid into Tui Mali's cup before moving to one side and clapping slowly three times.

Tui Mali, his hands visibly shaking, raised the crafted coconut shell and drained its contents. I had seen him drink many shells of kava but never before had I seen his hands shake. Was it simply nerves or was there something else going on? In the silence and stillness one hundred people were watching a Chief drink the cup that symbolised a new era for Vorovoro. Poques and I were next. Aware of its significance and of the eyes and cameras watching me, I felt the weight of the moment as I put the shell to my lips. The liquid was cool, bitter and actually pretty strong. The moment I finished it, I relaxed.

After the austere silence of the kava ceremony came the presentation of the pig. Freshly lovo'd that morning and wrapped in leaves, it was laid down at the far end of the shed away from Tui Mali, its roasted snout sticking out from the end of the hand-woven basket. God knows what the first footers were thinking by this stage. A few more ceremonial speeches in Fijian, and then Ulai nodded to me from the back of the crowd. I crawled forward so that I was about fifteen feet in front of Tui Mali, to perform what I knew was probably the most important speech I had ever made in my life. I was to ask Tui Mali in front of his people and our tribe members if he would accept us onto his island and into his community. As far as the people of Mali were concerned, if Tui Mali received the gift I presented on behalf of all our tribe members, it would be more binding than any signature on a legal document.

I knelt forward and looked up at our Chief. In my hands I held a loop of rope on the end of which was tied a tooth of a sperm whale. Known in Fiji as a *tabua* (pronounced 'tambooa'), the sperm whale's tooth carries significant meaning. Kava is the day-to-day symbol for passing messages, asking for favours, or showing respect. A tabua is the next step up and is usually presented to important people at weddings, funerals or on other special occasions. They're not cheap nor are they legal to buy. I had to go digging around for this particular tabua in Labasa market, and as soon as a deal had been agreed and the cameras arrived to film the giant tooth purchase, the seller had suddenly vanished. Eventually, and in a dark enough corner where buyer, seller and friends all felt comfortable, I paid $160 for the smelly tooth on the end of a dirty rope. I had been told that sperm whales are not killed just for their teeth, rather the teeth are taken from them when they are found washed up on the beach. I wondered where and how often that was or whether I was inadvertently supporting whale hunting. Why had they become so significant in Fijian society? I guessed it was a symbol of greatness, reflecting that of the whale. I looked down at the paper that I had slid out from under my knees and began to read out the few lines written on it.

Back on the mat I whispered to Poques, 'OK, your turn, Chief, good luck.' The carpenter from East London, dressed in a sulu, Hawaiian-style shirt, and with the salusalu resting on his shoulders, crawled forward until he was in the same spot that I had just spoken from. He knelt up and began speaking,

'Tui Mali, I come to you as the tribe's first Chief. We are here to work with you and to live in harmony with your people and environment.'

The *USA Today* article would later report that his speech was a 'tad over the top'. But in that moment I thought the sentiment was right. Sure, Poques was full of idealism but that was fine as long as he meant what he was saying, which he did. He spoke sincerely to Tui Mali before presenting a hand-carved wooden picture of Vorovoro, copied from one of the photographs I had taken of the island from the plane the day we flew over it. A talented local artist called Coco, one of compost-toilet designer Chuck's protégés, had crafted it. Tui Mali was surprised and pleased with his present, you could see it in his eyes and enthusiastic handshake with Poques.

Doug, our deputy Chief from Arizona, then crawled forward pushing a pile of books in front of him as he did so. Now in front of the Chief, he put his hand on top of the pile and explained: 'These books, Tui Mali, are from all of us who arrived on Vorovoro today. They are for the children in Mali and we hope that each tribe member who visits Vorovoro will also bring books so that we can help build a library in your school. Vinaka.'

Tui Mali, delighted again at the gift for his community, looked down at the pile of fifteen or so assorted books. Picking one up from the top of the pile he looked at it carefully, frowned slightly and put it to one side before picking up the next book and breaking into a big smile before showing everyone: *Alice in Wonderland*. I squeezed my eyes together to see if I could see which book he had put to one side and almost laughed out loud as I read the title: *Bournemouth Through the Ages: A Black and White Pictorial Guide*. Why did anyone think that was what a Fijian island primary school needed? I guessed it had been grabbed last minute on the way to Vorovoro but I wasn't exactly sure where from.

Tui Mali spoke at length in Fijian to his people before turning to the first footers and saying simply, 'You know, in most of Fiji there is a line in the sand. On one side is Fiji and on the other side are the tourists. On Vorovoro there is no line. On Vorovoro there will be no line. You are welcome home now, Vorovoro is here for you, we hope you enjoy your time here. Vina'a va'alevu.' He smiled at the colourfully dressed first footers, who I am sure by now were struggling, sitting there for what had been an hour or so after long journeys. The good news for them and all of us though was that the ceremony was over, and it was time for *lovo* (lunch) and *meke* (dancing).

Well almost time. Prior to Tui Mali's speech, and during a brief pause in the ceremony, an idea had popped into my head, and I had leaned across and asked him if it would be possible to gather everyone together after the ceremony had finished. 'Sega na leqa,' he said. So now, with the formal proceedings finished, we called everyone present into a circle outside on the grass. I encouraged everyone to put their arms around each other, men, women, children, Europeans, Americans, Fijians, and a Kiwi, all together.

Once as many people had joined the circle as I thought was possible I stepped forward, arms aloft and cried at the top of my voice, 'People of Mali, we are one tribe now!' Luckily for me there was no tumbleweed on Vorovoro that day and everyone seemed to react, as far as I can remember, by clapping and cheering before turning and greeting one another. Handshakes and hugs and backslaps and kisses all round. Why did I do it? Well, because I wanted to give everyone the chance to say hello to each other properly. The ceremony was so formal with only a few of us playing a part, and I guess I just wanted to do something where everyone could join in, even if it only meant standing in a circle and greeting each other. I wanted to celebrate what was, for almost everyone present that day, a pretty important moment.

Next, two lines of women dressed in matching white shirts and blue skirts, each with wreaths of fresh flowers and entwined leaves wrapped around their necks, ankles and wrists, performed a traditional Fijian meke. The men who had served the kava sat in their circle and clapped and chanted as one of them played out a rhythm with two sticks on a *lagi* ('langee'), a hollow wooden log. It was an amazing sound, a deep pulsing rhythmic harmony that rose and fell a note or two every few seconds. It was the first time I had heard this kind of sound and I loved its fast, driving rhythm. The women moved as one as they shuffled their feet to the beat and arched their arms and hands in perfect unison back and forth across their bodies and over their heads. There was even a little girl at the front of one of the lines doing the meke, a big smile stretched across her face.

I looked over at the first footers, some of whom were now on their feet, clapping and cheering along with the rest of the audience. I could see Becky interviewing Justin with the iPod to make a podcast that would go online the next day and I wandered over to hear what he was saying as the meke continued.

It made for interesting listening: 'You know we're so genetically associated with this,' Justin was saying in his strong southern accent.

'What do you mean?' Becky asked, intrigued.

'The simpler times. These people are just as sophisticated as us but they are closer to mother earth, and the skies and the sun and the sea. It fills and swells my heart. It's just amazing to be a part of this and for them to share it with us. Doug tells me that they are less fluent in English than we are. But there is nothing substandard about this whatsoever. If we could just recognise that, and embrace it, and express it, I think human kind would be so much happier, rather than our concrete and etcetera.'

Etcetera! What a brilliant word to describe the rest of the things in our lives which Justin didn't like aside from concrete. I'm sure the tiredness and heat played their part, but there was a lot of emotion that day, and I think people could really feel that they were part of something unique. None of us wanted to get carried away by it all, we hadn't actually done a day's work on the island as a tribe yet, but just getting to this point was an achievement for everyone involved and it felt really good to celebrate that.

The rest of the day passed in a bit of a haze for me as the adrenalin and lack of sleep took their toll. I wandered between people who were enjoying a buffet-style lunch of earth-ovened pig, Fijian vegetables – dalo, cassava and yams – baked and fried fish with mitti, an onion and garlic flavoured coconut sauce, and palusami, a kind of Fijian lasagne served in a coconut shell. Tribe members and the people from the neighbouring island took their plates of food and sat on the grass, on the sand, under the trees and on the logs and ate and chatted. Soon tents started to go up and I watched as several of the children ran from one site to the other helping the *palagi* (white people) set up these strange pop-up canvas homes. On the beach, Raina and Becca were dancing with the children, taking turns to perform 'taki taki', the most famous playground song in the whole of Fiji, which involves plenty of hip shaking. We would all get our turn to do that.

Back in the shed, the kava session was kicking in, as most of the men circled the bowl that pointed to Tui Mali, and passed shell after shell after shell to whoever cared to join. I don't think there was a moment that day or night (I left the tribe members and boys going strong at about 3am) when I didn't see someone drinking or hear the sound of the deep clapping that happens every time a shell is finished. The closest thing I can compare the event to is a wedding. There is that sudden release when the happy couple have tied the knot and it's time to hit the bar, eat, loosen the tie, and chase girls around the garden. I guess in our own kind of way it had been a wedding ceremony as well, uniting our global community with this island and these people. It was definitely a union and one that was full of romance, if not of the traditional kind yet.

As the sun began its descent towards the sea, I checked with Dan that the beers were on ice. I wanted to top the day off for the first footers and I thought a cold one at sunset would do the trick nicely. It worked. The chilled Fiji Bitters were very gratefully received, although the Fijians were more interested in the kava. Those who hadn't seen a Vorovoro sunset before began to drift down to the beach with the beers in their hands and stood in a group, silhouetted, as the brightness of the day disappeared into an orange, pink, yellow and crimson light show over the edge of the earth. The date line wasn't far from where we stood on that beach and I thought about how close we were to the edge of time on that island. To where it all began, and where it all ended.

There aren't many times in life where you can let yourself get lost in a cliché and be so completely and utterly happy about it. But then, on the beach, I knew that the people who had joined the real paradise isle from a virtual one were happy to be labelled dreamers, searching for a better way alongside a traditional tribe. Searching for perfection. Well, there and then we had found it. I didn't know how long it would last but I made sure I banked it in my mind for the times when it wouldn't be quite as perfect.

16
BULA NI YAVUSA
TRIBE LIFE

The realities of community life kicked in about twelve hours later when the pot of scrambled eggs was emptied before half the group had eaten. We had employed three ladies in the kitchen from the start and were working closely with them to make sure everyone would be well fed from day one. It was very much a camping-ground atmosphere where food, plates and washing up bowls were all laid out on one long table. Tribe members took the prepared food from the kitchen to the tables and, until Justin donated a bell to the island, someone shouted when the meal was ready. People then came running, grabbed a portion and left for a log or spot on the beach, to have their grub. Not a huge amount of order existed which is probably why food disappeared so quickly. I'm sure that one or two people were simply not used to living in a community and having due consideration for others. Anyway, there weren't enough scrambled eggs and if the community was going to work it should be able to deal with that challenge. So we scrambled some more eggs.

The first tribal project was the showers, followed by a dining area. Both were initiated by our new Chief, Poques. The carpenter was quickly in his element and barking orders in his late night love-in radio show way: 'Right, James mate, can you get two hammers and two more bits of bamboo? Dixie, you carry on sawing, that's it. Lovely jubbly. Paul, chuck me that bit of rope and hold this ladder, I'm going up. Safe as 'ouses. Gorgeous up here.'

Very much the organiser, Poques quickly marshalled willing members into sweaty action. The Fijian boys took a back seat for a couple of days and watched the palagi have a go. It was the weekend, after all, and they were all recovering from one of the biggest grog sessions in their tribal history so why the rush? Well, despite the close proximity of the ocean, the tribe still had nowhere to wash and nowhere to eat.

The bucket showers were first to be constructed. A path was cut into the bush behind the kitchen and toilets carefully winding between the trees until it reached a rock face, under the shade of some tall breadfruit plants. There, two square wooden platforms were laid onto old shower trays we found in Labasa. From the drain in each tray we ran an elbowed pipe underground and away from the showers to a pit which we filled with sand and rocks so that the greywater could filter away.

I had bought a box of coconut soaps, handmade in Chuck's school, so that we could start as we meant to go on and wash only with biodegradable products that would not damage the island environment. We wouldn't be able to buy coconut soaps for every visiting member but I thought it was a good message to get out there from the beginning. At the four corners of the platform, wooden posts cut from further inland were planted, pulled together and tied with rope above where people would stand. I remember watching as six lads held this very makeshift and shaky ladder and scaffolding as Poques straddled the frame above and attempted to tie the four corner posts together above our heads. Luckily the health and safety officer of Vorovoro was not in sight. Tui Mali was standing next to me at the time. I asked him what he thought about this new type of bathroom. 'It won't last,' he said straightforwardly and quietly to me. 'When the posts dry out they will pull back and break and the bucket will fall on someone.'

I thought about raising Tui Mali's concern with Poques and the gang but he didn't seem overly worried. There was a sense in those early days that we would work it out as we went along and give everything a go. Finally, the steel bucket was suspended on a rope and pulley system from the centre of the four posts. In the base of the bucket was a drilled hole with a shower-head attached. Walls were built around each platform with wooden posts and coconut palms to protect people's decency. I later heard that the bucket *had* fallen onto someone's head, although not because the wooden posts had dried and snapped. Not just anyone's head, mind you. The bucket fell on James from *National Geographic*. Route one way to poor publicity, I thought.

I tried the new tribal bucket showers early next morning. Coconut soap in hand, I filled the other bucket from the tap by the kitchen, walked down the shaded path, stepped onto the first platform behind the coconut curtain and lowered the overhead bucket down via the pulley. I then hooked the rope onto a nail that had been banged into one of the posts and poured the water in, only halfway up, mind. Holes had been drilled to make sure people would not use too much water. I then hoisted the filled bucket until it was above my head, wound it round the nail and looped it so it was safe before twisting the nozzle above my head. It was, I have to admit, the best shower I had had since I'd arrived on Vorovoro. OK, it wasn't exactly a power blast massaging my neck and the water wasn't warm, but I was outside with a view of coconut leaves, a lush green canopy and beyond it the brightness of the coming day. I washed myself guiltlessly with the coconut soap and sang out of tune. This is how all days should start, I thought.

Next up was the dining area. Poques had ordered in a decent amount of roughly sawn four by two, which had been collected from the local saw mill and which he was now starting to cut up into table-wide pieces. His idea was to build a pentagonal dining experience near to the beach that would symbolise the soon-to-be 5,000 members. He planted five of the cylindrical core posts to form the pentagon, each post representing one-fifth of the tribe, measuring the distance between each one precisely. Members would carve their names into each post as a lasting reminder of who had been to Vorovoro. Between the posts we would build long wooden tables with benches on either side. Each table would be able to seat twenty, so that we would eventually be able to have 100 people seated for dinner in a perfect pentagon shape on the beach at sunset.

I didn't want to point it out to Poques that we were still some way short of 5,000 and that one table would probably have been more than enough. We compromised on two. I was fast learning the art of diplomacy with our first Chief. He and his helpers had built the first table right in the middle of the path between the two villages. I could see why Poques wanted the pentagon to work and why it had to be there, but at the same time it did seem a little silly to have our main dining table slap in the middle of what was currently the only path on the island. It was like building an airport terminal in the middle of a runway. I think some of the onlooking Fijians probably agreed. I noticed Doug, Poque's deputy, also watching a lot and not saying much. I could see Doug had different thoughts to his Chief as to how things should be done; he had built his own house in the desert, after all. But he wasn't confrontational about it.

Doug liked to keep himself to himself. He camped down the beach, went for early morning swims, naked apparently, spent lots of time making friends with the local guys and was now building a recycling unit with them off the back of the kitchen. Within days, he and Epeli, the chainsaw godfather, were good buddies. Like Doug, I didn't want to get too much in the way of Poques, especially at this early stage. The end result, apart from its positioning, was a brilliant piece of craftsmanship. A great long table that comfortably sat twenty and would provide a central focus for eating on the island for all that visited it.

I spent almost all of those first few days of tribe life running backwards and forwards on the boat to Malau and then by car to Labasa. There was food to buy, materials to be ordered, paid for and collected, beers to be bought, online blogs to write, cash to be withdrawn, emails to answer and phone calls to make. I felt like I was leading a double life. On the island I was part of the fast-emerging new community of builders and decorators, of kava sessions and songs and campfires and warm beer under wild starry skies. But in town I was a frantic mess of lists and headaches and overflowing inboxes and not enough money.

Very quickly, with all the big spending of the first few weeks in Fiji and no real income at all, we were heading for a financial dead end. The press release sent out on 1 September had been picked up by a few sites but hadn't had the same impact as our initial media pitch back in April. None of the doubters online seemed to react either. Perhaps it was still too early to tell for anyone, including me, whether it was actually working. I did know, however, that, with *USA Today* leaving the island shortly, we would have a write-up within a couple of weeks and *The Guardian* was also planning to cover the story, although nobody knew when. James from *National Geographic Adventure* was on the island for two weeks but the feature would not be published until the end of the year at the earliest. I was getting nervous and MJ didn't have that much to say that could reassure me. He was still struggling with the personal attacks online and spent most of his time keeping tribe members in the loop with island life and answering questions. Communication was difficult. But all was certainly not lost at this stage, it was just finely balanced, I told myself. I knew it would just require a lot more effort.

Coming back from town in those early days was the best part, leaving one life to return to the one I preferred; the journey across the sea giving me just enough time to forget about the problems of the first. I remember one afternoon in that first week in particular. The sun was already setting and the rich light smothered the surface of the ocean like liquid gold. As Api and I pulled up towards the shore, I could see all these figures walking out from beneath the trees and down the beach to help unload the sacks of rice and cases of beer off the boat and head back into the village. The fire was already lit and nearby I could see Becky dancing with the fire-poi she had bought from home, carving perfect rhythmical arcs. Further down the beach, four silhouettes were throwing a frisbee, two on the sand and two up to their waists in water. I could smell garlic and fish cooking from the kitchen. Tribe life was happening. I had to pinch myself.

One important part of the first week was to talk to the first footers about safety on Vorovoro. It was a new place for all of us and one that we knew had lots of potential hazards. Dan was going to lead the meeting and I had told him to remember that, although we had to be professional about this, he wasn't in an outdoor training centre any more. My brother's style of leadership is similar to that of a good teacher: ask the questions and then encourage people to give the answers rather than simply telling them. So, under the shade of the shed where we had held the opening ceremony and kava marathon, the tribe all sat in a circle while Dan asked, 'What do you think are the biggest risks on Vorovoro?'

'Fire,' was the first answer. Then the sea, then the rocky, slippery and steep terrain, then snakes and sharks, before finally someone, quite wisely I thought, said, 'each other.' There was laughter. 'Anything else?'

'Ahhmmm, I p-p-personally would be pretty scared about f-f-falling coconuts,' J-dub piped up.

'Yes! Coconuts!' Dan said, like someone in the class had finally given the answer he was looking for. 'So how do we stop ourselves from getting hit by coconuts?' It was at this point that I could see one or two of the members look at each other as if to say, 'Come on, are you serious? Are we actually going to talk about how to avoid falling coconuts?'

J-dub, however, was playing teacher's pet. 'I for one won't be sitting under any of the numerous number of Vorovoro's coconut tree population.' Good, John. Gold star.

And so it went on. There were suggestions that, for the steep and slippery walks, we should build wooden staircases and hand rails, that we should have a book for people signing in and out whenever they left the village, and that we should even think about putting nets under the most dangerous coconut trees. I could see Doug rolling his eyes; I wasn't far behind him. There were no Fijians around at that moment. I wished there had been, because it would have been great to ask them some of the questions we were asking ourselves.

Dan managed the meeting expertly and took seriously all the suggestions that were put forward. It was going to be interesting to see how safe the island would become. I didn't even allow myself the discomfort of thinking too much about what could go wrong. All I could think about was the man who had lost his leg to a shark because he had fish tied around his waist. I decided what my safety priorities were, I'd take a risk on sitting under coconut trees but I wouldn't wear a belt of dead fish when I went snorkelling. Not yet.

Not only were we continually baking under a blanket of blue sky but it was also a full moon. It made for tricky tidal management, however, as coming and going from the island at low tide was not easy. This quickly prompted a discussion about the construction of a jetty to avoid damaging the coral. Each evening we would sit on the beach and watch the moon rise over the headland and arc over our island. Each night it became brighter and more spectacular, drawing a bigger crowd.

We worked out that the following night would be full moon and so it was universally agreed that we should have a party to celebrate the great night light. By the time I returned from town with bottles of Bounty, the lethal local rum, and the day's supplies, the tribe were already preparing for the party. Through the trees, I could see what looked like a new tribe member, someone I didn't recognise. I was wrong. It was Suzy dressed up as a pirate, something she liked to do sometimes. By day she was very much involved with the projects, passing on her engineering knowledge to J-dub as he fixed coconuts as counter-weights to the toilet doors. But by night Suzy liked to dress up, even on a tropical island, and tonight, wig 'n' all, she was a pirate. Fair enough, I thought, why not? I have to say I was a little more shocked when she turned up for dinner on another evening in full leathers, fishnets and stilettos. God knows what the Fijians thought. But it happened and, apart from a few chuckles, people, Fijian or otherwise, accepted it and got on with island living.

So, with Suzy the pirate, plenty of rum and a full moon rising, we all gathered around the long table for the night's main event. Divided by five roughly sawn lengths of wood, the table had been split into narrow tracks, and Dan, head torch on, stood at the far end of the table and began building the atmosphere:

'Tonight, ladies and gentlemen, I welcome you to Vorovoro's first full-moon crab race.' Cheers. 'These crabs are serious, this is like the hundred-metre dash for them, OK? And they are psyched. Now, as with all good stadiums we have stands. We have crab stand A,' more cheers, 'and crab stand B,' massive cheers. 'We're gonna do a bit of a run before we get to the fun.'

Who is this guy, I thought, as I watched my brother as the entertaining compere of the island doing the biggest build-up to the shortest race in history. It was hilarious. He was unstoppable. 'These are the crabs we're going to be racing tonight. As you can see they've got claws, be aware of health and safety, and don't put them anywhere near your face.'

And so it eventually began. Mickey Mouse beat Alien, before Predator started eating Mickey and Borat escaped. Poques provided the poker chips for the betting and everyone got involved. You will pleased to hear that all the crabs survived and, although Api was keen to cook them to celebrate, we persuaded him that they had earned their freedom and should be released back on to the beach.

I'd had a lot of rum by this stage, and as soon as I heard the opening bars of Gnarls Barkley's 'Crazy' on J-dub's solar-charged iPod speaker system I was off. I left the crabs and their racing and started strutting around the grass, doing what I imagined at the time was an impressive solo disco performance. John Travolta would have struggled to keep up I thought, as I beckoned to Va, our fantastic head chef, to join me on the dance floor. Little did I notice until I'd thrown a few more shapes that the attention and cameras and lights had switched from the crab-racing stadium to me. Luckily I wasn't on my own for long and soon Justin from Alabama was rotating his tie-died pants in circles around me. I was letting go, I could feel it and I didn't care who was watching. But that was enough, I decided, as I twisted my way out of the spotlights and down towards the beach.

I walked across the rocks beyond the sand and down to the water; I needed to cool off. I passed Raina, the American graduate, and thought it would be impolite if I didn't invite the girl in the bikini on the beach in front of me for a swim. 'Sure', she said. I found the drop-off to the sand and we dived in. The water was refreshing and I immediately felt more awake as it slapped me out of the dizziness brought on by the drunken dancing. Raina and I swam out further before stopping to talk as we trod water. Blonde and athletic, she was attractive, especially in the sea at night in the light of a full moon. I'm sure we talked for ages and sorted out a lot of life's big questions but my memory was dented somewhat by her body as it wrapped itself around me. Still treading water, we spun around, drifted, sunk, came to the surface, laughed. The hedonism of the night and of that place and of the girl in the sea with me was the perfect end to the start of new tribal life on Vorovoro. I even thought I could see phosphorescence sprinkled around us in the water, but that could have been the moonlight or the rum. Whatever it was, I was a lucky boy, and I knew it.

17
YAVU NA SAULA NI KORO
FIRE

The reef fish sped around in me in a giant knotted ball, turning in precise unison this way and that. How did they know how to do that, I wondered? I signalled to Dan, asking what his depth gauge was at. Not much, it was time to ascend from our eighteen-metre dive. It was only Dan's third dive, but already he was a natural. I had learnt to dive in Kenya and, after seeing turtles and sharks on one of my first scuba journeys, I knew that, whenever I had a chance, I would dive.

Dan and I were taking thirty-six hours off Vorovoro in Savusavu, a small diving and sailing town on the southern side of Vanua Levu, Fiji's second largest island. I had told Dan I really needed a day off. I'd been flat out for the last two months in Fiji and I was shattered. I needed to pause. I wanted to spend time off the island with my brother as well, to have a decent chat about how he thought things were going. We agreed that it would be OK to leave the girls, Becky and Sara Jane, on the island to run things while we were away and, anyway, Poques and Doug were there, older men with a lot of experience between them. Besides, we were only a phone call and a three-hour drive away, what could possible go wrong?

Dan and I had changed and were about to walk down the hill to the seaview bar for food and some cold beer, it was Saturday lunchtime, when my phone rang. 'It's the island. It's on fire!'

'Hang on, Sara Jane, what do you mean it's on fire? Calm down a second, tell me exactly what's going on.' Dan stopped and looked at me as I listened.

'I'm on the boat, we can't get onto the beach because the tide is too low, and I'm looking at the middle peak of the island and it's on fire, the whole thing is smoking. I can see a lot of flames on the far ridge.' Crap. Crap. Double crap. I wasn't going to get a cold beer after all. And the island was on fire. And Dan and I weren't there. We were a long taxi ride and boat journey away.

'OK, listen. Dan and I are on our way. Stay calm and find out as much about the fire as you can. The most important thing is to get onto the beach and do a head count of everyone. Call me back as soon as you have done this with an update of how big the fire is and how far the Fijians think it will spread.'

I hung up and called a taxi. Dan had already run back up the hill to grab our things from the dorm we had been staying in. Within ten minutes we were speeding past the seaview bar and back towards the hills and an island on fire. The reality of the situation quickly sank in as we sat in the back of the car and started to discuss all possible scenarios as we began our first bit of crisis management. We had no idea how bad the fire was, or how much of a threat it posed to the villages, but Sara Jane's comment that she could 'see a lot flames on the far ridge' didn't sound good. The far ridge of the middle peak of Vorovoro was some distance from where she would have been waiting on the boat. If she could clearly see flames, they were not small; this was a serious fire. I had two immediate concerns. The first was that fire would spread across the grasses covering most of the island at the end of the dry season and destroy our newly discovered paradise. Secondly, there was the danger that tribe members would tackle the blaze and that there would be a serious accident.

I knew any major incident now would extinguish our dream in a flash. I turned to Dan for a plan that would keep it alive.

'OK, we'll be back in Labasa by about 3pm. That means we can be at Malau by half past. I'll call the fire department in Labasa and put them on stand-by. After we've got a head count of the tribe members, we need to be able to advise everyone on what to do. Once we have a full assessment of how bad the fire is, we can decide whether we need to evacuate the island or not.'

Evacuate! We couldn't evacuate the island, we'd only been there a week! But my brother was right of course, If it was a large fire that was going to sweep through the villages, then it would be better to have everyone off the island. I didn't like the idea of trying to organise an evacuation but I accepted it might have to happen.

Sara Jane called. 'OK, I'm on the island now and the fire is just...'

Shit. The line cut out. This was going to be frustrating. I tried calling her back. No luck. I just hoped that the two Chiefs, Poques and Doug, and the two girls, Becky and Sara Jane, were calmly co-ordinating a sensible response. Thinking for a moment about their different personalities and how they might react under pressure, I suddenly realised that they might not be working all that well together. I leant forward: 'Hi, yes, we're in a bit of a rush actually. Would you mind driving a little faster to Labasa?'

'No problem,' an Indian-looking Schumacher said as he tried to accelerate from third into second up a steep potholed hill.

My phone rang with Becky's name flashing. 'Becks, how are you, what's the situation?'

She was out of breath. 'I'm now up on the hill fighting the fire as it spreads towards the valley. Everyone is OK. We're just trying to stop it.'

'Becky, listen to me. No one should be fighting the fire. It's dangerous, if the wind picks up it could spread fast and you could easily get trapped out there. I need you to tell everyone to return to the beach, do a head count, make sure the villages are safe and then call me back.'

'OK, but I don't think some of the members are going to listen to me.'

'Just tell them that we are asking them not to fight the fire because we are concerned that it could get more out of control. If they refuse, leave it. But you make sure you get back to the village and round up as many people as you can. Find Sara Jane and call me back in ten minutes with an update.'

'OK, I'll do that.'

'Before you go, Becks, just tell me how big the fire is now and what the family are doing?'

'From where I am it looks pretty big, it's spread across the whole of the main hillside and it's coming down into the valley. It's moving fast. The family are making fire breaks behind the village.'

'OK, thanks Becks, call me back and take care.' I looked at Dan who was noting down the time of each conversation so we had a record of what was happening and when, at least from our perspective. 'What do you think, Dan?' I asked. 'It sounds like it could burn all the way through the island.'

'I'll call the Fire Service now and see what they say. You should call Tui Mali.'

We made our calls. Tui Mali was already on his way to Vorovoro I was told, that was good. The 'fire service' said they would only come out – shipping a barge of water and a pump – if the fire was threatening the villages. My brother told them that it was threatening the villages but they told him that the village actually needed to be on fire for them to respond. This basically meant they didn't provide a service to the islands because once a village was on fire and a barge was mobilised it would be too late. So we were on our own.

Becky called back: 'They won't listen to me. Warren is screaming at me, he's lost the plot. He's saying we can't desert the family in their hour of need and that we promised them we would stand by them. It's a nightmare. I don't know what to do.'

'Becky, it's fine. If Warren or anyone else doesn't want to listen to us, that's their decision, as long as they are clear what we are advising. No point in getting into arguments. Tell them and leave.'

For the next hour we were out of mobile signal range and all we could do was sit and wonder. As we came over the mountain range I knew we would get a glimpse of Vorovoro in the distance. If the fire was bad I would expect to see smoke. We came round the corner and what normally was a view that would make me smile proudly now sent me into momentary shock. Far beneath us and out to sea, set against a deep and cloudless blue sky, was a long plume of black smoke that stretched from the brightness of the sun all the way down, narrower and darker until it hit land. Until it hit Vorovoro. Out of the centre of the familiar three bumps this black tunnel shot vertically up into the sky, dwarfing the tiny island from where it started. I wanted to cry. I was short of breath. If there ever was a symbol of a dream being smashed this was it, our island paradise was going up in flames.

I snapped out of my despondency as the phone rang: Sara Jane. 'OK, I think we've got everyone now apart from those that have refused. We've just met Tui Mali and he seems calm. The fire is still spreading but the Fijians don't seem too bothered, they're even making tea!'

'Good news, Sara. OK, here's the plan. If the fire is not under control and is still spreading at 3.30pm then we are going to evacuate the island. These are the reasons that you and Becky are going to give to the tribe members. Firstly, the personal safety of tribe members if the fire spreads during the night whilst people are sleeping. Secondly, to give tribe members the chance to rest until the fire is completely put out – it's been a stressful day. Tell Tui Mali first and say to him that if we can help the family in any way we will.'

'OK, that sounds fine. I think we're going to struggle to get everyone on the boat though, there are some real angry people here and they don't want to listen to us.'

'That's fine. Just tell them the reasons. What is the family saying?'

'It's a bit confusing. Some of them say we need to make fire breaks, others say we should let it burn, and Frances is just making lots of tea.'

'Call me back at 3.15pm and we'll make a decision then about whether we evacuate.'

I turned to my brother. 'Sounds like we are going to have some emotional flames to put out as well as the real ones.'

'Yes, I wish we hadn't left the girls alone with Warren and Doug, we should have known this might have happened. Also we really didn't have a proper procedure in place for when a fire on this scale started.'

I could see he was already blaming himself, and I didn't want that. 'It's not anybody's fault, we just need to deal with it as best we can from here on and then learn from the experience about how to manage a bush fire next time. First, let's get this sorted.'

Sara Jane called back on time. 'Right. The fire's still going strong and there is no sign it's going to slow up, so we've got everyone on the boat apart from Warren, Doug and Dixie. Oh, hold on, Justin and Suzy and James have decided they want to stay and fight the fire as well.'

'That's OK. Get going before any more decide to jump ship. Did you speak to Tui Mali?'

'Yes, he and the family are fine and understand the situation. He says the island is going to be OK.'

'Good, we'll see you at Malau in exactly an hour. Dan will then go back to the island and I'll take all of you to the Grand Eastern where we'll put everyone up for the night.'

'OK. You know there has been a lot of shouting here today.'

'I know, just get on that boat and Dan and I will be with you soon.'

We got to Malau an hour later, with bottled water, a fleet of taxis and tea and coffee and rooms booked back at the hotel. We had prepped everything we could to make the rest of the day relaxing. When the boat came ashore I could feel the tension hit me like a heat wave. Sara Jane and Becky stormed past me red-faced and got into the back of the car. The rest of the tribe got in the taxis. I smiled at them. There wasn't much to say yet, I just wanted to get them to the hotel. Sara and Becky were not happy. They had obviously had a falling out over how the incident had been managed on the island and about how some of the other members had reacted. I reassured them that they had done their best and the good news was that no one had been hurt. Dan would look after those remaining on the island and they should relax. They didn't look as if relaxing was something they were going to do soon.

Back at the Grand Eastern, after people had showered and had a drink, I started to talk to individuals, one by one, so they could vent their feelings and so I could piece together what had happened that day, both in terms of the fire and the fallings out. Five hours later, I was still listening as tribe members recalled how they thought it started, how it was managed and why they had listened to us and followed the evacuation. Most thought it was unnecessary to evacuate the island but understood the reasons why. They didn't feel under personal threat from the fire. I agreed but told them that I didn't like the idea of people sleeping while a fire spread across the island. There were sensible suggestions for future fire safety measures and the management of such incidents. The general feeling was that the girls did OK and that they had been unfairly treated by some of the members who had remained on the island. But at the end of the day, they all agreed that it was a stressful situation and, with so much confusion over what to do, people were bound to end up shouting at each other. As the night wore on, I could see everyone beginning to laugh about it as the cold beers and free hotel rooms helped compensate for the high drama.

I rang Dan on Vorovoro. The fire was still going strong but the feeling was that it would burn out by morning. We compared notes. He had spent the last few hours chatting with those that had stayed behind. We had remarkably different stories; different timings and different accounts of what had occurred. It was almost laughable how far apart some were. Anyway, the anger had subsided and the island vibe was more relaxed.

I asked Dan to put Poques on. 'How's your day been Chief?' I asked cautiously.

'Oh, no bother, no bother at all. I mean, I just think it wasn't right to leave the people when we promised to live side by side. We said last week we were one tribe and today we're not. But don't worry, everything's cool here now. Totally cool.'

I was going to mention the fact that as the island was still burning pretty badly things weren't actually totally cool, but decided I had best tread carefully.

'Listen Warren, I understand why you wanted to stay, and I don't have a problem with that or any of you that decided to do so. All I needed to make you aware of was the fact that we had good reasons to order an evacuation.'

'Yeah, no worries, I understand that you have a business to protect, that's fine, but this was our family and we should all have stuck with them. I just think the way the girls managed it was wrong. Doug and I have had a lot of experience dealing with these kinds of things and they weren't listening to us, there was a lack of respect.'

'To be fair, Warren, they were carrying out instructions I was giving them. But I hear what you're saying and we'll work out why communication broke down in time. This wasn't an easy thing for any of us to face in the first week, especially with Dan and me away. The main thing is everyone is safe. Listen, have a good night and I'll see you tomorrow.'

'Ben, you're too tired, go back on holiday and come back when you're rested. Doug and I have got this under control. The stars are amazing tonight.'

As much as I appreciated Warren's desire to help out in the situation, after today's conflict the last thing I was going to do was go away again. In fact, I swore to myself then and there that from now on either Dan or I would always be on that island at all times. I headed to Govinda's internet café and wrote up the news release about the day's events to the tribe, having checked it through with Dan and Warren and other members beforehand to make sure everyone was happy with the facts. I didn't want this incident to turn into an online gossip opportunity for bloodthirsty bloggers and any media following the project. We needed to play the Vorovoro fire story down as much as possible. Luckily only one paper picked it up a few weeks later and there was no knock-on effect from the amusing headline in the *Newcastle Sun*: 'Tribe almost toast!'

The next day, we all headed back to the island to be welcomed by Justin. Covered in charcoal, his clothes hanging off him in shreds, he was staggering down the beach gasping, 'It's OK, y'all, we put the fire out!' It immediately undid a lot of the previous day's tensions and was very funny but I could still sense some bad feeling between some members and the team. I chatted with everyone and we quickly put a bush fire procedure into place, with a fire alarm megaphone in the kitchen, a meeting point and a bullet-pointed plan for tribe members and the team in case it happened again. Everyone seemed satisfied that something had been done quickly and that we could now all get on with our island life.

I went to assess the damage with Dan. We walked up behind Tui Mali's village into the valley and towards the hill. Where there had previously been tall grasses, there was now black smouldering earth. The whole hillside had been cleaned out by the fire, as I had suspected from the boat. We estimated the burn area was at least five acres. 'So would you have managed it differently if you had been here, Dan?' I asked.

'No. I would have still wanted to get people off the island. I would have spoken to the family and taken it from there. None of us are used to dealing with bush fires and, even if we were, we don't know this island. Trying to fight it could easily have put more of us in danger, including the family.'

We walked behind the headland to where it had apparently started, still not knowing what the cause was. There had been various theories put forward as to why it started; that it was an out-of-control garden fire, that strange boats had arrived at dawn on the other side of the island or that a piece of glass left out in the sun.

FIRE

I sat down with Tui Mali that evening. 'So, everybody OK?' he asked. 'Yes, fine. It's just that none of us have really experienced a big bush fire before so I think some people found it hard.'

'But the tribe's OK?' Tui Mali was concerned that the incident on the island might have affected his new friends.

'Yes, they'll be fine. They all wanted to help but people had different ideas. I'm sorry I wasn't here.'

'Oh, that's no problem, the family was here. They knew what to do. It's good you take them off the island, keep them safe. Fires like this can be dangerous.'

'So, do you have any idea how it might have started?'

'Oh, no. When that story is ready to be told it will be told.'

Ah. So Tui Mali was not going to suddenly become a detective. He was going to wait for the truth to come out in its own time. I admired this strategy even though at home we wouldn't have had time for it. At least this way he was not accusing anyone of anything.

So that was the end of our first week as a tribe on Vorovoro. There hadn't been a fire in fifteen years and on the ninth day of the tribe's island adventure the whole island had almost gone up in smoke. It was a tough experience for most of those involved and one that redrew the lines of how the tribe would work. It emphasised the dangers of a business or organisation giving its members the feeling that they had a certain level of individual responsibility and that had created conflict.

Warren, the elected Chief, was angry that responses to the event highlighted the differences between a bunch of people who were trying to do the right thing for the people as opposed to the business. The community ideal and the legal operation had clashed. But, as the flames eventually died out, I was in some ways glad it had happened. It showed us an extreme situation where tricky decisions would have to be made if this whole project was going to work, especially with strong personalities involved. It forced us to take a step forward as a community and as an organisation that perhaps we might not have taken for a long time otherwise. It sparked conversations and debates that might have lain dormant for months. It was stressful, emotional and challenging but, in hindsight, it played a big part in the progress of the tribe.

And another thing, Warren and Doug, seemingly almost foes for the first week, who had so cautiously avoided each other in their differing approaches to work and leadership, were now buddies; bonded by the rebellion and firefighting. The Chief and his deputy were united.

18

TARA NA BURE LEVU
BUILDING THE GREAT BURE

I let the loaded vessel pass across the lens until it was completely out of sight before pulling back and capturing it again as it cut through the choppy waves towards the beach. I was filming the arrival of the reeds piled up high on the tiny wooden boats from the villages of Mali for a tribal TV episode. Leaving the camera on the tripod, I walked down to the boat, shook the hands of the six men who had arrived with the goods and started to carry the bundles a short distance up the sand to the building site. The reeds were the last of the materials to arrive and would form the roofing for our tribal HQ, the Great Bure, as it had become known on Vorovoro and online. Within a few days, the political and personal heat generated by the drama of the fire was subsiding as more and more projects sprang up and the goal of village building put any tensions or feelings of ill will into perspective. The tribe got on with it.

The building of the Great Bure had begun pretty much straight away as large groups of men had arrived early each morning to show off their traditional construction skills to the tribe and the world. First four pine posts about six feet in length were cemented into the ground to form the four corners of the house. Not so long ago, if you had been standing nearby when these posts were planted you might well have been thrown into the hole and buried alive. The belief was that whenever a big house was built its foundations should be held up by people.

Tui Mali later showed me the remains of a large Bure in a village on the mainland where people had been buried and it was surprisingly recent. It was odd and horrifying to reflect on these strange practices. And perhaps it showed us why Fijians put so much emphasis on ceremony and tradition when it comes to behaviour in and around these thatched houses. Luckily for us, times had moved on and for once I was grateful for the invention of cement. Corner posts fixed, the two giant six-metre pine pillars that were placed within the walls of the Bure to hold up its mighty roof came next. Pulling these giant trunks into place with nothing more than a loop or two of rope and a lot of man power was a spectacular building-site scene.

Ten of us on each rope pulled diagonally as the foot of the post dropped into the hole and men jumped underneath its great weight, holding it on their shoulders, until it passed its fulcrum and tipped precariously, threatening to topple into the kitchen, before settling into place. One of the boys then pulled himself up the full length of the post, gripping it like a monkey with the palms of his hands and the soles of his feet, before tying a Fijian flag to the top. There didn't seem to be any real order about who was directing the proceedings, just a lot of shouting and laughing.

With the main pillars in place, further core posts were planted down the outside walls, their purpose to act as further support for the heavy mangrove-wood roof. In the background we could hear the sound of the tribe's sole chainsaw working hard. I wandered back into the bush behind the village with other tribe members until we came to a clearing where the tree was being felled. There Tui Mali and a couple of other boys watched as Epeli, bow-legged and barefoot, in an old AC Milan football shirt, ripped denim shorts and a bandage around his knee, worked the base of the tall coconut palm like he was sculpting a piece of art. It was a heavy piece of machinery which this man was wielding one-handed with no gloves, glasses or worry that it might turn on him. He reminded me of Arnie in his classic Terminator days, a giant machine gun in hand that was obviously far too heavy and powerful for a mere mortal to hold, let alone fire. I skirted around the clearing until I was standing next to Tui Mali. I had an important question even though it looked like it might be too late to ask. 'Is it OK to cut this tree?'

'Yes, this is a good tree to cut. There is no more fruit. It is dead. It is good it is here for us.'

I was relieved as, for a moment, I had thought that our new village hall was going to contribute to the deforestation of Vorovoro's mini jungle. But the Chief said it was already dead so the beast could come down. And down she came, creaking until the vast trunk smashed to the jungle floor. One wipe of his brow and Epeli wandered forward and immediately began to cut through the vertical length of the trunk, all fifty-odd feet of it. This man was a machine. No measuring, no estimates, no rest, he just took on the task like he was cutting a piece of cardboard with a Stanley knife.

Once it had been separated into two clean halves, the tribes were called in. Lining each side of the cut trunk we squatted, wrapped our arms around them and, on the count of 'dua, rua, tolo', we lifted as one, pushing upwards from our legs, taking the weight on our shoulders. There must have been about fifteen of us on each split trunk. Still I thought I was going to be crushed and I'm sure I was not taking my fair share of coconut tree on my bony shoulders. Back at the building site, we laid the great log alongside the posts. Epeli, one cup of tea with two sugars and a long thin roll-up later, ordered the elevation of the flat side of the coconut beams so that they sat on top of the posts. He then walked forward and tapped a boy on the shoulder who promptly bent over so that the old warhorse could climb on his back and pull himself up onto the beam. As he straddled the freshly cut cross-bar – which by the way was the perfect length for the house – a large group of boys gathered around to watch the master in action, squatting in his shadow as sawdust flew off the blade above. Epeli carved notches into various parts of the wood so that it would dove-tail neatly over the posts, fixing it in place before five-inch nails were smashed in to secure the frame. All this happened within about two hours, and there was not one pencil mark in sight.

After a month of floating up and down with the tide just off the beach, it was now time to bring the mangrove wood ashore. We dragged the different lengths of wood, heavy with the water it had absorbed, into the shallows. Men with large batons would then sit astride each mangrove and bash the bark so that it fell away revealing bright red wood beneath. It looked like there had been a shark attack as a large area of water turned a deep red. The sound of the mangrove bashing was almost like a stunted drum roll, as one arm followed another smashing into the bark and the water. The noisy chainsaw aside, the sounds of the village building were fantastic and I liked hearing the noises before I could see what was going on. This was the sound of action, the sound of purpose. Once debarked, the naked mangrove wood was left out to dry for a couple of days. In the meantime, I watched as Epeli and Doug stood together in front of the emerging Bure and looked towards the top of the tall pine posts which now had a piece of string tied between them, mimicking where the top beam would be placed. I listened in:

'So does that look straight to you?' Epeli asked his American friend.

'What you want me to tell you? If that is horizontal, from down here with my own eyes, without using any level?'

'You have your own level, it's here. This is your Fijian level.' Epeli smiled, pointing at his own eyes. Doug cracked up.

'Jeez, Epeli, are you really going to decide how to level the top of the house with your own eyes from over fifty feet away? I guess that's just the way you do it here, right?' Epeli rocked back, bursting into a great gasp of laughter, slapping Doug's back with

BUILDING THE GREAT BURE

a heavy, leathered hand.

There wasn't a mangrove beam long enough to go the entire length of the house, so instead the boys lashed two together and winched them both up to the top of the posts. A bamboo scaffold had now been built across the centre of the house and it became a giant climbing frame for the guys as they leapt from one beam to another, regardless of how high off the grass they were. The beam in place, Epeli turned back to a head-shaking Doug.

'You see, the second mangrove is thicker at one end. So to make it level we just turn it around so that the thin end is the same as the longer mangrove. Now it's level.'

Obviously relishing Doug's fascination with this human-tooled measuring technique, Epeli delivered his killer line. 'Nothing hard in this world, Doug.' He smiled and walked off to find his chainsaw. This man was fast becoming a legend on the island. Where else are buildings of this scale built by human eye, muscle and a chainsaw operated by a 64-year-old?

The mangroves were then carefully laid diagonally on each side of the building from the outside wall up to the cross-beam where they rested. Nailed and strapped into place, they soon formed the skeleton of the Bure, the bare bones ready to be covered in an insulating skin. As about forty of us were admiring our fast-developing tribal home that afternoon with mugs of sugary tea and cassava cake, I noticed Tui Mali talking to an older man in a purple shirt I had not seen on the island before. The conversation looked serious. After a few minutes Tui Mali stood up. I walked over to him, anticipating the way in which he wanted to tell me something.

'This is Peter,' Tui Mali said, gesturing to the man in the purple shirt. I bent down and shook his hand. 'He says the Bure will fall down.'

I stood up quickly. 'Fall down?' I looked at Tui Mali in amazement. 'But how?'

'The posts, Peter says they're not strong enough. We need more pine posts to support the roof.'

'But the roof is already on,' I said, not meaning to state the obvious, as we stood in its giant shadow. 'Why does Peter think it will fall down?'

'You see, the ground beneath the Bure is sand and the roof is very heavy. So you need the stronger posts and you need to cement all of them, otherwise they will start to sink.'

'OK,' I said trying to soak up what I had just been told. Over sixty men had been working for nearly a month and now Peter, someone I'd never met before and who didn't speak English, had told Tui Mali that our great house, the symbol of what we were doing on the island, would sink unless we put in more solid foundations. I wasn't quite sure how to take this forward. 'So, why do you think no one mentioned this before?' I asked calmly.

'We didn't know. But Peter knows. So it's best, you know, it's best we fix it now.'

'I agree it's best to fix this now. Would it be OK to have a meeting with all the foremen this afternoon?'

'OK, you bring some grog and we'll talk.'

So after the day's work I took a bundle of kava to Tui Mali's veranda and sat down with eight men including Peter, Epeli and Tui Mali. After mixing the kava and sharing a round, I turned to Tui Mali again and asked, 'So have the men discussed what Peter was saying about the Bure?'

'Yes, we have talked about it and we all agree we need more pine posts.'

I looked around the circle and all the men nodded and smiled.

'You see, this man, he knows about these things. If he says we should put more posts in place, we should do that. It's better,' Epeli said, before sucking hard on his gargantuan roll-up.

I looked over at Peter who must have been a similar age to Tui Mali and Epeli, in his sixties at least. He was expressionless, looking away from the group, accepting the kava when it was passed to him and drinking quietly. It was pretty exasperating, to be honest. I was a little concerned that the viewpoint of one man who had only just arrived on the island immediately changed everyone's mind. But who was I to debate a decision made by such senior men? I accepted that it was a good idea and told the circle, 'OK, we'll go and pick up some more pine posts on Monday and fix them before the roof and walls are finished.'

'Vinaka, it's a good idea, Ben,' said Taniela, a brute of a man and captain of the Mali Sharks, laughing like a little girl as though the whole thing was completely hilarious.

With the pine posts in place a few days later, it was time to begin on the walls and the roof. The piles of bamboo were separated and each stick was smashed with a wooden club as the mangroves had been. This time, though, the aim wasn't to remove the bark but to partially break the skin of the bamboo so that it opened into long flat strips. You had to get your bamboo bashing just right otherwise you could easily break the whole pole and they were extremely valuable. Then the men would line up and begin to weave the flat strips between each other, creating a criss-cross pattern that eventually formed larger square and rectangular pieces that would become the end walls and the half-height side walls. There was a lot of bamboo weaving to do and you definitely needed gloves. A bamboo splinter is nasty, it can quickly cause infection and even grow under the surface of your skin.

As the walls went up, a few men were applying the final touches to the mangrove structure that the reeds would be fixed to. James from the *National Geographic*, as enthusiastic as any of the first footers, was going to all kinds of lengths to get *the* photograph of this great construction process. He had decided that he would lash his very expensive camera to a long piece of bamboo and swing it all the way up so that it was level with the boys straddling the spine of the building. He had to get it exactly right so that the timer would click just as the camera reached the highest point of the arc on top of the building. If ever photographing a building project could be called brave this was it. Tui Mali was fascinated by this journalistic desire to cover the story and spent a good hour helping James with his adventure photography.

A giant lattice was laid on top of the mangrove, providing a frame for the reeds to be tied to, and then the thatching began. Large bundles of straw were passed in a chain up onto the roof, which were then spread out until they were the thickness of a grown man's torso. A five-millimetre rope was fed through a hole in a giant wooden needle, about the length of your arm, and pushed through the straw. On the underside, boys sitting on bamboo scaffolding high up in the roof would pull the needle and thread around the mangrove and back through the thatch, giving a warning shout beforehand to make sure they didn't impale their partner on the other side.

Back on the outside, the rope would then be smashed with a club against a thinner piece of wood that battened down the thatch before being tied off again on the underside of the roof. It was a lengthy process, high up off the ground, which involved giant sewing moves, knot tying, bashing and a lot of shouting. There were no harnesses, no crash mats, and no one chose to wear a safety hat. If you fell, you just had to hope your mate was there to catch you. It was 11 October. My mum had just arrived on the island on my twenty-seventh birthday and watched as I climbed up the sloping roof to help finish the thatching. I straddled the spine of the house and banged in the knots when told to. The straw slope stretched out below me at very steep angle, like a ski jump. I had to concentrate to keep my balance whilst swinging the baton, carefully making sure I didn't slip or overbalance. That night Mum gave me a bag of presents and cards from home and the family dressed me in a black pocketed sulu and bula shirt before we settled down for a surprise lovo and cake.

Finally the Great Bure was complete with two Balabalas, kind of Flintstone-style giant black clubs that stuck out from each end of the roof. Inside we laid half the floor space with tongue and groove *vesi* (hardwood) and covered the remainder in sand, coconut leaves and Fijian mats, the traditional Bure flooring. There were three open entrances into the Bure, one from the beach for the Chiefs, one from the back, for the VIPs, and one at the kitchen for everyone else. Clearly the Mali community had become very proud of its work, that it had awakened a new-

BUILDING THE GREAT BURE

found interest in this traditional building process that a lot of the younger guys had learned for the first time. Over one of the many kava sessions during the building we were told it was the biggest in Fiji. I wasn't convinced of that but I was happy to go along with it. It was certainly big and it was the perfect home for the tribe. Tevita, Tui Mali's horticultural friend from the south, arrived and turned the surrounding area from patchy grass into a grand landscaped garden. Women decorated the inside with brightly coloured cloths and coconut palms. It was almost ready to be opened for business.

Stuart Kimberley, 24, had been working as a company vehicle administrator before coming to Fiji, and had been elected November Chief, beating a Belgian rival with his Steve Coogan-inspired Chief-cast. I picked up the fresh-faced, well-built lad from Royal Leamington Spa in Labasa and cracked open a cold beer on the boat journey back to Vorovoro. I told Kimbo, as he was known online, to sit at the front of the boat to balance the load, knowing it also gave the best view of the island. As we turned past Nakawaga, the sun was low in the sky, perfect light for showing off the island. I watched Kimbo watching Vorovoro, drinking his beer, shaking his head and smiling. I don't think he could believe he was going to be a Chief on this island for a month. It must have been a crazy realisation for him and I loved seeing other people being knocked back just as I had been.

That weekend we opened the Great Bure. Tui Mali arrived by boat dressed traditionally in tapa and walked slowly up the path that led straight from the beach to the symmetrically laid out garden between two warriors, who the week previously had been bamboo weavers. He cut the ribbon as the Mali schoolchildren sang, before we all went inside for the kava ceremony and the handing over ceremony from Chief Poques to Chief Kimbo. There must have been over one hundred people inside the house and everyone was lost in wonder at what had been built.

It made me consider why more Bures are not built in Fiji; they're such spectacular buildings and have a natural air-conditioning system as well as a calmness that doesn't exist in other places.

I hoped we would build more, just for moments like this, even though it had cost Tribewanted almost Fiji $22,000, with over $12,000 being split between the four Mali villages for whatever community projects they chose to carry out. I knew then and there we needed to find a way to control the spending.

But today I wasn't going to worry about money, I was going to enjoy this masterpiece of Fijian architecture. I had never really taken much time to consider architecture before but watching the development of this house made me think about how and why buildings are designed and constructed, beyond the practical reasons and towards the aesthetic and philosophical. The process of construction was so natural, rhythmic and sociable, I started to understand why man has always found building an important part of his development. Apart from the end result of providing shelter, the time it takes for the structure to rise from the earth to its final standing place is actually the most exciting part. Building a community was enthralling. We had started online and now we were doing it for real, and it was well beyond anything I had imagined when, sitting in the gloom of an English winter, we began to think about building a village 12,000 miles away on an island in the South Pacific.

19

BOLE BOLE LEVU NI VEILUTAKI
CHIEFLY CHALLENGES

'Do you think the prevailing literary trail reflects the reality or do you think a Utopia can succeed?'

It was a belter of a question at any time but at seven in the morning it was like suddenly being back in an exam hall about to begin a three-hour English Literature paper. Only this time I was sitting on Vorovoro's headland with James from *National Geographic Adventure* magazine giving what I hoped would be an interview that would inspire a lot of people to join Tribewanted. But even with the mental preparation I'd done I still didn't anticipate the questions that James was hurling at me at sunrise on the mountain top, dictaphone in hand. I paused and looked out to sea before answering. 'I would never describe this as an attempt to reach Utopia. To me Utopias are not something that happen physically; humankind is flawed. I think I understand evolution enough to realise that Utopia, in the sense of a perfect society where there are never any bumps or disagreements, cannot exist.'

'Why not?' James cut me off with a slam dunk.

'Because we're all in competition with each other to survive.' Hold on there, I told myself, just be careful where you go with this, you're not Richard Dawkins, let alone Darwin. 'Evolution is about survival,' I continued, 'and this is what's great here, because you learn a bit more about that rather than simply going to the supermarket every day. And ultimately therefore it's about instinctively wanting to extend and protect your own gene pool. And although you do think about groups of people and communities around you, everyone is, to some degree, an egoist in life, whether they like it or not. So to me this isn't about creating a Utopia, it's about building a community and finding a place that is physical – and probably also a state of mind – that you feel fits with you and who you are, and you get something out of it, a sense of freedom. But it's not about cutting ourselves off from the world on a tropical island, where a number of Utopian societies have previously been attempted. It's about giving people the chance to chase their dreams and realise some of them, get glimpses of perfection and then connect that with the rest of the world. But you're never going to get it throughout your whole life, every day.

'When I use the word Utopia, I don't mean nirvana, I mean a place apart where a set of ideals exist. Most of society doesn't work in this way, so I guess I'm asking if these ideals can coexist within a capitalist framework?' Ooh-yeah! 'Can ideals coexist within a capitalist framework?' Come on son, you know the answer to this one. I was getting peckish.

'Well, remember, if we run out of money on this project, if we don't sell enough memberships, then all the ideals go to waste. But the potential is there for some of these ideas to spread beyond this island, via the global community online. I mean, why can't every traveller deliver one book to one school in the world? It doesn't cost them anything and it can change lives.' I paused. I really wanted to get to the bottom of this, it was important.

'Let's go back to *The Beach*, because it appears to be the story that we're being compared to the most. There's a bunch of travellers, similar to the people here, and they discover what they think is paradise and, to be honest, what the author had in mind and what he describes is not too different from this place.

'The reason it all goes wrong is because the structure of that society is based purely on ideals and they don't consider the rest of the world. They cut themselves off. The problems occur when the world and the Utopian society meet, be it through the passing on of the map, the drug barons or the need for medical help because there has been a shark attack. It goes wrong.

'Now, we never set out to shut ourselves off from the world. Our ideals are based on what we understand a tribe to be, which in my mind is a community or group of people with a purpose, which in this case is working in partnership with an indigenous tribal culture. But things only happen if you've got the money in the bank or the structures in place or the boats in the harbour, and perhaps that's why this will work because we accept that you can't just run something based on purely Utopian ideals. You can't just expect to discover paradise and for it always to be perfect. If we did find our Utopia, our paradise, then after a while we wouldn't know it existed because we would have forgotten what an imperfect existence was like. So, yes I think dreams can be discovered but they must fit with the rest of the world, within, as you say, a capitalist framework. I don't want to burst the bubble here because it's fascinating, but this is a tourism venture, albeit with ideals bolted onto a business model.'

Satisfied with enough philosophical musings at sunrise, James and I climbed back down from the headland and walked along the beach towards the tribal village and the smell of pancakes.

During the six weeks it had taken to build the Great Bure, and in the aftermath of the fire, there were a lot of projects going on the island, with new experiences being had by tribe members and the Mali yasuva. It was also a period when the political and human structure of the project was being tested and shaped and measured against conversations like the one on the headland with *National Geographic*. Beyond the logistical challenges of co-ordinating boats, running a kitchen, buying and shifting materials, managing workers, team and tribe members, and making sure everyone stayed safe and healthy, the biggest tests came from within the power base of the emerging tribal community, from whence the Chiefs roamed.

When we began the project on the island, aside from the goals of building a sustainable village on Vorovoro, providing the visiting tribe members with an educational adventure, and supporting the local community in any way we could, there was no real structure. One had to be developed and the role of Chief was key. For the first two months of the project (as he had been voted in twice), it was up to Poques and I to find a system that worked for the online tribe, the local community and for the business, Tribewanted. It wasn't easy and in Poques I was finding someone who would push me all the way.

'We really need to have fixed budgets, Ben, for building, for labour, for running boats, the kitchen, to get the island online, for everything. Until we know what we've got to spend it's going to be very difficult.' Poques and I, with his deputy, Doug, were having a meeting in the aftermath of the fire and that event had made it clear to all of us that a lot needed to be sorted out.

'You don't need to worry about this stuff once you've handed it over to the Chiefs, because it will then be our responsibility with the tribe to make sure it runs smoothly,' Poques continued. 'We also need to have our role as Chief defined a lot more clearly, what we are and what we are not responsible for.' He was right, of course, boundaries needed to be drawn for what Tribewanted would look after and what the Chiefs would be expected to do. The reason I hadn't tackled this yet was because I wasn't quite sure how it would work; I had hoped we would find good leaders and develop a system together. The bottom line, however, was that if anything went wrong with the project then Tribewanted would take a hit. MJ and I were legally responsible. After all, it was our names on the papers at Companies House, on the island lease contract and in the newspapers. Poques and Doug had no legal obligations. If they screwed things up, they could walk away. MJ or I wouldn't be able to do that and the fire had shown that we had to find a balance between giving up some of that responsibility and losing control completely. If a Chief got carried away or the community voted for something that would damage the business, the island environment or the local community, there had to be a way of managing it.

'I agree with you guys, now is a good time to make things clearer to everyone. So how about this, we have a fixed monthly island development budget for each elected Chief which he or she is responsible for? For anything to do with development – building materials, labour, transporting materials, equipment and maintenance.'

'OK, how much?' Poques asked as he rolled a fag, not looking up at me.

'MJ and I have looked at the projected spending for the next year, based on the first month on the island, and we have decided we can commit Fiji $5,000 a month,' I said, preparing for a backlash of 'how the hell are we supposed to build a village on just over fifteen hundred quid a month!'

'Right, and what about our legacy as Chiefs? From the start, you and MJ said there would be something for the Chiefs to spend how they chose, something that they could leave behind?'

'Yes, we've discussed that as well. The idea was put forward online a few months ago that each Chief should have a dollar for every member of the tribe, to spend how they like. This will be on top of the $5k monthly kitty. So for you, Poques, your legacy fund would be $925, as that's how many members joined as of 1 September.'

'Good. I think this is a good move, Ben, and I think it will help the tribe see that you are committed to spending over the longer term and that Tribewanted is giving up more responsibility to the community. Can I have $600 from the legacy budget now?'

'Sure,' I said, still feeling pushed by the Chief I decided to call *Poques the Persuader*.

So that was that. We had decided to publicly commit almost $6,000 (£2,000) a month to the development of the island. The plan was well received online and members seemed excited at the prospect at seeing how different Chiefs would spend the money. The spending would all be recorded in a big red accounts book and would be available for anyone's inspection. Of course, it wouldn't be as simple as handing over the cash at the start of the month and coming back four weeks later to see what each Chief had achieved. We would have to manage the budget between us as projects overlapped and depending upon whatever other ongoing costs there were. I made it clear to members that outside this budget Tribewanted would cover the remaining costs in Fiji, like running the kitchen and the staff, the boats and the captains, the first aid gear, the internet connection when it was sorted, the airport taxis, the team wages, and all those other costs which you don't anticipate when you're doing something like this for the first time.

The next Chiefly debate happened soon after the first, around the campfire. We had just watched J-dub in a spontaneous, enigmatic and energetic performance of the 'Ying Tong' song from *The Goon Show*; the human-sized hobbit scampering back and forth for a good four minutes before he collapsed in a heap on the sand. Tribe members had tears rolling down their faces while most of the Fijians stared open-mouthed at what they had just witnessed, not sure if it was a joke or an crucial part of our traditional culture. Epeli simply sat there and rolled another ridiculously long smoke, ignoring the eccentricities going on around him. From where I was, leaning against a log, it was an entertaining scene and one that had become less surreal as the nights had passed. Poques leaned over, glass of rum in hand. 'You know we really need to sort the Chief's role out, Ben, it's just not right yet.'

This was the way Poques liked to approach work and what we were doing on Vorovoro, picking the moments you probably least wanted to discuss those issues, around the campfire. His passion for the project to succeed was beyond doubt but I was becoming increasingly concerned at the way he seemed to be pulling other tribe members into his view of the tribe's politics, into his way of thinking. I knew there was plenty to do in terms of structuring the project but I didn't like the way he appeared to be creating barriers between members on the island and the team that represented Tribewanted, the company.

'I know, Warren,' I responded as we sat by the fire. 'But don't you think we should sort this out in the morning?'

'Yes, but the thing is I think the members need to know what's really going on with TW Ltd.' What the hell did he mean by that? And what was this TW Ltd? I'd seen him write that online and I didn't like it. It seemed to make out that there was a board of directors in a tower somewhere cunningly planning the next way to exploit the island tribe; there wasn't, it was me sitting on the sand by the fire and it was MJ sitting online back in the Wirral.

'What do you mean?' I asked, now feeling uncomfortable.

'Well, the money, Ben. I'm not stupid, I know you must be running out of cash, but you need to tell people if this is happening. They will help. I for one am ready to put money into this and to come on board full-time. You know I've told the tribe members that I want to be on this island for the three years and I will.'

Whoa! From talking about the role of the Chief we were suddenly on a whole different level and, to my mind, this wasn't the time or place for that discussion. Poque's increasing determination worried me. I knew in the sober light of day it would be easier to discuss but around the fire that night I was angry and my confidence was taking a hit. If every Chief was going to challenge me like this I wasn't sure I would have the energy to handle it.

Of course, Poques was right about the money. It didn't take a genius to work out that, even though we had just celebrated hitting 1,000 tribe members six months to the day since we launched, it was not enough to keep the project going full-time for too much longer. The costs of renting islands, developing online communities, hiring people and building villages soon add up. But I needed the Chiefs and tribe members to support the project and attract new members, not to inspire in-fighting. We needed communication between all of us to be fluid and we couldn't afford to fall out. I know this was not what Poques intended. He genuinely wanted it to work and he cared about the place and the people but his approach was unnerving me.

In contrast to this underlying tension on the island, there were plenty of amazing things happening that did act as a motivation for me and everyone else involved. The first school trip with the tribe members was particularly memorable. Everyone was dressed in sulus as we walked up the sand to Ligaulevu village. The headmaster asked the children to put a line of benches at the front of one of the classrooms before gathering all seventy students into one room. The tribe members filed in and sat in a row beneath the broken blackboard facing the room of angelic faces.

'Today is a very special day for our school,' the headteacher began as the Shine cameras rolled. 'Today we are very happy to welcome our visitors from around the world who are currently staying on Vorovoro.'

Each tribe member then stood up in turn in front of the children, aged 5 to 12, who all seemed to be learning English very fast, and introduced themselves and the books and presents they had brought for the school. To thank the visitors for their gifts, the children would then sing. Not a quick nursery rhyme but a series of songs, hymns and anthems whose harmonies and pureness hit you like a breaking wave. Faces of utter innocence pouring out the most perfect sounds were enough to make most grown men wobble. That day I noticed J-dub wiping away a tear or two from behind his glasses, as many others have done since. The children's songs, much like the ones I had heard in schools in Africa, were stunning, memorable and moving. As one of the tribe said to me outside afterwards, 'I would have come from England just to hear that.'

After the greetings, everyone ran outside with the footballs that some of the members had brought and played games on the large playing field in front of the school. It gave the teachers a chance to rest and it gave the tribe members a chance to be children again, running freely in circles, singing, dancing or being on the receiving end of a tackle from a 10-year-old. Mali School became an important part of our weekly routine as the tribe visited every Friday, relieving the understaffed teachers for the morning, delivering books and reading, teaching and playing games with the children. I hoped that in time we could develop the relationship with the school more, to bring more long-term value to both groups.

That afternoon J-dub, recovered from the emotional impact of the children's singing, Raina and I decided we would make our own way back to Vorovoro rather than take the boat direct from the village. An unlikely hiking trio, we headed west from Ligaulevu and along the two-mile track that the children from Nakawaga village walked each day to school and back. Behind the mangroves, past the cassava plantations and over the hills of the interior of the much bigger Mali island, the path unfolded through the heat of the day. An hour or so later, we climbed the pass behind Nakawaga and stared down onto Vorovoro. It was the first time I'd seen our island from there and it looked as spectacular as ever. We felt like we'd just discovered it for the first time after days of hiking through the jungle. I told myself that we should make more effort to bring people to this village and climb the bigger hill, where the view of Vorovoro from the top would be awesome. J-dub decided the hundred-metre swim between Mali and Vorovoro was too much, so Raina and I left him with our cameras in the village. 'I'll send a boat over as soon as I get back.' So the American girl and I were back in the sea again, although this time it was broad daylight and neither of us had drunk any rum. I enjoyed spending time with her, she was adventurous, easy going and liked getting stuck into the project work. And she looked good as we waded between the mangroves onto Vorovoro, feeling like we'd crossed a great ocean to get there. I wondered if anything might develop between us. I knew she was going later that week so I guessed that would be it, our island romance would have to end.

We rounded what was now known as peak four of the four peaks, a challenge the tribe members had started that involved running and clambering along the spine of Vorovoro ticking off the summits as you went. Dan and I had run it a couple of times together, scaling the cliffs behind the tribal village before turning back down the hillside and charging through the bush and across the valley floor. Then it is up the highest peak of Vorovoro, where the fire had cleaned away the long grasses. Going down the other side, a steep drop with large boulders, meant levering yourself down carefully before crossing the next small valley and bouldering up a narrow ridge to the exposed third peak, my favourite, before fighting through the thick bush and tall grasses of the final peak and descending to the point between the mangroves and opposite Nakawaga where Raina and I now walked. The rest of the run was along the flat of the rocks, sand and stones back to the tribe village. If you timed it right when the tide was out you didn't have to wade through the muddy mangrove waters hoping the sea snakes wouldn't fancy your leg for lunch. It was exhilarating stuff, and a run that Dan and I did in a personal best of thirty-seven minutes, a time we were both pretty pleased with. That was until a long-haired Kiwi called Murray turned up and actually ran down the boulders we had crawled across and knocked three minutes off our record. Thirty-four minutes still stands as the record for the Vorovoro four peaks challenge and I'll be very surprised if it's broken.

The island hikes, swims and school visits meant escapism from the daily reality of what was going on under the surface of the happy tribal life: the money worries, the long-distance communications problems with my business partner, the relationship between the online community and the island and, of course, the Chiefs. But just as these island adventures allowed me to escape they also motivated me, like my running had done back in Devon earlier that year. They energised me for the days and weeks ahead. And I would need every ounce of energy I could find, because the running of this tribe was about to get a lot harder.

20
TACORI
TRAPPED

Becky was sitting by the pool at the Grand Eastern and looked upset. I sat down next to her. 'What's up?'

'I can't believe you did that, Ben. I can't believe you would do that to me. I trusted you.'

'Did what, Becks? I don't know what you're talking about,' I said, desperately trying to work out what she meant.

'The tape. I watched the tape of you talking to Warren and Doug after the fire. I watched you asking them about me and I heard you talking with them.'

Shit. That hadn't even crossed my mind. Becky had been making a video diary and had stumbled across the footage of the meeting between Warren, Doug and me that Dan had been filming for Shine. I remembered speaking to Warren and Doug about how the team had managed the fire that day and they said they thought Becky did not fare particularly well. I knew that Warren and Becky had clashed and, as far as I was concerned, that was understandable and we had moved on. But hearing that conversation had brought it all back for Becky and she felt that it shouldn't have been filmed.

'Listen, Becky, I'm sorry,' I said immediately. 'That meeting shouldn't have been recorded beyond the discussion of the fire itself, the conversation about people should have been off-camera. I was just focusing on the conversation and forgot about the camera. I'm not a television producer, sorry. It shouldn't have happened.'

Becky, crying now, continued, 'It really hurt me. I felt like you were picking me out for blame and on something that could end up on television as well, that's just not fair. I'm part of the team here.'

I could understand why she was upset even though I hadn't intended to set her up. I sympathised with her as she wasn't, after all, employed to manage fires and headstrong middle-aged men. She'd been employed to make online TV updates for the tribe members at home. She was also part of the team, and her trust in my ability to listen to everyone and their feelings and weigh everything up had been broken. I shouldn't have let the camera carry on filming once it became personal. I'd made a mistake.

'I don't think I can do this any more,' she said, 'I'm going to leave.' Aaah! I wasn't expecting that.

'Becks, you can't leave, we've only just started. We can sort this out, I'm sure we can.'

'Look, Ben, it's not just the fire and that tape, it's the project. I know how stretched you are financially. I saw that when you were bartering for water the other day and you were so desperate to keep the cost down. But I also know that I need the money, I need to keep my career moving, and you shouldn't be paying me ahead of buying water or employing local workers. So I think it's best if I leave. I've had an amazing few months and even now, feeling like shit, I don't regret it.'

She was right. We couldn't afford to keep her on and nor should we. If we had got the technology on the island and were churning out tribal TV episodes each week that she was presenting and producing - and if they were bringing a lot more people to the project - then her job would have been completely justified. But, for whatever reasons, that hadn't happened. And the videotape incident had pushed her over the edge. I was upset as well. I liked Becky a lot and I had really enjoyed working with her but in that instant I realised, I think properly for the first time, that I couldn't keep everyone happy all the time. There were going to be decisions throughout the project that some people disagreed with and others were upset by. It was a hard realisation, especially when the person getting hurt was someone who had become a good friend. I felt like I'd let her down. We agreed that Becky would work for another two weeks before heading off to travel around New Zealand and Australia, something she was excited about doing. After the emotion, there was a collective sense of relief between us and I hoped that, in the time remaining, we could salvage our friendship. But, for now at least, feelings were too raw and I felt like crap.

That afternoon, I went online in Govinda's to send MJ the news about Becky and check up on the finances. It wasn't looking good. Even with *USA Today*'s Travel Feature cover story and an article in *The Guardian* intriguingly entitled 'The Beach, the sequel?' – which said Tribewanted was a 'bold experiment' and 'difficult to criticise' – hardly any new members had joined. I'd been sure earlier in the year that this kind of publicity would bring in significant money. I had no doubt most travel companies getting the media exposure we were would have been laughing. By now I was convinced that what the Jem Report and the proliferation of bad gossip online was doing the damage, even though we had actually started the project and tribe members were writing up experiences online that were full of praise. One quote in particular grabbed my attention: 'I have been travelling for a year to Thailand, Australia etc... just following the tourist trail. Vorovoro is the first time that feels like I have found something unique, untouched and off the beaten track.' Nick Cresner was an environment graduate who had arrived shortly after 1 September and his Vorovoro experience was echoed by many others.

But the numbers did not make happy reading. If the income and expenditure matched the last two months, we would have just about enough cash to keep things going until Christmas. After that it would be unsustainable. It was a pretty perilous position and one that was keeping me awake at night. The separation between reality and my dreams was breaking down, my real-world fears spinning out of control in my subconscious, not allowing me to rest properly. MJ was due to visit Vorovoro soon and I knew it was going to be a pivotal time for Tribewanted, both in terms of coming up with some quick solutions for the cash problem and evaluating how we were working together. It had been tough maintaining close contact since I had moved to Fiji.

When MJ arrived, it was obvious things were not going to be easy. He seemed distant on the island, unable to join in with many of the activities and projects. He had lots on his mind. I knew we had to find decent chunks of time together to go through everything but it was difficult as I was pretty flat out. On the third afternoon after his arrival, we at last found a few hours and sat down on the veranda of the team's house.

'There are just a few things, Ben, that I'm concerned about that are going on here.' It was not the start I wanted. I guess I hoped the first thing I would hear him say was 'Ben, this is awesome, look what we've achieved.' Instead I just waited for him to tell me. 'I think you need to be very careful about the way you're managing things and people. I'm telling you this because I want you to realise the problem before you make a mistake, I want to help make this run well.' Not knowing what he was going to say next, I was already pretty riled. I had been working my nuts off to make the project work and the first thing my business partner did now we were face to face was criticise. But I bit my tongue and listened. MJ continued:

'It's just the way you are with people. You take charge and I think sometimes you do too much when you should be encouraging others to have a chance.'

'What do you mean? Can you give me an example?'

'Sure. Whenever there is a ceremony, you are always the one speaking and presenting the kava. I think other tribe members should do it.'

'I'm just trying to fulfil my role here on the island,' I said, thinking that what I was doing was showing people. 'But I see what you're saying. I'll try and give members more of a chance in future, no worries.' I wanted to argue my position but I didn't want conflict. MJ and I had never fallen out and now would not be a good time to start. We both knew that. The rest of MJ's concerns weren't all that serious, just little things he'd noticed. I listened, accepted what he was saying and told him I would try to do something about them. I would. I wanted MJ to see I was doing everything I could to make this work. Then I turned to him, 'So what about you? How are you doing? What are you thinking about *your* role within all this?'

'Coming back and seeing how amazing it is, I really just want to be here. It's so difficult sitting at home and reading all the negative stuff online. At least when you're here you can see all the good things happening. I really want to be here.'

'Yeah, it must have been really tough at home, hearing how much fun we're all having. But how do you see yourself fitting into the set-up and us working together?'

'My hope is that you can focus on all the logistical stuff for the project and I can be more involved with managing the team and running the online side of things. But I guess that's going to be a bit difficult without a fast internet connection in Labasa, let alone on Vorovoro.'

It sounded like it would be a difficult fit for sure and my instinct was that, in a real space and an intense one like this island, we would really struggle to work together on a par. It wasn't that I didn't want him there from a personal point of view. I really wanted MJ to get over the knock he had so patently received from the nasty online gossip and if coming to Fiji at least for a while was going to help, then that was great. But we would also need to be very clear in our minds about where our responsibilities and roles started and stopped. We agreed to think about it for a few days and make a decision before he left Fiji.

'Sorry to disturb you Chiefs, is now a good time to come and talk?' It was Poques.

'Sure,' I said, 'Come and grab a hammock.' It was early November and Poques had handed on his Chiefly title to Kimbo, but was staying on 'for a few more weeks'. Recently he had posted online to the tribe members that he was applying for the position of 'Project Manager' on Vorovoro and had offered to work for Tribewanted for free. The online members had reacted supportively, thanking Poques for his commitment to the project. Of course, it was a slightly different story on the island. Poques and I had had a conversation about the possible need for a skilled project manager who wasn't a local Fijian, and I had agreed with him that this might be necessary. I had told MJ before he came to Fiji, and he was interested in Poques taking on such a role. I told him my concerns and we had agreed to sit down and work it out on Vorovoro. But we had certainly not advertised a vacancy as Poques had suggested online. It was this that worried us.

'We really appreciate what you have given to this project and what you want to give,' said MJ, as diplomatically as he could. 'But Ben and I are concerned about how you are going about this, especially that you are informing members online before we have decided anything. It doesn't really show great communication between us.'

'Oh, I'm sorry. I thought you were going to tell everyone. But anyway you really do need a project manager, otherwise it's not going to work.'

'Well yes, we recognise that, Poques, but we need to agree this between ourselves and look at budgets and so on first.'

'But I've told you I'd work for free! You'd have my skills, energy and commitment for nothing.' For nothing, I thought. It was an attractive offer but how complicated would it be?

'OK. Give Ben and me a couple of days to think about your offer and we'll make a decision before I go home,' MJ told him.

'No worries guys, I just want you to know I'm here for you.'

MJ and I talked at length about Warren, about the pros and the cons, about how we felt about the guy. It was a tough decision. I think we both wanted it to work for Poques but, at that moment, with things looking increasingly fragile and good communication increasingly important, we agreed we didn't want to take any more risks.

Besides, in terms of the job position, I was keen to see Fijians take the lead on projects supported by whatever talents the tribe Chiefs and members brought. It was as important, in my eyes, to support their development as it was Vorovoro's visitors. I was also concerned with Poques's ongoing presence on the island. I felt like he was suffocating the new Chief, Kimbo, and that for the sake of the project and for Poques himself, it would be good if he left the island for a while. As for his desire to stay for three years on Vorovoro, a vote had now rather confusingly been passed online that members could stay beyond three weeks for an unlimited period of time. Of course we had hoped this would quickly bring much-needed extra cash to the project but, apart from one or two who stayed a week or two longer, virtually no online members bought more weeks. It was also a vote that opened up the very possibility that I had hoped our initial three-week limit would prevent, difficult members causing problems on the project. And here with Poques there was a case in point. If he was to remain on the island for the next three years, even as a paying member, something would have to change because, as he later admitted to me, he was now a 'thorn in the side of Tribewanted'.

MJ volunteered to do the dirty work and tell Poques he didn't have a job that wasn't advertised and that we were going to ask him to leave the island for a few weeks. I was grateful as the whole issue had drained me. It illustrated the advantage of having MJ on the island, too, and showed our strength as a partnership. Now we needed to deal with our biggest challenge of all: money. We would need every last bit of strength to work out a solution, otherwise we and the tribe were going down. My biggest fear of failure was letting down Tui Mali, the family and his people. There was hope and expectation amongst them that hadn't been there a few months ago. There was also a relationship that strengthened by the day between our two unlikely communities, the local and the global, that would be a great loss to both if it had to stop for something that seemed by comparison so trivial.

'So at this rate we have less than two months before this thing goes under. What do we do?' I asked my weary-looking business partner frankly as he sat cross-legged on a mat, spreadsheets scattered around him.

'We've cut back on everything we can – none of the team are getting paid any more – and we can delay quite a few of these payments for online stuff and the inland revenue.'

'Yes, but not for ever. We need to bring in cash soon, and we ought to be able to. I mean look at the first three months, we were flying, and we didn't even have an island then!' I said, not quite believing it myself.

'The main problem in my opinion is the perception online. People think there is a risk with this project.'

'So let's invite Jem and his online buddies who don't believe that what we're doing is real to come and see for themselves. Because what we are doing here is a good thing, for everyone involved. These people piss me off. If only they could see what is happening on the island, and what we're trying to achieve, they'd soon change their minds. We should get them out here, although I might have to go and stay on Mali for a few days.'

MJ smiled at thought of our virtual nemesis walking up the beach and me sitting on top of a hill in Mali with a bowl of kava and a pair of binoculars, cursing. But it wasn't funny, and MJ and now Tribewanted were suffering badly from what had been insinuated online.

We agreed we would encourage more members to write up their Vorovoro experiences and we would post them online. I would also try and spread the word in Fiji so we could start to pick up travellers who hadn't decided which island they were going to yet. And we would both start meeting potential investors. Even though we weren't in a position of strength as a business, we knew we had a great idea on our hands, one that had been recognised internationally, was up and running and had a potentially bright future. I had to travel to Australia later that month as my tourist visa ran out and my work visa was yet to make its way through Fiji's bureaucratic maze, so MJ would set up a couple of meetings for me with potential investors whilst I was in Sydney. I would also try to inject the city backpackers with Tribewanted fever.

Despite this increasingly desperate situation, on the surface island life was bubbling along nicely. Tribe members helped build a chicken pen and a garden with the vivacious Tevita where numerous vegetables and fruits had been planted. Kimbo had put his legacy money towards painting and reinforcing Poasa's house as well as building a recycling unit behind his kitchen, something I was pleased to see the family themselves had requested. Dan and Api had been running some successful fishing trips with tribe members catching yellow-finned tuna and barracuda from the Mali channel, and work had begun with the local men on building a jetty on the south side of the island, away from the beach, to prevent any possible coral damage at low tide. Numbers of tribe members on the island were low, between five and ten, but those that came were having the time of their lives, and the friendships being built between the family, the workers and the visiting tribe members were fantastic. The only hard thing was saying goodbye. From the first footers' departures onwards, everyone found it difficult. Those remaining on the island would form a tunnel on the beach and those tribe members who were leaving walked through it hugging, handshaking and kissing their tribe as we all sang the Fijian goodbye song 'Isa Lei'. There were almost always tears, and I could see that the Fijians especially found this difficult as more and more people arrived and departed. At some point we would have to look into having set days, otherwise it was going to become an emotional strain and I was sure people would not continue to let themselves open up to get hurt week after week as their new-found friends left.

The view from the boat as you waved goodbye with a leaving tribe member was memorable every time. A crowd of people would stand arms aloft on the beach, waving bamboo posts and coconut fronds until you disappeared from view, when they would all turn and walk back up the beach to get on with their island existence.

The night before MJ left, we sat up late in Ulai's sister Vani's house, the family home on the hill behind Labasa that the team used as their chill-out space away from island life. It was a difficult conversation. We knew we were at a crossroads both for the business and as partners. Since we had met less than a year ago we had been through a rollercoaster experience and we had stuck close, supporting each other even when we disagreed. And that night I told MJ the news he didn't want to hear. I told him that I thought it wouldn't work out if we both lived on Vorovoro together. I told him what he knew already, that we were too different and there was too much at stake with the project to risk falling out with each other. The only other option in my mind was for me to leave the island and for him to run the project; something both of us knew would not make sense. We were both visibly upset that night but we remained friends and agreed that we had to stick together to get Tribewanted through this, whatever it would take. We would do everything in our power to keep the dream alive.

21
VUAVIRI
COUP

Kimbo and I sat down on the mats in the open shed under the 'Mali' banner and began the ritual kava and cake-eating session which appears to be a national obsession in Fiji. We all leaned forwards as a fleet of shiny tinted-window 4x4s pulled up at the other end of the field. Out stepped a very large man. He made his way forward with two men on either side of him dressed in dark blue shirts and bright white sulus with a crocodile tooth finish. I could just about see Tui Mali kneel in front of him on the grass and present the tabua. One of the big man's attendants received the whale's tooth and the party moved across to the main shed, the stage.

We were in Nadori ('Nandoree'), a large village fifty miles up the coast from Labasa, for Macuata Day (Mathuwata), a fundraising event and celebration for all the villages from up and down the northern coastline of Vanua Levu. Tui Mali had just been chosen by the people of Macuata to be their new representative on the Great Council of Chiefs, the traditional body of Chiefs in Fiji, which advises the President and the government of the day on tribal matters. The closest thing I can compare it to is the House of Lords. It was a great honour to be one of only a few dozen Chiefs on the Great Council out of hundreds in the country and Tui Mali had presented the first tabua to the chief guest that day, the Vice-President of Fiji.

Kimbo and I had gone along to show our support for Tui Mali. We were part of his community, after all, and we wanted to see how some of the money raised from the Great Bure project was going to be spent, as well as to experience Fijian culture beyond Vorovoro. Tui Mali came and sat down with us and the fifty or so members of the Mali community who had taken the two-hour journey to be there. Kimbo and I shook his hand, and I smiled as I saw what he was wearing: a Winnie the Pooh tie. I imagined his wife choosing it for him that morning. 'Now dear, we want you to look your best for the President, so I think this should do the trick.'

We drank kava, ate more cakes and watched a whole parade of Fijian tradition unfurl on the grass in front of us and the thousand or so other people that had gathered to watch the spectacle. And the Vice-President did pretty well as he received eight tabuas from various Chiefs, a whole pile of woven mats from the different villages and, most amusingly, a dance with about thirty women. The traditional dances, the mekes, vary in pace and style, and each one tells a story of Fiji's past; some even allow a glimpse into its future. The women's meke started in a tight circle in the middle of the field before opening out and shuffling towards the Vice-President who was sitting cross-legged on the main stage. I could see Tui Mali had a mischievous look in his eye. 'Did the Vice-President eat all the lovo himself?' I whispered. Tui Mali's laugh was high pitched and giggly, not what you expect from a Chief, almost childlike in its infectiousness.

'I think he must have eaten the pig's head himself,' Tui said, joining in the fun.

The gaggle of women had danced to where the big man was sitting and were now on stage, pulling him to his feet. He shuffled backwards and forwards, ten women either side of him, arms linked, obviously delighted by the benefits of being the Vice-President. Oh yes, he was the daddy.

The fundraising donations made, Mali making a significant contribution I was proud to see, Tui Mali went to have lunch with the chief guest and it was time for us to leave. As we walked past the building where the VIPs dined, I wondered what the chances would be of having a quick chat with the Vice-President. I wanted him to know about what was going on here in the north. I spoke to one of the guards and said I was with the BBC (I had the camera from Shine), as I thought it might lever us some access like they had told me it would back in London all those months ago. The guard returned five minutes later and said it would be fine, but I wasn't allowed to talk about the political situation. No problem, I said, I'm not a reporter, I would just like to meet the main man.

The President was supposed to be there that day but, because of current political problems, he was unable to leave Suva. A country whose recent history had seen not one but three overthrows of the elected government, most recently in 2000, was rather suddenly sensing another unstable political situation. Apart from the newspaper headlines that said the army commander was putting pressure on the government to meet certain demands, I wasn't entirely sure what was going on. But I knew I wanted to talk to Tui Mali about it, especially if the Vice-President's guard was wary of anyone talking to him about 'the current situation'.

The Vice-President climbed down the steps as I waited ready to intercept him before he got into his car and sped off.

'Pleased to meet you.'

'Are you doing the *Survivor* thing?' the Vice-President immediately asked.

'No we are not, we are doing Tribewanted. We are on Vorovoro island with Tui Mali,' I explained, then told him a bit more about how Tribewanted worked, before asking him how his day had been.

'Oh, it's been lovely.'

'I saw you dancing with the ladies.' I'd clearly had too much kava.

'Yes, well I thought I needed the exercise,' he said laughing. 'Well, thank you very much and good luck.'

'Thank you, and it was a pleasure to meet you,' I said, trying to control myself. Exercise! Fronting a campaign as a role model for a healthier Fiji was probably not going to be his most likely legacy, but still. Off he went with his tinted windows, back to Suva and the boiling pot. I turned to Tui Mali and asked him about how the money that had been raised by Mali was going to be spent.

'The money that has been given today will be spent in building a hostel for children coming from outer islands and out of Labasa, which is very hard every day.'

'And I have been meaning to ask you. What is going on in Suva at the moment? Do you think that everything's going to be OK?'

'Yes, yes everything will be OK,' Tui Mali said confidently.

'Because you have to go to the Council of Chiefs meeting next week?'

'First time.'

'First time, and it is going to be a serious meeting. So Tui Mali is going to sort everything out?'

'Yeah, I think so,' the smiling Chief replied. Talk about a baptism of fire. Tui Mali's first meeting with his council was an emergency one, to try and resolve the developing impasse between the government and the army.

'We have had a few people emailing us, asking what is going on here and is it safe to come to Fiji. You do not think that we will see a repeat of what happened in 2000?'

'No, our commander is just talking,' Tui Mali said, doing a hand-puppet motion with his fingers.

'Just talking it up. Let's hope so. We have enough challenges, we don't want another,' I said.

'The big question he is asking is, what is wrong with the bill that the government want to introduce now?'

'The Qoliqoli ['Golly Golly'] bill?' I said, not quite believing I had remembered what I read in the papers.

'Yes, the Qoliqoli bill, which the commander says is not good.'

'What does he not like about it?'

'He says it will cause fighting amongst each other, you know, and he tries to stop it.'

'Why does he want to? The Qoliqoli bill is trying to give landowners more power in terms of ownership of the sea, and fishing rights.'

'Who owns the Qoliqoli as you own the main land, as you would the dry land,' Tui Mali clarified for me, rather mysteriously. 'Now, I have got the right to go and fish but I do not own anything there. If you find oil or something else anything under the bottom of the ocean it would not be mine.'

A problem, I thought, after reading more about it. And, as the last three coups subtly suggested, something the people in Fiji didn't seem to be prepared to compromise on. I hoped Tui Mali was right, that it would blow over, that this 'clean-up campaign' that the army commander was threatening would come to nothing. Because if there was one thing we didn't need now it was a negative story about the country we were operating in. I had seen the impact of bad news on tourism and projects in Africa. Foreign Offices advice against travel means insurance companies invalidate your protection - and mums worry big time. The end result is that people stop visiting. I realised that day, as we travelled back from Nadori, if things deteriorated in Fiji then we were in even deeper trouble.

The following week I headed to Australia to see if I could find that briefcase full of cash we so badly needed. I met two investors in Sydney and one on the way back, in Fiji. All three seemed very impressed by what Tribewanted had achieved in so short a time, and they all liked what we were doing and the potential of the idea and the brand. And of course they loved the fact that the BBC was going to broadcast the story. The problem came when they asked about the financial situation.

I was frank, there's no point wasting anyone's time in these meetings. I told them we were short of money and needed investment now. I told them why the money wasn't coming at that point but how we would get over that. I told them I was confident we would succeed. And I think they believed me. They all asked for a detailed breakdown of the cashflow and business plan for 2007 and then we would go from there. But by the time I got back to Vorovoro, things in Fiji had deteriorated and preparing business plans for potential investors was not my first priority.

The army commander, who by now everyone on the island was calling Bananaman because it was easier to say than Bainamarama, had given the government a deadline to meet his demands, otherwise the army would begin their 'clean-up campaign'. It expired at midday on Friday 1 December. Tui Mali had returned to Vorovoro and Tevita, a Fijian traditionalist to the core, had organised a big welcome home reception for our Chief, as it was the first time in Mali's history that any of their Chiefs had been on the Great Council. We had a big lovo, a kava ceremony, and mekes performed by tribe members themselves, this time in the Great Bure. It felt like a really important community occasion and one that would have happened regardless of our involvement. It was great to see Tui Mali visibly relax after what must have been a stressful week. He had come home to his family, and we were part of that. I think we were all beginning to feel as if we really were part of the community in Fiji, not simply special visitors. I didn't talk to Tui Mali that day about what had happened in Suva, as I thought I should let him enjoy his homecoming, but the following morning I had tea with him on his veranda. 'What do you think will happen now?'

'Ben, it doesn't look good. I think this man will do what he says he will do and I don't think the Prime Minister will back down.'

'So what does that mean?'

'We have to wait and see, but there may be difficult times ahead. You know the Chiefs tried but the army doesn't want to listen and these people are very determined.'

Riah, a 20-year-old from Oregon, was our December Chief and our first *Marama*, female Chief. She was a happy, self-proclaimed hippy with a wide smile and a lot of energy, and was working on the village aesthetics, building bookshelves, weaving mats and making cushions. I don't think she expected to be a Chief on an island in the South Pacific in a country where it looked like it was all about to kick off; she had never even left her home state before that very month!

Kimbo had done well with the jetty project. I had been impressed with his commitment to the community and his gentle approach to leadership. He was keen to stay involved, so with the need now there, we invited him to remain on Vorovoro as an 'island gapper', a position we had created to help support the main team and work in the village. I saw potential in Kimbo and, although he was quite a shy lad, he was fun to live with and obviously cared a great deal about the project. He would be a good asset, to my brother especially.

So as the tribe, now only a handful, sat on the grass in the sunshine weaving mats for the Bure, I was preparing for what might happen on Friday. The British Foreign and Commonwealth Office was already advising against travel to Suva unless absolutely necessary and Australia was advising against all but essential travel to Fiji itself, which I thought was a bit much at this stage. I registered the names of our current members and team with the British, American and French embassies, and was sent an email the next day from the British Embassy saying they had prepared a camping ground within their compound for those who needed it if the situation got worse. Camping in the Embassy! We weren't in a war zone, we were on a tropical island in the sunshine. The Australians, furthermore, had now deployed a couple of warships off the coast of Suva in case they needed to evacuate their citizens. This was all getting a bit too full-on and the bad news had begun to spread as the world turned its attention to Bananaman and his Friday lunchtime deadline. Online tribe members were starting to link the articles in the local and national papers about Fiji, and already Sara Jane and I were having to calm emailed concerns from members who were due to be visiting over the next few weeks. I posted a message online to reassure people:

> There may have been reports abroad regarding the political situation in Fiji. This impasse has continued for some months now but with little effect on people's everyday lives. However, concerns shown are genuine. That said, some of the reporting may be a bit over the top and far from the reality of what life is all about in Fiji. On Vorovoro, tribal living is normal. Arrival processes and procedures are normal at Nadi, with assurances given by the responsible agencies of no extra procedures or disruptions for inbound travellers. If needed, further information on this can be viewed from the respective country travel advisories through the embassies. We will keep you all updated, but there is no cause for alarm.

I headed to town on the morning of Friday 1 December feeling like I had lost control of our future. In a way I had. If things kicked off today and the country shut down, no one would want to come to Fiji, and the last legs that we were standing on as a business would surely buckle beneath us. I sat at my laptop with the radio on, following the *Fiji Times*'s regular online updates. Midday came and went and nothing happened, but then about an hour later, an announcement was made on the radio:

> Commodore Bainamarama has just been spotted at the Police vs. Army rugby match in Suva. This is what he has just told Fijivillage.com: 'I maintain my demands and the deadline still stands and I will make a commitment to my stand after the rugby match.'

A rugby match? What about his threats to take over the country, were they empty? Soon a picture appeared of him on the *Fiji Times* website, wearing a baseball cap and sharing a joke next to my old mate the Vice-President! Was the future of the nation seriously less important than a game of rugby? If it was, to Bananaman, then I for one was pretty worried about what kind of man was threatening to take over this country. No one really seemed to know what was going on.

This guy was funny, and either making it up as he went along or cleverly drawing it out to get maximum attention. It must have been the best advertised coup in history! Back on Vorovoro, tribe members and local Fijians also thought the whole thing was pretty amusing. No one could quite believe that the first thing he was going to do as the ultimatum to the government expired was go and watch the rugby with his mates. And not just any old game, but a symbolic contest between the army and the police. I hoped the rest of the world would laugh along with us, and say, 'What a funny little country. We should go there for our holidays, those guys have a great sense of humour.'

The rugby match affair, although an entertaining respite for all of us, only delayed inevitable. I posted the following message to the tribe online on Tuesday 5 December at 6.30pm:

> Fijian Military Commodore Bainamarama has just claimed that he has taken control of the country. There is no violence in Fiji and business is carrying on as normal. The takeover means that Fiji will feel unstable for a while, mainly around the capital Suva, before a new government is elected. But it is very unlikely to affect day-to-day life, especially up here in the north. What does this mean for Vorovoro? Vorovoro is probably the best place to be in Fiji right now, especially when the radio is off! We will be carrying on as normal and welcoming new tribe members as and when they arrive. We are not considering closing or suspending the project unless the security of the tribe members or the people of Mali is compromised. We don't expect that to happen. We would just ask you to continue your brilliant support for this project by posting online and gathering around the world as we, and others in Fiji, go through this testing time. Vinaka, Ben and the tribe.

'Meet the President' was the headline in the newspapers the next day, stamped on a picture of the head of the army commander.

I was putting a brave face on a very difficult situation. If the travel bans stayed in place, which everyone expected for at least a number of weeks, and if the bad headlines kept rolling – the news had made the front pages in New Zealand and Australia that week – then getting new members to join the tribe from anywhere in the world was going to be near impossible. This was not a good moment to do our sales and marketing push but it was exactly the time we needed to do it. The impact showed immediately. Before the coup, we had had at least one or two members joining a day, but as soon as the coup happened not one new member signed up. And what chance did we now have of an investor backing a venture in a country where there was no government? I didn't know how long our own membership impasse would last, but I knew what it meant for us; unless MJ and I found some money soon it was goodbye Tribewanted, goodbye Fiji and goodbye to our beloved Vorovoro. The dream was almost over.

22
SOLESOLEVAKI NI KIRISIMASI
CONSOLIDATION AT CHRISTMAS

'Hey Dad, you've seen the news I take it?' I was on Skype to the old man back in Devon.

'Yes I did. It was just on the ten o'clock news.'

'Really, it's getting that much of a profile?'

'Yes it is, but I don't think people will take too much notice, there's no violence. So what about the project, what are you thinking?'

'We're going to be fine on Vorovoro, there's never going to be any danger there. But no one is signing up. We've already had a couple of cancellations over Christmas and you know how much we need the cash now. I'm just feeling pretty stuck.'

'Why don't you think about closing the project for a while until this passes? Come home and cut all business overheads until you have some cash coming in. I think people would understand if that happened, and it would give you time to regroup and get the business organised for when things get better in Fiji. You don't know how long this is going to last.'

My dad's proposal, although it made sense from a business

perspective, was not something I wanted to do. In fact, shutting down Vorovoro just over three months into the project was the last thing I wanted as it would send the wrong messages to Tui Mali and to the tribe members. But would it save us in the long term? Did we actually have a choice? It was definitely a good plan if we wanted to save as much money as possible. Back on Vorovoro, I found Dan. 'What do you think, Dan? Do you think we should head home until things improve?'

'I guess it would be the best answer for the business but we need to think about everything else. I'm not sure. What was your first reaction to the idea?'

'Well, I don't want the tribe to leave this place. We promised to live and work with the family and, if we leave now when it's still safe here, I don't think most people in Mali would understand. I want Tribewanted to stand by them.' I heard myself echo Warren's words from three months earlier when he fought the fire. Now, in the heat of the situation myself, I knew how he felt. But I needed to find a way to save the business as well as standing toe to toe with our neighbours. I told my brother what I hoped might be the solution. 'How about I leave the island, go back to the UK, try and find some cash and work things through with MJ? You stay here and manage the project. I know Tui Mali and the community trust you, and so do I.' He was the only person in the world at that moment that I would completely trust with the running of the project. Sara Jane was already heading back to the UK for a break, MJ was at home, and the only other person out here was Kimbo, a week into his role as a gapper. If anyone was going to manage Fiji, it was Dan. He agreed.

I borrowed the money I needed to buy a plane ticket and a week later I was sitting in the departure lounge in Nadi watching the sun set over the mountain range they call the Sleeping Giant, named after the shape of a man lying on his back. I hoped that when I returned the country would be back to its sleepy old self and not making headlines around the world because it couldn't run a democracy. Although I was very much looking forward to going home to see friends and family, I also knew I was on

CONSOLIDATION AT CHRISTMAS

another mission, a mission to save Tribewanted and our island dream.

Back in wintry Devon, Vorovoro life seemed so distant. But I didn't have time to daydream and enjoy the build-up to Christmas, I had a lot of work to do. I had been on the phone and on emails with MJ pretty much full-time since I'd landed back in the UK. We had already started talking about what to do with the business and we both knew that we would need to find the cash in the coming weeks. After the investor meetings I was aware we wouldn't have time to go through that process now. I had been on my own money hunt and had found access to a decent loan that would save the business and get us through two or three months of no income. It was not a loan I wanted to take but we had no choice. I was, however, not prepared to invest in the business this time unless MJ could match me. This may sound harsh, but it was a serious situation. I had happily put the few thousand pounds I had saved since graduating towards getting Tribewanted off the ground but if I was going to take any more financial risk I needed my business partner to do the same. But it was also clear MJ didn't have any cash to put in. So we began to reach our own impasse, one that we both realised was going to quickly reach a crunch point.

We also talked about the situation beyond the black and white of the finances. Communication between us had deteriorated since I had left for Fiji earlier that year. We had found it virtually impossible to run the business between us at a distance and with a back-to-front time difference. But it had also become clear from when MJ had visited Fiji that we would find it difficult to work on Vorovoro together. Until that point, we had seen our differences not as a source of conflict but as a reason for success. On Vorovoro, however, we would stifle each other.

On top of this, I knew MJ was keen to quickly develop some of his further online ideas, some of which looked pretty good, and that being either in Fiji or a director of Tribewanted in its present state would restrict him. Of course, all this would have been different if we had better numbers and more cash, but we didn't and we had to work it out within the current situation. MJ had also had a number of approaches from different media companies interested in talking to him about some of his other creative brainwaves. He was worried that staying involved with Tribewanted would mean that he lost these opportunities.

Through these conversations, although hard for both of us and especially for MJ who cared about Tribewanted immensely, it became apparent that we needed to find a way out for him. And so we began the process of talking to lawyers and drawing up an agreement to satisfy us both. It would release MJ from the stress of Tribewanted, help him break away from the online criticism and give him freedom to pursue his other ideas. And it would give me the opportunity to invest cash the business needed and take the project forward without the challenge of communicating with a business partner on the other side of the world.

A week later, I drove to Liverpool with the share buy-out contract on my lap. It was the first time I had seen MJ for a couple of months and it was under difficult circumstances but it was good to meet him. We still got on pretty well and we both accepted that it had come to this although, all logic aside, I could see how upset it made him. It went against how he felt. MJ signed the contract that would relieve him of his responsibilities as a company director, pay him for his shares and give me the control of the business. We went to the pub for lunch. 'So what's next for you, a year after this all began? Are you planning to have as exciting a year in 2007?' I asked my now ex-business partner.

'I hope it will be exciting, sure, but I really don't want to go through that kind of stress again. I'm really happy I played my part in getting Tribewanted off the ground, and I know you will turn it around from here. As for me, well, I'm already talking to other people about the next idea, so hopefully it won't be too long. But right now I just need to rest, it's pretty difficult to accept this is happening.'

'I know. But I'm sure there are plenty of people out there who want to hear about what Mark James Bowness has got in his head. You'll bounce back. You will. One more thing. I was hoping you would stay involved as an adviser in online development. You know more about it than me and I'd like it if you would stay involved at least in that role, although I have to tell you it doesn't pay particularly well. Actually, it pays bugger all.'

'I'd love to, thanks. You know the hardest thing is about letting go of something that was much more than just shares in a business. The idea I had a year ago really has turned into something amazing.'

'I know and I'll make sure I keep it going, I promise. Remember, you're still in the tribe, you just don't have to worry about it any more.' He smiled wearily, disguising an intensity of emotions.

We walked outside the pub, where we shook hands and wished each other luck before I drove off into the December mist. I was very relieved that I now knew where I stood and that, although there was a massive challenge ahead of me, I could now crack on with it. But I also knew the responsibility now rested squarely on my shoulders, and my shoulders only, and that certainly tempered the sense of release I now felt.

MJ and I had also written a statement to be posted online for the tribe. We were concerned about what the reaction might be if we told members that one of the main reasons MJ had left the company was because of finances. We were worried that the online tribe, already feeling a bit out of the picture over the recent poor communications from us, and nervous about what was going on in Fiji, might start to lose faith in the project. If we revealed the full extent of the financial situation now we would probably have a coup of our own on our hands. The message we sent the tribe talked about the need to focus on Fiji, and MJ being unable to do that, both of which were true. I felt bad that we hadn't been completely open with our members but knew that it was the right decision.

Next stop was Chester with MJ's sister, Sara Jane. It was 23 December. Shine's camera followed me as I walked up the steps in the freezing night and into the bar by the river. Sara and I had to make the decision about whether it was a good idea for her to come back to Fiji and continue working for Tribewanted. I told her over a hot chocolate in a very different setting to the one we were used to – her hair was styled and she was wearing make-up for starters – that I would like her to come back to Fiji and how much Tribewanted could afford to pay her. She accepted and gave me a hug, telling me how much she missed the island. The whole episode with MJ over the past few weeks had left her caught in the middle between a career, her family and an island she loved. It can't have been an easy situation. And although for me at that point it might have been tempting to say I didn't think it would work out for her with Tribewanted, she had proved herself over the past few months, was incredibly committed and I wanted it to work for her. Although brief, it was a good meeting, 'See you on Vorovoro,' I said as I climbed back into the car - and that's a good thing to be able to say to anyone.

I've had better Christmases, I have to admit. For most of the next week I was passed out on the sofa, exhausted from the last few weeks and full of cold. I knew the New Year was going to be a busy time and I wanted to get back to Fiji as soon as possible, so I just slept. Ate and slept. My family must have been ecstatic. I hadn't been home for months and the moment I arrive I pass out in a snotty, coughing mess. Happy Christmas, Benj! I didn't even make it out on New Year's Eve, but I'm glad I hadn't because shortly after midday the phone rang. 'Hey Ben, happy New Year from Vorovoro!' Being twelve hours ahead they had already celebrated.

'Happy New Year, Dan. How's 2007 looking?'

'Awesome Ben. Awesome. We've just come back from a mammoth session in Lingaulevu, the whole of Mali was partying hard and throwing people in the sea, and now everyone is round the fire dancing, with sparklers and coconut cocktails. Everyone's feeling a lot of love on the island tonight.'

'And who is on duty?' I asked, slightly worried suddenly that if something went wrong no one would be sober enough to sort it out.

'I am. I haven't had a drop and it's one of the best New Years ever. Wish you were with us.'

'Me too, Dan, me too.' I could hear the laughter and singing in the background and I felt like crying. Not because I was desperate to be there, I'd knew I would be back soon, but because I was so happy that we had stayed, that we had stuck it out with our family in Fiji.

'Here's Dad, big love to the tribe and family. See you soon, Dan,' I said before there was any chance I did start crying. I found out later from Dad that there had been a wedding that week on the island, well, a kind of a wedding. Toni and Chris had arrived on Boxing Day and asked if Tui Mali would bless their recent marriage, so a short traditional ceremony was organised on the beach and Tui Mali read from the Bible and blessed them. A large turtle had also been found on the island, and the tribe had persuaded the local boys not to cut it up but instead release it back into the sea. It was all good news from our island home, just what I needed to hear. I didn't go out to celebrate the New Year that night; instead I sat up with Dad and Frances, and drank a good bottle of wine before falling asleep by the fire, dreaming of my return to Vorovoro.

23
BASIKA NA DUI TIKINA
ENTER THE TIKINAS

Our online community, our tribe, had been ignored and the first thing I was going to do in 2007 was make sure I spent a decent amount of time talking and planning with them for the year ahead. This was going to be a great year for the tribe, of that I was sure.

The first thing I did was write an update of where we were with the project and what I thought we needed to focus on over the coming year. A sustainable water solution, for a start. There was enough rain falling on Vorovoro now, we just needed to work out the best way to harvest it and conserve it. Further accommodation was needed. The Great Bure and the shed, which the January chief, Stuart 'Wildgeeza' Wild, was turning into a super-shed, or proper house, were currently our only real sleeping spaces. What should we do next? An improved farming plan for fruit, vegetables and livestock; a look into how we could introduce green power on Vorovoro and finally how we might support local projects in the school and communities in a more structured way.

Online, I said I would like to see further structure in the way we made decisions as a tribe and to see more involvement from members in the weekly newsletter. I also told the tribe that it was my aim to find another 1,000 members by the start of 2008. I knew this was a big call, but I wanted to set our goals high and I wanted the tribe to come with me on the journey. I said I would be online at 8pm on Sunday 7 January GMT if anyone wanted to discuss any of these plans.

Alongside my written address to the tribe I also recorded a podcast that I thought might help give more confidence to members for the year ahead. It took me five or six takes to get the message and words across in the way that I wanted. Curiously, I found it much more difficult than most of the TV or press interviews I had done over the last year. I felt like I was doing a state of the nation address from my own bedroom. I knew I was talking directly to people who had invested time, money and dreams in this project and I wanted them to know I was working my hardest so they could be confident in the tribe and continue to enjoy the adventure. I was fully aware of the gossip flying around between some members as a number of emails ended up being forwarded to me. I didn't want to get involved with that, I just wanted to crack on with the future. But from what I read there were quite a few doubters out there within our own ranks. Doubters whose faith I was determined to restore.

I also set out some personal and business goals for the year ahead. I rewrote the business plan and cashflow for the year, tightening things up as much as I could within the constraints of the commitments we had already made. Membership sales targets were drawn up and I even managed a graph or two. I had to remind myself not to get too carried away. One of the big aims for me was to get Vorovoro online as soon as possible. We had failed so far and to take the idea to the full extent of MJ's original conception we needed that connection. I knew we didn't have the cash to do it so we would have to find a partner who saw the benefits of being involved. It was one of the first things I would tackle when I got back to Fiji.

I also looked at how the team might develop. My short-term aim was to have both a sustainability manager on the island (we at least had the UCL team working on a sustainability plan from now on, which would be a great help) and a web 2.0 developer to reflect the two core aims of the project. I put aside some money to recruit these people. Everyone else would be on a very basic wage and I would not pay myself until we were easily clearing our sales targets and had paid off all our debts. I realised this might be a long way off, but it was good motivation for me. On a personal level, I wanted to focus on my fitness and my knowledge of sustainability. I would swim regularly, I told myself, when I got back to Fiji, and I would start reading more. I also wanted to start surfing, and as soon as we beat our first monthly sales target I would buy a surfboard for the tribe.

I logged onto the Tribewanted chatroom just before 8pm on Sunday night, and by the time we had all said hello to each other there were six of us. I think the number grew to about fourteen at one stage. Not massive, I know, but it was enough people to talk through some of the plans with. The tribe members I spoke to were enthusiastic and just pleased to see some action again. J-dub was there as usual, full of energy and online acronyms like IMHO, which stands for 'in my humble opinion'. The idea of forming councils around each of the project goals was put forward and I said I thought that this was vital. My dad was in the kitchen with me and I was bouncing the chat off him as he prepared one of his 'look what I've just cooked' M&S classic dinners. When I mentioned the councils idea he asked me what the village councils were called in Fiji. 'Tikinas,' I said, already typing it into the chat room. The members loved the idea of forming Tribal Tikinas, so we quickly agreed the main ones we would need.

The Voting Tikina would organise the voting system online, gathering the important points of the debates and writing the proposed wording for each vote before sending it to me to post in the 'voting booth'. Yes, we had our own online voting booth where you put an 'X' in the box just like you would in an election.

ENTER THE TIKINAS

Why general elections aren't done online yet I don't know. Mind you, if our 'unlimited time' vote was anything to go by, there is still a lot of trial and error before online voting becomes the norm. We would also try to form an Energy Tikina, a News Tikina, a Tech Tikina, a Sustainable Development Tikina and a Dream Foundation Tikina. One of MJ's ideas at the start had been that we should set up a charity alongside Tribewanted that would raise money for projects in Fiji apart from Vorovoro. It would be called the Tribewanted Dream Foundation. We had all had the chance to realise a dream by being part of Vorovoro so we, as a tribe, should in turn try to help those with less opportunity to realise their dreams, whether this was through health, education or sustainable development. I knew there were several members who were keen to take the Dream Foundation idea forward and I hoped the Tikina might spark this.

I posted the proposed Tikina ideas on the forum and we had a great response with a number of members putting their names forward to help. It felt good. The online community was springing back to life and, although I knew we had a long way to go with the technology as it wasn't exactly Facebook in terms of being easy to use, that was less important than getting more content, news and ideas on it. People were thirsty for information about Vorovoro and it was the team's job to quench that thirst.

I met with STA Travel that week to see how much they could push Tribewanted in 2007. They were keen, they told me, and set out some strong marketing ideas. I left the meeting confident that things would take off with them as, in terms of membership sales, they were our key partner. If they got the marketing of Tribewanted right and well placed, I was confident we could bring in lots more members.

I was aware that there had been a shift as well in the reasons why people would now join the project. The initial buzz had obviously gone, there was no need to worry that the memberships might sell out. Now the focus had to be much more now on what was going on in Vorovoro and targeting those already on the road. I rewrote a lot of the website that week and, with Komodo, redesigned the homepage to show the different aspects of tribe life from island news to gatherings to recent votes to tribe member's profiles, as well as making the whole project look more credible. I think it was a good step forward and the members agreed.

I also met with our sustainability advisers who, amongst others, included Jodi from MTT Sustain, Michael from Climate Care, Helen from Global Sense and Dr Bell from UCL. I told them about the tribe's green dream, of how we wanted to work towards sustainability on Vorovoro, to cut our carbon emissions; those that we couldn't cut, like flights, we would offset with Climate Care, pumping valuable funding into renewable energy projects. I was particularly excited about UCL's imminent work on the project especially after I met the post-grad students who were all looking forward to working on Tribewanted. It was a good team and I knew how lucky we were to have their support.

A few days before I was due to fly back to Fiji, a package landed on the doormat. I ripped it open and pulled out a picture of Vorovoro with Becky and Ryan Smith (another first footer romance), snorkelling towards the headland. It was a stunning picture with the contrasting blues of the water and the sky framing the rocky outcrop that was so distinctive of our island home. But what made the picture make my hands shake and my eyes blink in disbelief was the bright yellow box that framed it. The photograph was on the front of *National Geographic Adventure* magazine. Vorovoro was a cover story. I honestly couldn't believe it. 'Wild Islands!' and 'South Seas Utopias, Welcome to Internet Island' were the headlines splashed across Vorovoro's azure waters. Inside, the 9-page, 5,000-word feature was a fantastic adventure story. I had been brought up on *Nat Geos* at home and at school and to see our project, our island and our dream framed by the iconic yellow rectangle was incredible. At that moment, as I stood in the kitchen looking at pictures of me and the first footers in the magazine, I felt a renewed sense of energy for what we were doing. If we had made the front cover of *National Geographic*, there was no way this was going to fail.

24

KACI MAI VALE-MOCE TANIELA
GOODBYE, DAN

Raijeli and Kesa grabbed me by the arms and dragged me down the beach before dunking me unceremoniously in the sea.

It was mid-January, and I was back on Vorovoro and on the receiving end of the New Year tradition of 'getting wet', which would apparently last all month. The water was like a bath, and I lay on my back and floated for a few minutes, staring at the big blue sky. I couldn't quite believe I was back in this place. I was having one of my Utopian glimpses again.

The first thing I noticed about the island was how green it seemed. The heavy rains of the previous month had not only kept replenished the tribe's water supply but had also transformed the island foliage from the browns and golds of the end of the dry season into a rich, lush blanket. The tribe's village was immaculate, the gardens were better kept than those of an English stately home and work on the shed and Chief's Bure was coming along nicely. I'd only been away for a month but now I knew again what it felt like to be arriving in this place for the first time. It really was like entering another world. People don't really live like this, do they, I thought to myself, smiling.

The political news in Fiji had begun to subside and, although no new government looked like getting elected any time soon, at least the negative headlines overseas were disappearing and the travel warnings receding. From what I could pick up on what the Fijians call the coconut wireless, it seemed that the budget travel market might bounce back pretty quickly. Those in the know in the travel industry will tell you the two most resilient groups are the backpackers and the Brits. 'There's been a coup in Fiji and you can get completely high on this kava stuff. Let's go!'

Bragging rights seem to be as important to a lot of travellers these days as actually travelling itself and the combination of what they could blog to their mates about a lawless land where drug-taking was a national pastime was incentive enough to change for a stopover in Fiji.

We didn't, of course, want to start attracting that crowd although I suspect that there are some members out there who joined just so they could let it slip out over dinner that they had, um, joined a tribe. 'Yeah, that's right, I've joined a tribe, and we've, well we've got this island in Fiji you see. Yeah, that's right, an island in Fiji, and I'm going to go there some time and help develop it.' A few braggers would be acceptable, I thought, if they helped the cashflow graphs lean in the right direction.

The advantage of being up in the north, an extra plane or boat and bus adventure away from Fiji's international airport, was that we didn't attract the kind of backpackers who turned up looking for the nearest party island. No, people who came to Vorovoro had thought it through and could see that it wasn't going to be a resort experience. I'm sure that's why we've had virtually no trouble as yet from tribe members on the island. But to be honest none of us, including Tui Mali, who had the news direct from the Great Council, really knew what was going to happen to Fiji. The situation might deteriorate at any moment. The army road checks could easily become road blocks and the clean-up campaign, which was in full swing, could turn nasty. But there

GOODBYE, DAN

was nothing any of us, including Tui Mali, could do about it.

Dan was sitting on the floor in Poasa's house and, knowing he was only with us until the next morning, I went and sat with him. He had stayed on an extra two weeks in Fiji to give me more time in the UK to plan for the year ahead. He was desperate to get home to see his girlfriend, Mollie, and I know staying in Fiji this long had put a lot of pressure on them. There's no way you can keep a relationship strong for more than a few months on opposite sides of the world so Dan had chosen to go home. If he stayed in Fiji he would probably lose her and he didn't want that to happen. We had less than twenty-four jet-lagged hours together to hand over all the project stuff and to hang out. It wasn't enough. The family were giving Dan his leaving presents.

'These, Taniela, are for Mo, your nou [Mum],' Frances, Poasa's laugh-like-you're-going-to-cry wife said to him, handing over a large woven basket with several smaller baskets inside. Dan thanked the family before looking at this new gift set. He turned to me.

'What are these?' He held up the mini-baskets that were actually stitched up so you couldn't ever use them for anything.

'I think they're for decoration,' I said, trying to help him out.

I gave the family the Christmas presents and cards from Mum. Poasa opened the parcel and held up a Malvern Hills tea towel. I couldn't believe Mum was still giving tea towels out as presents. Poasa immediately hung it on the wall next to the blown-up picture of my brother, Taniela, sitting on the side of the boat looking a bit too cool for my liking. The only other pictures in the room were one Becky had given the family of a Vorovoro sunset alongside framed portraits of Her Majesty Queen Elizabeth II and Princess Di. Dan was in serious company on the family's living room wall and I hoped he realised what it meant. It indicated that the family had fallen in love with Taniela, that he was very much their brother, their son and their best friend. I could see that Raijeli and Kesa especially were going to miss him. Even within a few hours of being back on the island, the impact he had made whilst I was away was obvious. The community, the team and the tribe members all looked to him. I really didn't want him to go; it was painfully clear that this was what he was good at, motivating, organising and looking after people. He, Kimbo, the recent visiting members and the family had kept the tribe spirit very much alive when they probably all knew things were touch and go with Tribewanted and with Fiji.

That night, we drank kava on Tui Mali's veranda to *Bula* (welcome) me and *Moce* (goodbye) Dan, but the jet lag kicked in after the third shell, and I was out for the count as a full grog session ensued. The next morning, as we waited for Dan to walk through the tribal tunnel onto the beach, I heard the Shine cameraman ask Api, our Taniela-trained boat captain, what he thought of the boy he had been working and fishing with over the last six months. Api turned his honest eyes to the camera and said: 'He is my best friend.'

Dan walked down the line handing out envelopes of photographs to the family and workers, pictures he had taken during his time on Vorovoro. There were a lot of tears as I waited on the boat for my brother to leave. We didn't say much on the journey back to Labasa. I knew he didn't really want to leave a place and a people he had fallen in love with, just like the rest of us. But he was in love somewhere else and, as I told him, 'Vorovoro will always be here for you, Dan but if you stay here any longer Mollie might not be.'

At Labasa airport he promised to help with anything that needed doing from the UK and I knew that would be important. He had given up a lot to come out here and had made such a difference and, as Sara Jane and I hugged and waved goodbye, I knew Vorovoro had lost one of the good guys. Dan had gone.

25
CAGILABA
CYCLONE

Mosquitoes were everywhere. The big rains had brought full water tanks, green grasses and also an explosion in the insect population, the least favourite of which seemed to be constant companions. They were really one of the few things that came between the reality of island life and perfection. Fijians, of course, had learnt to deal with the problem and we quickly followed their lead. Don't leave buckets of water out where they can breed. Do keep the village areas clean and empty of piles of dead leaves. Do burn coconut husks in the Bures, around the kitchen, showers and dining areas – the best repellent is smoke. Do cover yourself in Epeli's homemade coconut oil slick mixed with various leaves. The mosquitoes will not come near you. Neither will anyone else.

The first week back on Vorovoro was a good one. Wildgeeza, our Chief for the month, wasn't perhaps quite as wild and crazy as his tribal name suggested. He was a 29-year-old motorbike enthusiast from Oxfordshire, a brilliant technical draughtsman, sketching out plans for the new super-shed he was working on and even helping some of the locals with their own home-building plans. The showers were upgraded and a smaller Chief's Bure was getting close to completion. The jetty posts and walkway were now finished, and it was simply a case of fixing the floating pontoon in place. The Chief's budget system seemed to be working nicely and even though we had lost Tevita, our horticulturalist, since he hadn't returned from his Christmas break, the garden was flourishing and I was surprised to see that Kimbo seemed to be developing a rather special relationship with the chickens.

In Lingaulevu, the tribe had helped construct a *Mokka*, a traditional way of catching fish by building a stone and coconut weaved wall in a semi-circle in front of the mangroves, that trapped fish as the tide went out. Island life was ticking along nicely. We just needed more people.

Online, meanwhile, the Tikinas were forming and a tribe member who called himself Gilligan, an enthusiastic and colourful American German-teacher, had taken the lead in the Voting Tikina. He was busy organising the wording and structure of votes and seemed to be making a lot of progress, from the number of his Tikina supporters and the amount of emails I was being copied in on. A few votes on the structure of the Voting Tikina – voting on how to vote was something that always confused me slightly – had passed through relatively smoothly, although Gilligan was a little unhappy that I hadn't quite posted them on time as per his request. I apologised and said I would do my best to make sure it didn't happen again.

Next up was a reworking of the previous botched 'extra time' votes. The wording of the earlier vote meant that tribe members would be able to buy an unlimited number of weeks. The result, however, had caused controversy. There were three options if the initial vote for extra time carried, which it had. The first was that tribe members could buy an extra four weeks of island time; the second option was to be able to buy an extra six weeks; and the third option was that tribe members could buy an unlimited number of weeks on Vorovoro. The result was that 46 per cent said that members should be able to buy an unlimited amount of weeks (option three), whilst the first two options of some kind of limited vote made up 54 per cent of the vote. The tribe argued, and I had to agree in hindsight, that the 'unlimited' result could not be carried as more members had voted for some kind of 'limited' option. If you're not confused already, it got a lot more complicated, but the point was we needed another vote, and Gilligan and his Tikina were sorting it out. My job was simply at this stage to post the vote online.

When I received the three new votes that needed posting I could not actually fit all the wording of the second vote within the given space in the voting booth. It was late on a Friday and I knew that Gilligan would be miffed if they didn't go online tonight as requested. So I took the option which I thought was the lesser of two evils and posted all three votes, including the second vote in which I had to cut the final seven words because of lack of space. I didn't expect, when I logged on again the following morning, to be on the receiving end of a tirade of abuse. My inbox was full of anger from Gilligan telling me I had changed the wording of the vote without his permission, and that I always changed everything, and that I always manipulated everything to my advantage, and that the only person I was in this for was me! He had also posted a similar rant on the forums entitled 'I apologise, but today was the last straw for me', which included this explanation of why he was so unhappy with me:

> He has taken out the words 'and in observance of Tribe enacted rules' without ANY warning ... without ANY discussion ... without saying so in the forum and, in my opinion, with complete and utter disrespect for the process of democracy or our opinion as Tribe Members and I refuse to be involved in this kind of deception.

The omission of the seven words, which I was convinced had no effect on the way the wording of the vote could have been interpreted was, according to Gilligan, a step too far and he was quitting the tribe. I immediately responded online, for the first time dropping my diplomatic shield and told him he was overreacting. But that was that, he vanished from the forums and Tikinas and inboxes. I supposed he had another agenda which he wasn't prepared to raise with me. Instead he took a petty issue and threw his toys well and truly out of the pram and all over the pavement. I had been told he was a nice guy, a great host, and I knew he was a strong supporter of Tribewanted. But I was really disappointed to see this response. I didn't know what I'd done to make him react like that. It frustrated me and, as I returned to Vorovoro that afternoon, with dark clouds gathering, I wondered if we really were ever going to get this online community working well.

We dropped Va back at the Malau jetty for the weekend. It must have been about five in the afternoon and, by the time we had stopped on Mali in the small settlement of Vuni Moli (the orange tree), it had started. At first sheets of rain lashed down on us as we skimmed across the flat water. But as we skirted round the Mali headland waves began to take shape. Frances, Poasa's spectacularly happy and rotund wife, was screaming and yelping with each wave we hit. You wouldn't have guessed that she had lived on an island all her life. Captain Api ducked and dived the small fibre punt between the peaks and troughs with the expertise of a man who was, as he himself told us, 'born in the sea'. The crests of the larger waves were now breaking over the bow of the boat. Water washed over my knees as I sat cross-legged on the plywood deck. I looked up at Poasa who was laughing at his wife's wailings as he leaned back casually against the roller-coastering side of the boat like he was having afternoon tea. The sky was getting blacker by the minute, but there was still a good hour until dusk.

I could see waves breaking high up the beach as we bounced around the headland of Vorovoro. It made me think of the landing crafts on the Normandy beaches in the Second World War, boys much younger than me ducked down, looking forward, waiting to face their enemy. I couldn't begin to imagine the fear.

I shuddered as a wave slapped my face. I could only be grateful that all we had to do was get to that beach, that there wouldn't be any bullets to dodge. Adventure takes many forms, I thought. We hauled the boat high up on the land then body surfed the beach breaks, scraping our chests against the coarse sand. Why does a change in weather make people go nuts?

I woke early on Sunday morning and walked down to the tribe village. I was happy to see it was still raining, and even happier to see the 1,000-litre tank overflowing with water caught by the guttering from the toilet, shed and kitchen roof tops. I started pumping. The hand-pump we'd bought off Chuck must have been nearly a hundred years old. Sure, it did the job, but each push and pull required, for me at least, my full bodyweight behind it. Each pump (one push, one pull), sent about two litres of water up the pipe and the hill into the big 10,000-litre tank. After about twenty minutes of pumping, Kimbo appeared.

'Yadre.'

'Ready for some shift work?' I asked. '100 pumps each then swap. I reckon we can fill the top tank today if we go for it.'

By mid morning it was looking good. As Kimbo pushed and pulled his way through another century stand, I hiked up to the big tank and clambered carefully via the adjacent rockface onto its slippery roof. Clinging to the rim of the opening as my legs dangled over the edge, I peered into the darkness. I was shocked, it was almost full. The water Kimbo was pumping was pouring in more than three quarters of the way up. In my life before Vorovoro and rainwater catchments, a nearly full tank of water wouldn't have excited me. But after a few months on a very dry island it was the kind of thing that made my day. Water scarcity was a real issue, and when it wasn't so scarce life was brilliant. Kimbo and I were doing our bit, harvesting the rain for the tribe. It felt good. I even drew a *Blue Peter*-style pump-o-meter on the small blackboard to notch up our centuries. I don't think that Kimbo cared about the pump-o-meter but I like to measure progress. It was like a test match, accumulating runs (pumps) which required more and more concentration as we tired and got closer to three figures. Two sessions – morning – lunch – afternoon – and we were well on our way to victory. The tank would be full by afternoon tea and the Ashes would be ours! But then the wind came. It blew the tarp off the roof, the matting off the table, and soon trees began to bend and break. Kimbo and I had to retire early.

Api and Poasa were busy banging nails into sheets of corrugated iron across the windows of the three houses when we got back to the Fijian village. The wind was getting a lot stronger and the blue wooden boat bounced around in the sea like a kid being pushed around in a circle of bullies. The rain stung as it pelted us horizontally. Raijeli shouted through the storm: 'We have to get everything from the kitchen and bring it up here! It's raining inside!' So we all ran back down to the kitchen and started ferrying containers of vegetables, flour and sugar to the safety of Poasa's house. The hundred-metre stretch between the tribe village and the Fijian village is normally a pleasant walk, running parallel to the beach, shaded by coconut palms. Not today. The coconut palms now blocked our path where they had fallen and we either had to hurdle or duck under them to get past.

On the second run, I was carrying a large bucket of rice when a pair of coconuts thudded down two feet away from me. I stopped dead in my tracks. It was like a stun gun. If those two little things had landed a couple of feet to the left at exactly the same time I would have been in trouble. There is nothing quite like the sound of a coconut thudding to the floor. It's scary. They're dangerous, predatory coconuts. They do, after all, kill more people a year than sharks. The only advice I can offer is don't stand still. I didn't. I continued down the coconut gauntlet as fast as I could go with a three-kilogramme bucket of rice in a storm until I made it to the other end. It was like a nasty version of a game from 'Takeshi's Castle', the extreme Japanese TV game, without crash helmets or the smiling contestants, of course. The sound of the tree's branches whiplashing against their own trunks was painful. Like some form of natural masochism, the trees were beating themselves and being torn apart in the process. There was nothing we could do for now. The houses were safe, the food was dry. It was time to sit it out.

I lay on my mattress and read a chapter called 'Love Miles' from George Monbiot's *Heat* about how to stop climate change and possibly more devastating storms than the one that was rattling the window next to me. By now I was sure it was a cyclone. The reading distracted me from the creaking of the corrugated roof as each gust of wind threatened to lift it. In this chapter, Monbiot's aim was to find a solution to the amount of carbon the airline industry was pumping into the atmosphere before it was 'too late'. According to the author, and his extensive research, there is no technological solution: bio-fuel, more efficient fuel, alternative means of travel – all out. The only way for air travel not to be the cause of civilisation collapsing was to stop flying. By stop, he had calculated the world needed to cut the amount of flights by 96 per cent in the next few decades. I was angry. Even if Monbiot was considered a radical thinker, I knew a lot of the facts he was using were accurate, even before I'd heard any counter arguments.

I was angry because I knew giving up or cutting down on flying was the right thing to do. One of the freedoms I value most is travel and flying. But here I was, experiencing my first tropical island storm, perhaps having helped cause it, and Monbiot was telling me I had to give it all up. Perhaps we shouldn't be here, we shouldn't have responded to that NLTB webpage advertising Vorovoro. I was confused, frustrated and for a few minutes I didn't know if I had the strength or the determination to deal with the bigger, longer-term picture.

But, before I could sink any further into despondency at the state of the world, the immediacy of the cyclone stole my attention. The roof had started to leak and the end of my mattress was getting wet. Kimbo, Sara Jane and I hauled everything from the front room into the back room of the house and onto the newly built storage shelving. Kimbo skewered a fishing knife between the panels in the ceiling, water started to seep through. We put plastic boxes under the leaks. I was pretty concerned that the roof might not last the night.

I suddenly remembered I'd said I'd be online by 3pm on Sunday afternoon to run through the problems that the missing seven words from vote two had caused. Obviously I wasn't going to be online at that time as it was already well past 3pm and we were in the middle of what we now understood to be 'cyclone season'. My phone battery was low but I needed to get a message out. I knew that when I wasn't online that afternoon or the following morning for the weekly tribe meeting, people would start asking questions and then someone would post the hurricane headline and no one would know what was going on. I couldn't call anyone as the only areas with phone reception on the island are all outside and even if a call connected they would not be able to hear a word I was saying. So I typed out a text message in the house, saved it as a draft, and lined it up for five recipients, hoping that it would get through to at least one:

> Storm on Vorovoro. All OK, but stranded. Will be online ASAP. Ben and tribe.

I ran down the path to the tribe village, praying that all the coconuts that were going to fall had already fallen, and turned left onto the path that cuts inland towards the other side of the island and the jetty. More fallen trees, branches and debris to be hurdled. The run-off from the hillside had also flooded the path. I waded waist deep in fresh rainwater until I got to the 'phone box'. Now, if you're expecting a classic English red phone box, the sort you see in *Postman Pat*, when you come to Vorovoro, you're going to be disappointed. The Vorovoro phone box is a bench with a sign saying 'phone box' hanging from a tree. It just happens to be a good place for mobile phone reception.

I crouched down behind the bench and sent the message through the dry bag I had the phone in. Message sent. Brilliant. I continued along the path, as I'd just remembered that the pontoon was tied to the mangroves and I wanted to check that it and the mangroves it was tied to were still there. It wasn't. Shit. I couldn't see it anywhere and dark, mangrove muddy waves were breaking hard on the stony beach.

I sprinted down the connecting path back to Poasa's house like I was in some kind of jungle war movie. I was charging, I desperately didn't want to lose a pontoon we had spent a lot of time and money on before it had even been used. A small army consisting of Raijeli, Sara Jane, Api, Kimbo, Chief Stu and Kesa all ran back with me and a rope and a video camera to try and rescue the pontoon. Api dived into the dark waves. Even standing in the shallows, my shins were taking a pummelling from the stones and wood being hurled at the beach. Api disappeared behind the mangroves, and for about two minutes we lost him completely. I knew Api was a good swimmer but even by his standards this was pretty choppy. It was also dusk and the storm was no less intense. The whole situation reeked of danger. If I had been making the decision, it would have been a red light. But not for Api. And just as we were starting to get worried, Api and the pontoon emerged into the gap between the mangroves. I waded in and tried to surf the square structure onto the beach. We tied it to two trees with a rope and retired. Pontoon rescued. Job done.

We all slept in Tui Mali's house that night. It was the driest, safest place to be. I gave Api a miniature of Grants Scotch Whisky I'd brought from home and we drank tiny capfuls of it and laughed as it melted in our throats. After the day's adventures, we all slept in a line together on the floor of our Chief's house, sheltered from the storm.

I woke early. The corrugated iron over the windows was still rattling but there seemed to be less intensity than yesterday. Outside, the rain was heavy rather than ferocious and the sky was no longer full of flying debris. I walked down to the tribe village, clambering over fallen branches as I went. You could hardly see the sand on the beach for the amount of wood, seaweed and rubbish that had been washed up. The dining room had half a fallen tree leaning on its roof while a line of pawpaw trees behind the kitchen that we would collect fruit from daily were no longer there at all. Along the beach four or five large trees had been ripped completely out and lay on the wet sand with the white water frothing around their lifeless branches.

But the Bure and the other structures in the village were still standing. The Great Bure stood proudly, like it had just handed off an aggressive tackle with a flick of one outstretched arm. The thatched colossus hadn't flinched, a testament to the Mali builders and a building tradition that has evolved in the face of such battles. Back in the Fijian village, I walked past the chicken coop to where our garden was. All the beds, makeshift shelters, nurseries, and plants were gone, wiped out by the wind and the vast amounts of rain that now flooded the valley. Three months' work had been destroyed in a flash. I walked over to where we had tied up the pontoon and was relieved to see it was still there, undamaged.

Unfortunately, the same couldn't be said for the jetty. Lying on my stomach from the cliff above I could see that the cemented rocky walkway that Murray, Kimbo and a good number of Mali boys had put hours and hours of heavy work into building was smashed to pieces. The angry sea had reached out a claw and ripped out days of labour in a few hours.

Kimbo was due to fly back to the UK that night, before his return in a month as an island manager, Dan and I having decided that he was ready to step up to the plate. But, until about an hour before his flight was due to leave, it looked like he wouldn't be going anywhere. However, later that day, the wind finally began to settle and we all jumped on the boat for a bumpy ride to Labasa, to shelter there until the remainder of the storm passed. Later we could return to Vorovoro for what would be a very big clean-up.

A fire, a coup and now a cyclone; not six months had passed since the first footers had landed on Vorovoro and already all this. I wondered if the tribe could take any more. I also wondered for the first time if there was some force beyond all this that was very simply and regularly saying, 'This is a bad idea, give up now.' Of course, I had doubts every time we were seriously challenged, both on the island and online, and these challenges had been frequent and each one had threatened to finish the tribe off, to smash the dream on the rocks before it had been fully realised.

But I also had a sense that morning as I stood on the littered beach with waves breaking around my legs that so far we had survived and, because of this, it would work. I knew the clean-up work on the island would set the project back, and for all we knew more cyclones were on the way, but we were too far into this to back out now. I had a plan for the year ahead. There was a tribe online who wanted to work and who were going to come here and make it work. And we had Tui Mali and his yasuva who, through all the upheaval, would smile and say, *sega na leqa*. No problem.

III
NIU KEI NA VAKANANANU VOU
THE COCONUT EVOLUTION

26

SIGA DAMU NA VANUA
SUNSHINE AFTER THE RAIN

'Hi, you must be Craig?' I said as I slushed my way across the very muddy Grand Eastern courtyard and extended a hand to the 20-year-old with the shaven headed chap wearing glasses, baggy shorts, flip-flops and a vest. Craig had been travelling and you could tell.

We had been lucky during the cyclone; it had been our first weekend since the start of the project that we'd had no tribe members on Vorovoro. We had also been lucky that we didn't live in Labasa where the cyclone had caused serious flooding, smashing the banks of the river and taking mud and debris about a mile inland. Boats had replaced cars on the streets until the waters began to subside. There had been little warning on the radio. It was a Sunday afternoon when the storm ripped in off the ocean, through this little Pacific civilisation. Now the town and the surrounding sugar cane crops it was dependent on were a swamp. The whole of the ground floor of the hotel had been covered in a thick layer of mud that had risen two feet up the wall. I was very grateful our laptops were stored on the second floor. I took pictures for the hotel's insurers before jumping in a taxi with Sara Jane and Craig, our newest tribe member.

Heading through the town it became clear we should have stayed on the island. The place was a mess, sewers were overflowing and anything on the ground floor (where most of Fiji lives) was pretty much ruined. As we edged our way through the brown sludge, I looked on as families and shopkeepers dragged their livelihoods outside and piled them up in stinking mountains on the side of the road. Food, clothes, books, businesses, all ruined. Unlike the hotel, I expect few of these people and their properties were insured. From the vantage of Vani's house, high up above town, we could see where the flood had swept inland and the extent of the damage and destruction it had caused, including the loss of two lives. For these people, who were dependent on so little for so much, the effects of the cyclone were utterly devastating. Many would have to start again. For us, by contrast, it simply meant a day of sitting out of the wind and rain before venturing back to Vorovoro. But I wondered how much all this damage that the path of the cyclone had left in its wake, to the infrastructure in Labasa and on the island itself, was going to set the project back. Would people want to come here while fresh memories and pictures of cyclones and coups still hung in the air?

Over the next two weeks, Sara Jane, Craig, an Australian tribe member called Kirsty and the family and I stayed in the Fijian village on Vorovoro and, under grey skies and more rain, started the clean-up. In a way I was glad it was such a quiet month, we wouldn't have been able to do much in that weather anyway.

Dad and my step-mother, Frances, arrived a few days later. They were on a pre-planned holiday in New Zealand and had changed their travel plans so they could spend a few days with us on Vorovoro. I was disappointed the island didn't look its best but at least it meant I had some time to spend with them. One morning we all decided to go out to the reef for a fishing trip. It was drizzling as we left the driftwood beach but, by the time we had chugged out to our favourite spot, the rain was sheeting down, the swell was building and we were cloaked with a thick mist.

We dropped anchor and Marau, one of our very reliable workers from Nakawaga village, dived off the front of the fibre punt, spear gun in hand. This was Marau's domain. We watched as he ducked underwater for at least a minute at a time before surfacing and bringing his catch back to the boat. He worked fast and, within twenty minutes, we had eleven fish on board. On the way back, chilled by the wind and rain – a novel feeling in Fiji – we dropped a couple of hand lines with shiny spinners and trawled. I didn't think we would catch anything in the murkiness that morning, but just as Vorovoro came into view, Kirsty, who was holding one of the lines, flicked her arm back as the force of the bite spun her round. Api grabbed the line and began to help haul in the catch, which, after we had photographed and weighed the Sanga back on the beach, came in at a cracking nine kilos. Enough to feed us and the family for a good few days. We wouldn't have to rely on Labasa after all.

'So what do you think of our island life, Dad?' I asked, sipping hot, salty fish soup from a coconut shell in Poasa's house.

'Well, Benj, I don't think you should have any trouble once you get people here. Even in the rain and with hardly anything going on it's fantastic. In fact we're quite glad it's not too hot.'

'That's the thing isn't it, getting people here? I mean even with the *National Geographic* cover story, we still didn't get a big surge in numbers - and you don't get better PR in the travel industry than that.'

'For sure. But remember the coup had just happened and, if you're not in Fiji itself, most people would still be wary of coming here. After all, if you're looking for an island escape there are plenty of other options.'

'True,' I said with a sigh.

'But look, what you and the tribe are doing here *is* unique and word of mouth will spread. You just have to keep pushing. If I were you I would put more time into local marketing if you can.'

Dad was right and it was something I had already been looking to do before the cyclone had hit. I decided that, as soon as we had cleared up the villages and beach, and when the sun had begun to shine again, I was going to head south, and start to put Vorovoro on the traveller's map in Fiji. I was also pondering another theory as to why our continued excellent PR and glowing word of mouth reports were not bringing in swathes of new members. It was one that came from the author of the *National Geographic* feature himself, my fellow Utopian debater, James.

I had emailed him after the picture of Vorovoro on *Nat Geo* had stared out from the Times Square news stands for a few weeks and asked if he thought that the poor response in terms of new memberships was purely down to the current political mess in Fiji. James wrote back and outlined the basis of what we would call the Demystification Theory. He suggested that, in our attempts to show the critical bloggers and those that read them, this was not a scam we had gone too far. We tried to prove that the project was credible by plastering the homepage with links to news articles, tribe member island experiences and all the latest Vorovoro news. The desire to prove doubters wrong was understandable. But, in doing so, we were also removing the very element that had brought both critics and the flood of early members in the first place.

Remember the man in his car who pulled off the side of the motorway when he heard about Tribewanted on the radio, desperate to be part of the dream? And the journalist at Reuters who insisted on putting the story online instantly for fear others would beat her. The hundreds of tribe members who had joined despite warnings from friends and family had all been looking for an intangible something to believe in. We extracted that element of mystery when we started for real on Vorovoro, showing precisely what was happening. With detailed toilet talk, tide times and morning menus we replaced risk with mundanity - and we also removed part of Tribewanted's appeal. We took away the subconscious attraction of a possible 'no strings' life in paradise that had also sucked me in from the moment MJ's email landed in my inbox on that wintry day in Devon. The Utopian dream and the real world had met and, although it was beginning to find a working balance on Vorovoro, it was much more complicated in the minds of those following the story online and in newspapers and magazines. The thought made me want to head back to my hammock, for ever.

'I'm a hob-nob, the marine of the biscuit world. Dunk me!' Craig, now fully immersed into island life, was giving his audience, which included Dad and Frances, Kirsty, Sara Jane, Api, Raijeli, Kesa and me, a series of pretty good Peter Kay impressions that he had obviously been reeling off for months to British backpackers around the world. Peter Kay-ed out, I sat down next to Craig on the sand by the first campfire we had managed to get going since the cyclone, and asked him how he was enjoying his time on Vorovoro.

'I absolutely love it, mate. I mean, I know there's hardly been anyone here but it's just been brilliant to get to know the family so well. I've not found a place like this on my travels yet.'

'So why don't you stay?' I asked.

'I can't. I'd really love to but I'm on a budget.'

'Look there's no Chief standing for March yet, and it's only two weeks away. I don't think we're going to have anyone apply between now and then, so why don't you stand? I think you would do well, and although there's a lot of work to do here, it would mean you would have a free stay for a month.'

Craig knew he had nothing to lose so the next day he posted his manifesto for March Chief of the Vorovoro Tribe to the backdrop of Hare Krishna chanting and the smell of freshly cooked samosas in Govinda's internet café. If he pulled this off, he'd have bragging rights well beyond any of the skydiving DVDs or scuba-diving photographs he had stashed away in his rucksack. He would be a Chief!

I had pushed Craig for two reasons. Firstly, we needed a Chief, urgently. We hadn't had one in February, which was fine as there had been a cyclone and it was a short month. But now, with March fast approaching, we needed to get some momentum back in this project and Craig was our only real chance. Secondly, I was interested to see what would happen if someone who pretty much fitted the current backpacking cliché was given a bit of time and responsibility on this project. Would it change his perception of what he was doing or what he wanted to do? Would telling people about jumping out of aeroplanes every night around the campfire be as important to him? And so, two weeks later, with a character reference from Kirsty who had played a big part in the online community so far, Craig Enderby from Wiltshire was elected Chief for March. I don't think his mates at home believed him until they saw it on the newsletter.

The rain clouds finally began to clear and, with a full water tank and a plan now to build a second, permanent and much larger tank, the sun began to shine again on Vorovoro. And with the sunshine came the tribe, one or two at first then quickly a steady trickle of members began arriving on the island. With them the adventure flickered back into life.

And Raina came back as an Island Gapper. When she applied for the position I was both excited and concerned. I knew she would be a great gapper, but should I take her on, given what had happened between us in September? What would the gossips say? I wanted to be as fair as possible with the tribe. I thought about it for a while and decided to give her the job because she was the best applicant. I didn't know what would happen between us when she came but I knew she would do a good job on the island.

Craig matured overnight and, after a vote online, led the building of two lofts at either end of the Great Bure to provide extra sleeping areas. It used the large roof space really well and was cheap. With simple driftwood stepladders to climb up onto the plyboard deck, the loft at the eastern end was named *Cabe na mata ni siga* (sunrise) and at the western end *Dromu na mata ni siga* (sunset). Chief Wildgeeza's super-shed was given bamboo walls and, after a few days weaving with the boys from the village of Matailabasa who were doing the job, Craig had been renamed Tui Bitu, the Bamboo Chief!

Jonathan Segal, having witnessed with his own eyes the two

planes crashing into the New York's twin towers on 9/11, had decided in the paranoia-heavy aftermath of that event to move away from New York with his family. His young daughter had discovered a tabua in a box in the family loft, and it had sparked Jonathan's memory of backpacking through Fiji. He returned with his family to the small Pacific country where, after a stint at Telecom, he set up Fiji's first web design, marketing and communications company, Oceanic. Being both in Fiji and an online addict, Jonathan liked what Tribewanted was trying to do and was impressed that we were up and running so quickly. He knew the challenges of setting up a business in the country, especially when coups are almost as regular as leap years.

Keen to help, Jonathan emailed and we began chatting about the importance of an internet connection on the island in order to make this idea fly online, something which to date we had struggled to do through lack of funds and time. I remember saying on *Good Morning America* the year before that the three things we needed most on Vorovoro were water, toilets and broadband. Well, we had our toilets and water was being sorted out but we were nowhere near getting broadband. I'd had interest from a few internet providers, including AOL, in becoming partners with the project but unless I was going to go and pitch to them directly, it was going to be tough getting a corporation on board.

Jonathan had an idea. One of his major clients was Vodafone Fiji, and he talked the marketing director into the idea of supporting this oddball community tourism and technology project in the North. The company agreed to help. So on 1 March, as Craig officially became Tui Bitu, we welcomed a boat load of Vodafone execs and Jonathan onto the beach, where they handed over a brand new laptop and GPRS card to the tribe. Excited, I scampered up the rocks behind the tribe village where I knew we would get the best phone signal. Sitting between Ulai and Jonathan, I flipped the laptop open and slotted in the slim GPRS card. It connected. I wrote a post on the Tribewanted forum, and although the page took about three minutes to load I knew it was an important moment for the tribe and for the project.

I spoke to the assembled tribe members, Mali villagers and Tui Mali about what had happened. 'We are not just marking Tui Bitu and six months on Vorovoro today, we are also celebrating the connection of Vorovoro to the world permanently, not only through visiting tribespeople but through the internet.' I remembered what Tui Mali had said to MJ and I on our first visit to Vorovoro almost a year ago, about the world being able to see Vorovoro, even though Vorovoro couldn't see the world. Now he was even more right, although his amusing response to my announcement was simply, 'Good, so what next?' I'm not sure many of the locals really understood the significance but they were excited nevertheless. Or maybe that was more to do with the smell of lovo and a big bundle of kava roots lying on the mat.

Either way it was a great day and Vodafone even threw in a free Blackberry for me, which would mean, even with the tiny signal around the village, that I would always be able to pick up emails on Vorovoro. I could stay connected to the tribe and the world from the island. That evening we raced crabs and Jonathan and I drank a smooth single malt to celebrate. The island, the business, and the weather were at last just beginning to look up.

27
TEKIVU VUA NA TADRA
LIVING THE DREAM

I rolled over and stared at the picture of the island in the sunshine that lit up the blackberry screen and my face through the blind-broken shadows of the room. And, as the automatic light faded on my lifeline, taking the postcard-perfect Vorovoro with it, so the sound of six men breathing deeply reminded me of where I was. I had been lying on my back sweating for what seemed like for ever; a single ceiling fan was unnoticeable in the sauna-like conditions of the men's surgical ward of Labasa hospital. They had already operated on me the night before. They were due to do so again the next morning.

I could vaguely make out the flower-patterned red surf shorts in front of me. Raina leaned over and kissed me gently on the forehead. 'You sure you're gonna be OK?' At least I think that's what she said, so I tried to respond – 'yeah, sega na lega,' but was later told that it sounded more like very drunken drivel. The anaesthetic was only just starting to wear off.

Why was I in hospital? My little toe. Yes, the tiny one on the end that you never ever use except when you stub it against something and it reminds you it exists as you wince in pain. But this time it was really angry. I hadn't just stubbed it, rather I'd sent it the opposite direction to the rest of my toes. It had been the busiest week we'd had on the island so far with getting on for twenty-five tribe members staying. The beginnings of the dry season were pushing heavy clouds out to sea as a blanket of blue descended over our idyll. We were having a weekend of island Olympics to celebrate the Easter holiday and we were in the middle of an event well known for its physical dangers – charades. I was thinking about making up a shark attack story here because breaking your toe playing charades is hardly the stuff of legend, but it is what happened. And, besides, an aggressive encounter with the sharp-finned fish is something I hope I never get the chance to brag about.

I wouldn't have minded breaking my toe during coconut bowling, hockey-sticks or even musical flip-flops (a much more physical contest than you might guess from the name), but charades – come on! I picked the folded piece of paper out of the bowl and read 'Mr Bean', knowing that I could not use any words to describe the famous fool. I jumped up and ran around limp-wristed trying and failing to impersonate the silent comic. Unfortunately for my toe, Mr Bean accidentally snapped it running into a rock in the dark. I guess it's the sort of thing Mr Bean might do so, in that sense, I wasn't too disappointed with my impersonation. I didn't realise it was fractured until I went to the kitchen to get some ice for what I thought would be a nasty cut. When I tried to pull my toes apart to examine the cut the little one just flopped to the side, at right-angles to my foot. Bugger. Kimbo and Sara Jane patched it up as best they could but I knew it was fractured, and the next day I dragged myself to hospital, angry at the prospect of not being able to run around for the next few weeks.

Over the last month, with more people and projects, life had really started to take off on Vorovoro. Tui Bitu (Craig from Wiltshire) was turning into a cracking Chief, building a really great relationship with the local boys who were working there that month. The mutual respect was evident. His time for skydiving stories was behind him as he spent his days talking about four-by-twos and organising sevu-sevus for the arriving members. It was satisfying to watch the transition and I could see the positive impact the experience was having on him.

Aside from the Great Bure lofts, the bamboo walls, vesi floor and driftwood beds for the super-shed, and the finishing of the smaller Chief's Bure (yes, if you are elected a Chief on Vorovoro, you get your very own little house), Craig and I launched the construction of the 40,000-litre water tank on the hill behind the village. This was a big and expensive job but it was absolutely necessary if we were going to have enough storage for all the water we would need during the dry season. University College London's Environmental Engineers had by now delivered their Sustainability Plan, a great file of ideas, research, and suggestions for minimising our human impact on Vorovoro. We had taken their advice on rainwater harvesting as having the least negative impact of all forms of water management and were quickly trying to get this tank built before the rainy season stopped so that we could partially fill it. We all knew we might have left it a little too late. But build the tank we would and in came the boatloads of stones and bags of cement. It was all shifted by hand and created fifteen jobs for the strong Mali men for a few weeks. Tribe members helped where they could but it was pretty physical lugging the 50kg sacks up the slippery hill, before building the thing itself.

It rained heavily during construction, which, despite the muddy condition, the boys insisted was a good thing as it kept them cool. I just hoped it would rain a couple of weeks more once the tank was completed so we could collect as much rainwater as possible. It didn't. The day the tank was finished the clouds parted and the sun shone.

Back on the island now, hobbling round in Tui Mali's house on the only pair of crutches I could find in Labasa, I gingerly made my way up to where the tank had been built. The gang had done a good job and, although materials, transport and labour had set the tribe back over Fiji $12,000, it had been agreed that the Chiefs would spread the cost out over the coming months. I half-climbed, half-hopped up the ladder and sat on top of the tank so I could peer down through the small opening inside. There was about half an inch of water in the bottom. Kimbo, having returned from England as our island manager looking after day-to-day logistics on Vorovoro, joined me.

'Not much rain caught then,' I said, needlessly.

'Nope.' His monosyllabic answer hardly reassured me that there were a whole host of other fall-back options.

'So, any thoughts on what we're going to do about water during the dry season then?'

'Tevita reckons the reason we've got no water in the tank is because you forgot to bless the land before we started building on it. Tui Mali's tank is full.'

'Oh, you're joking.'

'Nah. He also said it's the reason you broke your toe.'

'What! I broke my toe and we have an empty water tank because we forgot to bless the ground before this thing was built?'

'No, *you* forgot to bless the ground.'

'Oh, thanks Kimbo, I'm glad it was me that forgot. Bloody hell, when am I going to work all this out?'

It was true, we were well into the project now and I was still learning on a fairly regular basis the differences between a Fijian perspective on why things happen and our own. Now whether I did break my toe because I hadn't instigated the blessing and not because I was trying to win a game of charades, and whether this was also the reason that the tank was not now full, unlike Tui Mali's, was starting to piss me off. Why didn't Tevita tell Kimbo, if Tui Mali or I weren't on the island? Why didn't one of the workers do the blessing? The communication process is complicated in Fiji, I knew that, but the moment I was out of action, it seemed to break down. Anyway, I decided to forget about the blessing cock-up and reminded myself that from now on when any new kind of construction on Vorovoro was about to commence I would be there with a bundle of grog and a scar on my left foot. As for water, I would have to head back to the government department in Labasa and no doubt argue about how much tax they weren't going to charge us before delivering a barge load of water for our new tank. I turned back to Kimbo who'd been smiling too smugly at my misfortune.

'From now on water is your responsibility. If we run out, I'm going to blame you. If you want this job in the long term then make sure we always have water.' That should motivate him, I thought, as I lowered myself carefully back down the ladder, noticing that I was a lot more angry when I was on crutches.

Earlier that month *The Guardian* and *The Observer* somehow both managed to make it to the island and, although I got into trouble for apparently coordinating this tête-à-tête, it was great news for Tribewanted. Both pieces were extremely positive, measuring the project's success from where it began a year before. Tribewanted was also featured on no fewer than five separate occasions in the *Fiji Times*. It seemed there was a collective recognition in the media at least that the venture was now not simply 'let's wait and see if it works,' rather 'it's started to work.' I was particularly pleased to read Benjy Lanyado's assessment in *The Guardian* of what we were trying to do on the island in the context of eco-tourism, even if the piece was entitled 'TheBeach.com':

> The idea that members are encouraged to engage in the project before and after visiting the island is a deliberate and laudable departure from other 'voluntourism' projects, where visitors satisfy their (usually gap-year) altruistic itch, then flee back home, make the photo collage and promptly forget all about it. The ability to take part in the democratic decision-making process is, for want of a better word, revolutionary. It means thousands of participants can take a daily break from office drudgery to have their say on a desert island thousands of miles away.

And important voting there was. Probably the most important to date was on what we should call the space Tui Bitu, the Mali boys and tribe members had cleared of long grass behind the village. They had built goalposts out of driftwood and hung old fishing nets over them. It was our very own jungle sports stadium. Hidden from the village and unsighted from either side of the island, the area was comfortably big enough for a bumpy game of four-a-side and was a dream come true for the lad who grew up spending most of his school days playing 'yarda' with his mates. 'Tanoa Park', where things go into the mix, won the vote and soon became the place to hang out for after-work matches between Vorovoro and Mali, or the Internet and Fiji. Tribe members even built a Tanoa Park scoreboard where you could drop a coconut on a piece of string every time a goal was scored. I've played footy on flatter grounds but not on tropical islands where I could bang the ball into the back of a fish net and where, if I missed, I would be wading through the sea to retrieve the ball.

The increased numbers on the island were in part due to the start of the dry season, but were also down to word of mouth and the poster campaign I'd organised with Jonathan's help around the Nadi backpackers' bars and internet cafés. I was starting to get calls like these:

'Hi, is that Tribewanted?'

'Yes, it's Ben, are you on your way to Vorovoro?'

'Well, we hope so. I'm Laura and I'm travelling with four friends and we've just arrived in Nadi and met this guy called Spud in the bar and he told us about Tribewanted and we'd really like to come and stay.'

'No problem. Come tomorrow,' I'd say, and they would. It worked well and, in April, despite the twenty per cent cut the Nadi agents would take, we beat our sales target for the month because of it.

So I bought the surfboards I'd promised myself and Tui Bitu and I paddled into the offshore break a few metres above the Cakalevu reef, three miles north of Vorovoro and the third largest barrier reef in the world. There was a peach of a left hander curling over the turquoise reef which I could see very clearly as the five foot wave rose and the swell hit the wall. It was very shallow. I shouted across to Tui Bitu who told me he had surfed in Australia. Well, I had surfed in Devon, but it wasn't exactly like this, on short boards, over a sharp shallow reef, with a shifting swell and current, and, hello, a series of sharp-finned shadows switching back and forth beneath our sea-lion-shaped surfboards.

'When you come off the board, fall flat on your back or front. Don't dive head first, its very shallow!'

I hoped Craig had heard me as he paddled ahead to the drop and disappeared over the lip. I paddled hard after him and onto the wave, wondering if it had ever been surfed before. I held the board tightly as it momentarily dropped through the air before the power of the wave pushed me forward. I wasn't even going to attempt to pop up, knowing I would come off straight away. Unable to paddle back past the wave and try and surf it again - that's how novice we were - we simply carried on through the breakers until we were spat out the side onto the flat sea. We lay on our boards until Api and the rest of the snorkellers came and picked us up to tell us about all the sharks they had seen swimming beneath us. We had virgin-surfed the Great Fijian barrier reef. Well, kind of. I called the break *Bitu*, 'the Bamboo Break', after its round shape, the colour of the reef and the name of my mate who I'd paddled with.

We would arrive back from these reef trips and all head down the beach to the end of the island where, beneath a small crack in the cliffs, rainwater poured, creating an endless freshwater shower. While it lasted, up until about a month after the rains stopped, we encouraged all tribe members to wash there just as we encouraged the members who hadn't been involved online to use the biodegradable soaps that more knowledgeable members had brought to the island. A platform was built under the little waterfall and I remember on one Sunday afternoon when we had all spent the day at the beach down there, getting six in the shower at once. And with more girls than boys on the island for the first time I was very happy to spend all day in the shower.

Things between Raina and I had kind of kicked off again

although it was difficult for us to see where it might go, as we knew she would only be there for four months as an island gapper. We were both conscious that we didn't want it to impact on the team or the island atmosphere in a negative way. It was already creating some tension, so I made sure we kept it low key and I made a point of not talking about anything to do with work or people on the island when we were alone together. But we still had a lot of fun, with most people who came to the island not even realising anything was going on. It was kind of a secret, which I think made it better in some ways. Looking hot in her surf shorts aside, Raina was a great girl and I'm glad she had come back to Vorovoro; I would definitely miss her when she left.

And there were other more lifelong romances that took place under the shade of the trees of Vorovoro. Doug from Arizona, Poques' deputy Chief in September, was due to return in July to marry his fiancé Mary Lou on 7/7/7. He had asked Epeli to be his best man for the day and was bringing eight of his family with him for a traditional Fijian wedding. Everyone was looking forward to it. We had also had Toni and Chris's wedding blessing and were expecting other honeymooners to come and spend their week of romantic bliss with the tribe. But perhaps the biggest surprise came when I received a phone call from an old friend:

'Hi, Ben, it's Becky.'

'Becks! How are you? How did the rest of your travels go?'

'Amazing. Anyway look, I can't talk long, but there's something I need to tell you.' She sounded like she did that day when I told her she would be moving to Fiji.

'What is it now, Becks?'

'You remember Ryan?'

'Of course I remember Ryan, you were stuck to him for most of the time he was on Vorovoro.' Becky had been in denial about getting together with Ryan, the young Californian lad who was among the first footers. I think she was concerned it might be unprofessional.

'No I was not. Well look, we've kind of been seeing a lot of each other…'

'Oh yeah.' I was sensing but not quite believing where this was going.

'And anyway,' she blurted out, like she couldn't hold it back any longer, 'we're engaged, and we want to come to Vorovoro to get married.'

'Becky, that's absolutely amazing news. Really, amazing. Congratulations to both of you. Of course you should come and get married here. It's the only place you can get married. Let's arrange a time next week when you can ask Tui Mali.'

In fact, family circumstances finally stopped them from coming. But Becky and Ryan were to be the first couple who married after meeting through Tribewanted. And by the end of the first year four couples that had met either online or on Vorovoro were engaged. There was definitely a lot of love in this tribe.

The Chiefs continued to arrive and each in their own unique way made a difference to the project and moved the community forward. Micki Bradshaw, 43, a home-care worker from California, became Mika Marama as our April Chief and oversaw our busiest month for tribe members on the island. Tom Buttigieg, 22, an economics graduate from Warwick, was our May Chief who became known as Tui Tomasi, and led the construction of the family Bure and a library building project in the Mali school. In June, Ryan Garcia, a 24-year-old from Hawaii, landed on Vorovoro with two large bags of fishing and free-diving gear and began to teach the tribe how to dive and spear fish, and the local boat captains how to teach. Tui Wasi (the Ocean Chief), as he quickly became known, also marked out a line with buoys for where boats should come in and out of the island, to prevent reef damage. The kitchen was extended and gardens were cut, cleared and planted. Such was the tribe members' involvement with the projects and the people on Vorovoro that they quickly became very attached to the place, with almost half extending their stays, and of course staying in touch and contributing online once they had said their teary goodbyes. Walt Flood, an enthusiastic member from Chicago went a step further in showing his passion for the tribe:

I have travelled to many places and had great experiences, but I have never had a difficult time leaving somewhere. Vorovoro was the first. I had been thinking of getting a tattoo even while on the island, but didn't have a good design. But I got back and, honestly, was incredibly depressed for quite a while upon returning. I couldn't get enough of the island and couldn't stop thinking about everything that I had experienced while there. Now I have the tattoo the depression is gone and I just want to help as much as I can and count the days in excitement until I can return to the island, hopefully as a Chief. I guess I just needed a little bit of Vorovoro in my life. That's why I titled the tattoo 'My Vorovoro'.

Online meanwhile, the tribe was starting to make longer-term plans for Vorovoro. It was voted that from the beginning of the second year, 1 September 2007, we should have three set arrival and departure days. The majority of the members that voted (now over one hundred on each occasion) were prepared to sacrifice their own travel flexibility for the benefit of the project. Fewer boat journeys would mean less fossil fuel burned, fewer dollars spent and less of an emotional strain on the now almost daily Bulas and Isa Leis the full-time islanders were having to endure. Tribe members had also voted that members should be allowed to retain their voting rights for the length of the project, regardless of their membership status. This again made sense to me, as I knew that the more members were involved online over a longer period the stronger the online community would become and the more accountable the tribe would be to the project.

The accountability was already improving as more members who had visited the island started to share their real island experience and thoughts online. OK, so it was happening on a smaller scale than we had hoped when we launched the project but at least it was happening. The online tribe was collectively and responsibly making decisions about a holiday destination and the democratic majority was putting local community and environmental considerations first. After more than two months of debating, the tribe voted to limit the number of visiting members to thirty at any one time.

As the owner of the business, the thought once would have petrified me, but as I got to know them and they got to know Vorovoro and me, we learned to trust each other. I think all this has some really interesting implications for company and customer relationships in the future, even though I would struggle to ever see the relationship between those that work at Tribewanted full-time and the tribe members themselves purely in those terms. We're all in the tribe, together.

Finally, tribe members have voted to scrap the now mythical 5,000 target. My feeling was that, since we hadn't reached that tipping point a year ago, our goal of 5,000 had become less important. Yes, it was a useful way of getting the thing off the ground, but now with the benefit of hindsight and the perspective of a year's real-world challenges behind us, it seemed much less significant. Besides, 5,000 individual members was now an impossibility within the three years of the project, especially as members could stay a lot longer (one 26-year-old London escapee had booked eight weeks and was extending her time). We have 1,300 members from over 35 countries, 250 of which have already been to Vorovoro, and I know many will never come.

Tui Mali turned to Kimbo: 'So tomorrow at sunrise you will kill the pig.'

Whether Kimbo liked it or not, tomorrow he was going to do it in front of the tribe. Tui Mali had told him this was his job, and it was a great compliment to the company car fleet manager who had come such a long way over the last few months. His Chief had now recognised that he was one of the men of Mali and must therefore do as they do, which tomorrow meant killing the pig.

The next day was Mother's Day in Fiji and Tui Mali had told all the men that we must prepare a lovo for the mothers, despite the fact that nine out of the ten female tribe members on Vorovoro that week did not have children. 'It does not matter,' Tui Mali said matter-of-factly, 'they will be mothers soon.'

So before dawn a small group of us men, both tribe members and Fijians, woke early and began husking and scraping the coconuts, skinning the dalo and cassava, and preparing the lovo. The firewood now lit beneath the pile of rocks that would cook the food, Kimbo was almost ready for his moment of transition to Mali manliness. Sitting on the grass opposite the happy little pig, he seemed to be thinking about what he was about to do to this little nose-twitching pink creature of destiny. I wandered over and stood next to him, hands in pockets, staring at Mother's Day lunch. 'Remember mate, this could be on the BBC one day, just think about that.'

'I know, I know. I don't have much choice do I? The Tui has asked me.'

'Nope,' I said, returning the monosyllabic answer he had given me on top of the water tank when I was hoping for reassurance. Epeli held the pig, which clearly knew the end was nigh and was making a lot of noise.

'Now,' the old man said. Bang. Kimbo swung the wooden club down and clipped the pig's nose. The poor animal looked up slightly bemused but certainly very conscious as the onlookers gasped. Bang. Kimbo didn't hesitate and with the second swing caught the beast on the back of the head and knocked him out cold. Epeli did the rest, cutting the throat while the pig lay motionless, and within ten minutes had it roasting in the lovo. I asked what the watching mothers (or mothers to be) thought.

'It's a bit shocking to watch, but it's good to see where our food comes from and anyway, he wouldn't have felt anything,' said Mirjam, one of the Swedish girls who made up an ever-increasing mixture of nationalities on Vorovoro. I agreed. We'll see what impact it has if ever it's shown on television. I know it makes me appreciate a bacon sandwich more, and that's a good thing.

We dressed the girls with flower wreaths and served them their Sunday feast. Tui Mali stood at the end of the table:

You know this food is for you, to thank you for looking

after us, for feeding us during the year. But this is also to thank Vorovoro, the land, that looks after us and provides for us. The island is our home and she takes care of us and gives us everything we need.

It was classic Tui Mali and, just as he finished speaking, someone shouted: 'Look, in the grass!' We all rushed over and there, a few feet from the dining table, we could clearly see movement between the blades of grass. As we crouched we saw dozens of baby turtles instinctively clambering from their nest in the bushes towards the sea. Their eyes still closed, they didn't need to see where they were going, they swung their juvenile paddles back and forth to carry them over the twigs, long grass, and sand, until finally a tiny wave broke on them like a tsunami and sucked them out into the blue. It would have been an incredible sight on any occasion but to land on cue just as Tui Mali had finished thanking the earth for providing, it was a remarkable moment.

I saw Sara Jane crouching by the sea's edge, watching as the tiny dinosaurs prepared to face the riskiest hours of their life. 'I wonder how many will survive?' she said without looking up at me.

'Hopefully some will, there must be well over a hundred.'

'It's sad to think so many will die.'

'Are you getting all maternal on me, mother-to-be?'

'Heh! That's a long way off. No, that's another adventure. This one is enough for now.'

'You OK?' I asked, as she seemed a little distant.

'Yes, I'm good actually. You know I am. I mean, it's hard sometimes, I miss my friends and family a lot, but I have a lot here too. I know how lucky we are to live here. This just reminds me of those kind of things,' she said, flipping a tiny turtle over as he got caught on his back.

And as we sat there I thought about how far Sara Jane had come on this journey as well. She wasn't always in the limelight, on the front line, but she was always there, doing much of the donkey work on the administration in our temporary and resource-short

Labasa office. On the island too, she had played an important role in helping organise the kitchen and the women that worked there and, although it was an ongoing challenge, she always got on with it. I was proud of her and pleased she had come back to Vorovoro after that difficult time with MJ at Christmas. We had been through a lot together and it was good to have someone on the team who had been there for a while, who knew how far we had come. I hoped she would stick at it.

Plenty more column space had been taken up by the Tribewanted story over the previous few months and, as with the UK and Fiji papers, it was really satisfying to read the positive stories being written about was happening on Vorovoro. It started to undo all the negative things that had been said online last year. And, although we still had plenty of challenges to overcome, it seemed that the media were recognising what the tribe already knew, that we were living out a dream, and we were very lucky. Here's a favourite quote of mine, written by Steffan Kraft and translated from *Der Taggespiegel*:

> In the proximity of the tourist areas in Southern Fiji, the local natives are not even allowed to step upon the beaches or enter the tourist enclaves. On Vorovoro, however, the Mali clan have invited the members of the internet tribe community to kava rounds and carry the white ones forward in village celebrations. The Fijians will again welcome the next selected Chief in the coming month. Then the iron pestle will swing again towards the sky to meet the hollow trunk to create the quake of a large dream from a small village. The Pacific will calm and inside one of the small huts another group of people will sit in a circle. The Fijians will fill the bowl with enough kava for the next Chief. It will be a solemn moment, and in this moment, a few people will feel as if they have returned to the Garden of Eden.

28
NA GONEDAU VOU
THE FUTURE FISHERMEN

I knelt carefully in front of the old lady lying on the woven mat. Auntie's eyes were alive and she held my hand tightly without letting go, as she always did. It was obvious her condition was getting worse, she could no longer sit up. I sat with her whenever I visited Nakawaga on Mali. And, despite her fragility, she always gave me strength. She was fighting, you could see it in her eyes. And today her mind was alive. Smiling and talking gently as her daughter translated.

'She said she likes it that you always visit her before school.'

'I like visiting her too. It's the only rest I get all week,' I replied, smiling.

'You know I didn't always live in this house,' Auntie began. 'Before I lived over there, but then things changed.'

She was pointing out of the window and towards the sea wall in front of her small house.

'You mean your house used to be out there, in the sea?' I asked.

'Yes. My kitchen was out there, level with that boat.'

I looked out through the shutters to where the small punt was bobbing twenty metres or so off the beach.

'How long ago was your kitchen there?'

'Twenty years, no more. The sea is coming in. We used to sit under the big tree for village meetings. Now the sea has come in and we can't.'

And so I discovered at first hand the changes going on in the world's oceans and what they mean to island communities. It wasn't scientific but it was real. The old lady could clearly describe the time a generation ago when her home was above water. I looked out to sea and imagined the dwellings. I looked back into the village and the hills.

'Now more people in the village and less places to be buried. The hills behind us, more people every year, and the sea coming in. Nowhere to go.'

It was a moment of sudden clarity for me. It was a wake-up call. The old lady that I guessed didn't have too long to live had opened my eyes to the future.

Knowing I would be returning to the UK soon, I wondered whether I would ever see Auntie again. 'See you at Christmas, Auntie,' I said as I shuffled backwards.

'Make sure, make sure you come back for Christmas. I will wait for you.'

'I will, I promise,' I said quietly, and left.

What had I hoped or expected when we launched Tribewanted.com on that frosty April morning? An avalanche of success? A 'revolution in tourism'? Thinking about it in the tree house that afternoon, I remembered I had been looking for an adventure that would benefit some people and might even educate us all in how to live more simply, not to mention a business that would work.

Like many of those who had joined the tribe, I was also searching for a connection. And on Vorovoro we were connecting with the people of Mali and with each other. In Tui Mali's back garden we were living in sun-drenched dreams, a village on an island whose ever-changing community existed pretty much in harmony with its permanent neighbours and spectacular environment.

But perhaps most important of all the questions and challenges this tribe has and will continue to confront, is what to do in the face of a fast-growing crisis in a changing world. Before MJ and I started out on this adventure, I was only slightly aware that the world's climate is hotting up and that it is our fault. Of course there are still plenty out there who don't believe climate change is man-made or potentially catastrophic. I, for one, am not prepared to take that risk. Besides, we should always be looking for ways to lessen our polluting impact on the Earth, shouldn't we? Regardless of the complexities of the science, it seems common sense to me that we should be trying to do more to protect our planet rather than trash it.

If you look simply at the crap pumped out from all the flights to and from Fiji, we have done more harm than good. So far, 300 people's flights to and from Vorovoro from Australia, New Zealand, Europe and America have emitted approximately 1,000 tonnes of CO_2 into the atmosphere. That's 1,000 tonnes more of damaging gases that are heating the world, melting the ice-caps and changing weather patterns. That's 1,000 more tonnes towards game over.

Like the world's climate itself, it's not that simple, of course. What we are doing on Vorovoro can reconcile the damage caused by the long-haul flights. Here are three reasons why I think Tribewanted is in balance with the impact it makes.

1. Vorovoro is green
On Vorovoro, we are aiming to have a carbon footprint so small you can't even see it. Cutting our emissions at home is the first place to start. Composting toilets, collecting our own rainwater, growing our own food, catching our own fish, reducing, reusing and then recycling our waste, no electricity, just renewable energy generated by ourselves, building with local materials, washing and cleaning with biodegradable soaps, and converting our boat engines to bio-diesel.

Most of this was already well under way nine months into the project and is now being enthusiastically driven forward by James Strawbridge, a phenomenal 22-year-old environmentalist. In the last two years, he has helped build a sustainable farm with his family in Cornwall and then moved around the country in a biogas-powered van with his dad, helping others green their homes. His passion for sustainability is infectious and he is already making a significant difference on the ground in Vorovoro. Fruit, vegetable and herb gardens that tribe members now maintain have sprung up around the village. A compost for all the kitchen scraps and a reed bed has been installed so we can reuse greywater from the showers on the gardens.

We are minimising the number of plastic bags coming onto the island as much as possible and we are reusing the rubbish that does make it for whatever we can: plastic bottles become guttering, bags stuff cushions, cardboard lights fires and so on. A simple, sustainable education programme is being kicked off in Mali School and on Vorovoro itself. Gardens have been planted behind the primary schools in Mali, and Kia and James led a rally with tribe members and schoolchildren down Labasa's main street chanting in Fijian: 'Keep our rivers clean.'

We also began weekly debates on the island and online covering topics like self-sufficiency and sustainability versus tourism. It's not exactly the Oxford Union but, between us, we've covered some big topics.

In August 2007, Ecotricity, the world's first green energy company, which invests in wind power in the UK, provided the tribe with a wind turbine and solar panels, to help us generate twelve volts of electricity. At last we had light and somewhere to charge our laptops and iPods. Hurricane lamps and kerosene were things of the past.

After a kava blessing on the ridge, thirty tribe members and Fijians put up the turbine which now turns proudly above the village. For me the electricity generated is less important than what the turbine symbolises. It shows those who visit Vorovoro that a simple, stunning technology exists to improve the lives of our communities. This is what we call the coconut evolution, from a palm swaying on the beach to the blades of the turbine spinning in the ocean breeze, pointing to a future without fossil fuel.

2. *People are learning*
I would be surprised to hear if many of the tribe members who have got stuck in online had read or taken part in in-depth discussions about climate change, carbon offsets, compost toileting, chicken farming or rat catching before Tribewanted. I certainly hadn't. The island adventure has captured people's imaginations, a thousand-odd tribe members and a barrage of international and local media have been swept up in this fascinating experiment where a search for paradise meets a twenty-first-century online community. Those that watch *Lost*, *Survivor* or *Shipwrecked*, those that have read *The Beach*, *Lord of the Flies* or *Gulliver's Travels* – Tribewanted appeals to them.

But, beneath the surface and beyond the unattainable idealism of full-time perfection and pure democracy, lies the real purpose of Tribewanted. It can educate and inspire people into living and travelling in a more responsible and sustainable way. Sure, the green machine is growing fast and I for one am getting caught up with it. But it will take time for more people to join. With the Tribewanted adventure more are, at least, watching.

Most people who have come to Vorovoro so far aren't eco-warriors. They're like me: they recognise that something needs to be done and they want to learn. The real springboard for all of this learning, however, is online. It's taking this story to the world, it's the tribe's vote for fewer boat journeys, it's the debate about carbon offsets, it's sharing and reading UCL's sustainability plan, it's thinking about what we do on Vorovoro and asking if we can do it at home. As a community made up mostly of people who are working this stuff out for the first time, we are also learning from our mistakes. If UCL's plan had been written and implemented before the project began, how many of us would have followed it?

Locally as well, the sustainability bug is spreading. Villagers have visited Vorovoro to see our skyscraper – the compost toilets – impressed that this very simple system needs no water and leaves no trace. The Vorovoro family have cleaned up the plastics and cans that were dumped in large piles when I first arrived and have asked if they, too, can recycle their rubbish. We are beginning to start simple sustainability classes in Mali School and we hope that children will teach their parents. Change will take time, but it is better, I think, that they follow us, rather than we impose ourselves on them.

The local Fijian reason for being greener is, for the most part, not through an understanding of global climate change (how can it be when they've never left their own island?). Rather, it will motivate as a way of being more resourceful, of saving money and of looking after their homes. Reducing and reusing already plays a big part in the lifestyle here and that is something we are learning from them. If we get it right on Vorovoro, and we are going in the right direction, then we can get it right beyond Vorovoro, in the villages in Mali, and in the lives inspired and educated through the online network. I mean, how difficult is it really to change a light bulb or put a compost bin in your backyard? Surely we're all capable of that?

3. We are investing dollars into renewable energy
After we've done everything we can to reduce the carbon dioxide we emit, the best and currently only way of combating the problem is to offset. We are not going to cut our CO_2 emissions in half overnight – we need to be realistic about that. Changing our own lifestyle, let alone that of towns, regions, countries or planet, is hard. Paying money to organisations like Climate Care to invest in renewable energy projects to balance out our carbon habit may seem slack. Didn't people once pay someone to pray for them as they committed murder? It feels a bit the same. But that attitude is for people who already live carbon-free lifestyles or who don't believe climate change is happening.

For those who do recognise it is happening and that we should do something about it, supporting the switch from a fossil-fuel dependency to a renewable energy grid (solar, wind, tidal, biogas, etc) is a good thing. I don't see how tree planting is the answer but I can understand that investing in renewable energy may be. So if I, or Tribewanted, can help with that, can afford to do that (which surely anyone who can afford a long-haul flight to the other side of the world can), then that is a step in the right direction. A technological fix would be brilliant with planes run on coconuts, trains on cooking oil, cars on water. It could happen but we don't know if it will.

We're reducing our footprint, we're educating people and each other as we go, and we're offsetting the rest. That, for me, is good enough for now, it is a start. Tribewanted has taught me that doing nothing is not an option.

But what about travelling itself? Today you don't need the exploration agenda of Captain Cook to find yourself culturally immersed. You just sign up to a volunteer programme or 'off-the-beaten-track-adventure' and whack it on a credit card. And it's the ease of access to those complex worlds that, it seems to me, is making travel today both increasingly fascinating and contradictory in its impact.

Yes, thanks to the huge growth in tourism and experiential travel, there is more money going to people who previously didn't have it. Yes, there are more jobs. Yes, there are fantastic social benefits. But the balance is not there. Yet. Too often the traveller gains perspective and develops, but at the expense of the people they are drawing upon. I think what I've learnt as much as anything from living and working in Fiji and amongst the yavusa of Mali is that, whenever developments happen in the world that bring different cultures together, we must be committed to spending a decent amount of time on them. A few days, even weeks, is not enough.

The people that live on Vorovoro and in Mali were there before we arrived. They will be there long after we have gone. And it has taken a year for me to begin to understand what growing up and living here is about. Attitudes, ways of living and beliefs take longer to change. That's not a good or a bad thing; it's just how it is. Through the development of the project, we have realised that if we protect the local community, culture and island, and don't exploit it for our own ends, then it will be preserved for everyone for a lot longer.

So that someone just like me a thousand years from now can spear a fish under the same rock on the Vorovoro reef and enjoy their lunch.

My lungs felt as if they were going to burst as I clung to the rock on the seabed. Finally, after what seemed like minutes, I reached the target number in my head and let go, kicking the fins behind me as I sped to the dancing lights above. Fresh oxygen poured into my body, bringing with it a smile to my face as the contrast of stunning views above and below the water reminded me of how lucky we were to have access to both of these beautiful worlds.

Ryan, a 25-year-old from Hawaii, was our June Chief, and he was teaching me how to free dive and spear fish. He was remarkable underwater, holding his breath for a minute or two at a time, lying flat on the sand six metres below the surface and waiting for the fish to come to him. Then, just as they became comfortable with this big new life form in their back garden, he would pull the rubber band up the shaft of the aluminium pole until it was taut with tension and point the three sharp prongs at his pick of the school. Release. A mini underwater earthquake would erupt as all the fish flew in opposite directions away from the impact. All except one, left quivering with the three prongs puncturing its scaly skin. Ryan would swim to the surface and cut the gills with a small knife before clipping the fish to his belt. Like a set of accessories, this was the fourth fish he wore around his waist that morning, their different colours making for a fantastic fashion statement.

'OK, you saw that?' I nodded. 'Your turn. Here, look at that same coral head, the red fish with the big eyes, you see it?' I ducked my face under the surface and, through my mask, I followed Ryan's arm to the rock where a small red fin twitched slowly back and forth.

'I see it,' I said, before tucking my body under and kicking one fin out of the water as Ryan had taught me so I could dive vertically. Equalising on the way, I pulled the rubber band taut as I approached the place where the red fin was giving its owner away. I got closer and it wasn't swimming away. I held out the weapon in front of me. I was two feet from it now, I didn't want to miss. I was a hunter. I let go and speared the fish just behind its big eye. I had my first kill.

I had taken its life in an instant, its fins flickering fast for a few seconds before they fell limp, lifeless. How much guilt can you feel when you take a life like that? For me the feeling is countered by the reason for the sacrifice: if the fish feeds us so that we are healthy and intelligent and make responsible decisions about how to live then there is no guilt. The fish became my lunch and gave me a sense of purpose that day that I had been lacking for a while. Fried in garlic, its tasty meat and skin reawakened me to the cycle of life. We, at the top of the food chain, are duty bound to care for everything we can so easily spear, farm, fell or burn. I am never going to hug trees like they were members of my family but, with the Vorovoro experience in my back pocket, I hope I will always respect the natural environment, do my best to conserve it, the atmosphere and all the different species.

29
YAVUSA KACIVI
TRIBEWANTED 2.0

Api and Epeli were sitting on the earth in the shade of the bamboo wall. I walked over to them, crouched, and shook their hands. 'I can't believe this *vale* [house], it's perfect. It's my first house. Vina'a va'alevu,' I said, thanking them in the local Mali language. They smiled, pleased I was so delighted.

A month earlier, I had *kere kere*'d (asked) Tui Mali if it was OK for me to build a small Bure on Vorovoro where I could live. I had also asked the tribe online, telling them it would come from my kitty and not the monthly Chief's budget. Both my Chief and my tribe had given me the go-ahead, so I went to visit our old friend Epeli in his village with a bundle of grog to ask if he and his gang would build me a home. He happily agreed and, after a week of harvesting mangrove, bamboo and reeds just as they had done with the Great Bure, he and six boys arrived on Vorovoro to set up camp and a makeshift kitchen on the beach. We cleared some long grass halfway between the two villages and back from the path. I had decided that I would like to live halfway between the tribe and the Fijian village, that seemed to be the right spot. And the view of the sea wasn't bad either. Three weeks later, and with the help of a lot of tribe members while I was still on crutches, my first house was complete. It had set me back about $1,500 – not bad for three years' rent, I thought, deliberately forgetting about the $150,000 island lease so I could enjoy the moment.

Api looked up at me and said, 'This place is Eremoni. E-ri-moo-nee,' he pronounced slowly for me.

'E-ri-moo-nee,' I said slowly back. 'I like it. What does it mean?'

'Eremoni is the place that connects people.'

Connect. It's a word that I've heard a lot over the last year, and now, sitting outside the little thatched house that had been named 'the place that connects people' on an island in the Pacific I wondered what all this 'connecting' really meant and what is the potential for current online technology to change the world?

We only have a basic internet link on Vorovoro. It's not what I had hoped for when we started but it is something. But the internet has already reached the next level. It remains the platform upon which this project was built.

The most fascinating aspect of the relationship between the online and island communities is their collective attitude. Tribe members who have participated online before coming to Vorovoro have arrived on the beach with a certain understanding of the place, its people and what we are trying to do here. They have already contributed to the island community's development and they have built friendships, virtually at least, with people who are swinging in hammocks and fishing on the other side of the world. For those that have followed the project online before they leap into the real world, it is an exciting moment and, for some if you read the thousands of posts that have accumulated on the forums, it is a moment that can't come soon enough. I worry that the expectations built by this fervent online conversation will never be matched but, this hasn't been the case. Expectations have been exceeded. Every time. Our friend Walt with the tattoo is a good example of this:

> Any expectations I had before going were just dead wrong and totally undershot. The island is about twenty times more beautiful than I ever expected. The people are just infinitely more friendly and fun to talk to and hang out with than I ever expected. The food is delicious. The smells are amazing – the sea, the dampness of the near-constant rain (until today), the pine that I was chiselling to build shelves, the palm leaves coating the ground in the Bure … And the sounds are just as good. The rain bouncing on the tin roofs, the roosters trying to out perform each other, the people laughing – always laughing – the sound of axes and hammers on rock, and behind it all, just audible, the sea pounding into the reef just at the edge of sight on the horizon and adding a deep and constant bass to the whole thing.

Walt's blog is by no means a one-off. It seems that the more people are involved online before they come, the more they gain from the experience once they're here. This is a generalisation, as I also know that there have been others who haven't even logged onto the community until after they have left Vorovoro and have also utterly immersed themselves in island life regardless. As more have visited Vorovoro so the online community has started to work better, with increasing numbers recalling their time on Vorovoro and presenting their thoughts on how the island should develop with the benefit of real hindsight.

Where the online project hasn't met our expectations or initial goals as yet is in its scale. We have just over a thousand members and not five times that amount as we hoped. And out of those thousand only about two hundred are actively involved online while currently an average of just seventy-five take part in the voting process. So why the apathy? Was the online side of Tribewanted unimportant to most members? Well, yes and no.

For almost all members the reason for joining was because they would be able to visit Vorovoro and take part in a real-world island community. The problem has been that the initial online community we have developed has been, for want of a better word, clunky. With many of its members used to the speed and ease of Facebook or Flickr for social networking, Tribewanted hasn't hit the mark. It's hardly surprising and, looking back, I wish we had invested less time and money on trying to build something from scratch and focused more on using what was out there, tagging the tribe across the web to spread the word and take advantage of the best free tools available. I've seen that the web 2.0 platform is still so new that even the fastest-growing communities and sites are still researching and developing their technologies so how we can compete with these guys is beyond me.

But the ambition, naivety, and give-it-a-go attitude that led to rushed, even flawed decisions have also brought success. Now, after some breathing space, we have recruited our very own talented web Chief, Aaron Wheeler, who has taken on the challenge of developing the online community. Unlike other web developers, Aaron gets to live in Fiji so, when he's had enough of the screen, he can always take the boat to Vorovoro.

Contrary to the disappointing part-time participation of the tribe so far, the success of Tribewanted as a social network for its members is proven. The number of tribal gatherings, Tribewanted on Tour or TWOTs as they are known, that have taken place around the world and on a regular basis reflect this. Hopefully the recently formed Tribewanted Dream Foundation can give these gatherings a purpose. The Foundation has been set up by seven tribe members, voted in online as trustees, and will aim to support and promote sustainable development in rural communities, starting in Mali. This is where the online community as a fundraising force can really fly. The future is definitely bright.

Yet Tribewanted, from where I sit, is not something spectacularly different or revolutionary. It is rather, as the web 2.0 community say, a 'mash-up' of ideas and trends, the internet plus sustainability plus fairly traded tourism plus postmodern politics plus Utopia. It is global village meets human village -

and on a bloody tropical island.

As far as mash-ups go, and others would agree about this whether they come to Vorovoro or not, Tribewanted is as compelling as anything out there. With over 50,000 pictures, 30,000 online posts, 1,300 paid-up members from 35 countries, 5 hours of BBC television, 150 employees in its first year (if only for a couple of weeks), 50 votes and over a dozen elected Chiefs, and this book, it does suggest that this mash-up has a future.

We've learnt that the trade-off for ambition and bravado are sleepless nights and a lot of sweat. I don't see Tribewanted being pigeon-holed as an eco-tourism company. I think that it could be anything, as long as it keeps community, sustainability and adventure on its front line and continues to explore the relationship between a physical and an online tribe.

And how does Tribewanted fit with the bigger online picture? Well, that there appears to be a proliferation of social enterprises from all corners of the world, using the web as a platform for communication and to spread their big idea. I realise that this web platform is complex, uncontrolled and has many risks.

But the bright side, the sunny side, is full of positive opportunity. Twitter, the latest form of online chatter, uses instant messaging to take us beyond the endless garbage of our inboxes. It is simple and it's a platform of untapped – but I'm sure planned for – potential. YouTube came in eighteen light-speed months from being assembled in a garage to an £884 million 'Do no evil' Google acquisition. All power to the geeks in the garage, I hope they invest their overnight fortune wisely.

I-genius and StridingOut are networks that I belong to, connecting social entrepreneurs to help grow their business and have a positive impact on society simultaneously. MakeTravelFair, ResponsibleTravel and YourSafePlanet are travel sites that are pushing for a more sustainable form of tourism through online networks. Treehugger (bad name, brilliant site) delves into every aspect of green living in the twenty-first century and, with its own version of Digg (which allows users to decide what becomes the most newsworthy item), you can Hugg green stories and issues you like, helping spread positive ideas in an instant. Similarly, WorldChanging is a vast evolving guide to living sustainably in an age of global responsibility. StyleWillSaveUs (now there's a great name) is a magazine community focusing on greening fashion styles, giving sustainability sex appeal. Or if you want to see what happened to Mark James Bowness, the guy with the online island dream that we're now living, well he's back at it and his story and his latest ideas can be read at PeoplePassionPlanet.

Business can now exist yet be driven for social as well as financial ends. With our giant online shopping centre now accessible to so many, creating so much competition and opportunity and choice, a unique ethical or social selling point is surely the last great marketing differentiator. In capitalist chat, it's got to be the ultimate win-win. Business has to take social issues seriously because a significant number of consumers are telling them so.

But the pressure has to come from above as well as below. Governments must give incentives to businesses and organisations that put social impact near the top of their list. Social entrepreneurialism, supported by governments, investors and consumers, can change the world.

I am only in the second year of running my own business, one that took off overnight, almost burnt out in the same amount of time under the strain of its own ambition before recovering and building something more sustainable that I hope will grow.

The web platform is the technology of our generation. It brought us to Vorovoro and it offers unprecedented opportunity, barely a decade old and already revolutionising the way many of us live and work around the world. It is a tool that, used creatively and responsibly, really can improve lives and protect the planet. At least, on the cool woven mat inside Eremoni, I can roll the wheel on my Blackberry and, with one bar of reception, connect to the world.

30
SEGA N KA E DREDRE ENA VURAVURA OQO
'NOTHING HARD IN THIS WORLD'

Epeli looked me in the eye as he banged a five-inch nail through the roughly sawn four-by-two and into the underside of the mangrove. He laughed as, after five blind perfect hammer-to-nail shots, he missed. The Vorovoro legend's party trick was something I had seen when we were building the Great Bure and it was one I never tired of watching or seeing people's reactions to for the first time. Tribe members would stand open-mouthed at what they had witnessed. Epeli, brimmed hat, bow-legged, leather-hands, would turn and say, just as he had to Doug before, 'Well, nothing hard in this world. Only you or me hard in this world.' Then he'd burst into a great rip of wheezing laughter, usually slapping one giant hand on your shoulder until you felt like your upper body might crumple under the weight of his playful blows.

Of course, Epeli, like so many Fijian people I have met on Vorovoro, was right. We are the only real obstacles in our own paths. If we can negotiate ourselves we can negotiate life. He had a brilliantly simple way of saying things without a classical command of the English language. In five short words, he had the oratorical impact of statesmen like Churchill or Mandela, on me at least. I know others who've met him who would agree.

Epeli is just one man in Fiji who made me think about life differently. There were many more – men, women and children – from Vorovoro, Mali and the world. The place and community culture and what we initially presume to be a simpler lifestyle seem to provide a great space for people to open their minds while their bodies adapt to the rhythms of island life. Too often, I think, we judge developing countries as less sophisticated simply because the former don't have the financial means to live as the latter do. What I continue to discover in Fiji and on Vorovoro is that the wealth and richness and diversity of life here is more apparent in the open-armed, respect-driven tribal cultures of the Pacific than any city I have spent time in around the world. From what I have seen so far, you rarely observe alienation, detachment or loneliness in a Fijian village. There is, however, a support network for everyone and a hierarchy of respect that points upwards in age.

I have realised that I must make every effort to respect, nurture and protect not just the environment but also this way of living. One of the aspects of the Tribewanted project I am most proud of so far on Vorovoro is that it seems to have rekindled a local interest in Fijian tradition, be it bure building, meke dancing or a heightened emphasis on the culture of ceremonial respect. This isn't down to us, it's down to a few strong-willed people within the Mali yasuva who have bravely said, 'Let's welcome the world to Vorovoro and show them that the Fijian way is a good way.' We as a global community have been sensitive, as well as lucky, to embrace that opportunity and celebrate it. Long may it last.

But community harmony didn't always exist on Vorovoro. The big cultural differences between the visitors and those that lived and worked on Vorovoro sometimes led to tensions and at worst deceit. Alcohol was usually the main culprit. Although there was no pay bar, tribe members brought beers, wine and rum to the island. On three separate occasions in the first year, bottles of beer and wine went missing. The result was investigation, council meetings and, in one case, a sacking. I was later told by Tevita this was too strong a reaction to theft and that every one of these incidents should go to Tui Mali. Mistakes were made. Because Vorovoro exists somewhere between a Fijian village and a normal backpacking resort, it is often difficult to find the right cultural and social balance. It requires constant work. On another occassion, the issue of wages was brought up by the ladies in the kitchen and, although they were being paid a better rate than people in similar jobs on the mainland, the stress of working in a basic outdoor kitchen was creating tension. We increased the wages, brought in some young chefs from Suva and extended the kitchen space.

There were also issues within our own team. A 24-7 working and living evironment led, at times, to moments of 'island fever'. Kimbo, who was on the island more than most, suffered particularly with this. We made efforts to bring in extra gappers and work closely with the elected chiefs so that a work-island-life balance was struck as much as possible. I never expected this project to be easy and it will always require strong and sensitive leadership from Tribewanted, its visiting members and from the Fijians themselves. When you're trying something new, things are bound to go wrong. But the good thing about living on Vorovoro is you know that a new sunrise or Fijian smile is bound to get you quickly back on your feet.

I could see that Epeli and the boys on his team were just about finished for the afternoon. The family bure project was only a day old, but already all the posts were in and one of the bamboo walls had been woven. On Fiji, it takes two months to get everyone to agree on a job but only two weeks to complete it. I'm sure before I came to Fiji I would have expected it to be the other way round.

As I walked past the Great Bure, I could see a dozen girls from the tribe sitting in a circle inside weaving flowers into garlands and headdresses. They were preparing to perform a meke for Tui Mali. I was supposed to be performing as well, in the men's meke, a kind of warrior dance in coconut skirts. I could see some of the boys on the grass practising the moves. I would have joined them as I wasn't sure of the extra section that Tevita, our meke coach, had added that day. Apparently this particular meke was written just for Vorovoro and so it was very important we got it right. Especially as, alongside our visitors from Mali and Tui himself, we had the *Getaway* film crew on the island for twenty-four hours, as well as the Meke Appreciation Society, which had recently popped up on Facebook.

Getaway is Australia's leading weekly travel show and they were on Vorovoro to film a five-minute feature on Tribewanted. It could give us great coverage in Australia where so far Tribewanted hadn't had much exposure and I was keen to make sure that their short stay went well. At dawn that morning, they had joined us on a fishing trip and Jason, the host, had been filmed pulling in a seven-kilo barracuda two minutes after dropping a line off the back of the boat. I think it was only the third barracuda we'd ever caught.

The rest of the day ran smoothly as the crew got shots of tribe life in the village. There was a surreal moment when Jason and I were being filmed by *Getaway* talking about the family bure and Shine were filming us being filmed. And someone else was taking photos of the whole scene. Talk about postmodern island living. Anyway, as long as these big camera moments were just 'moments', I was sure it wouldn't spoil the spirit of Tribewanted.

Finally, everyone was settled and we all sat cross-legged on the mats on the sand in front of the Great Bure listening to the high tide shaping the shells on the beach a few feet away. It was that perfect light about half an hour before sunset where the brightness of the day begins to fade, taking its intensity with it, and everything is drenched in a golden wash. Rocks, trees, faces, sea, skin, all glowing effervescently, celebrating another day in this remarkable place. The sevusevu ceremony performed, it was time for the mekes. The girls filed out in their grass skirts with red flowers tucked hanging round their necks and tucked into their hair. Tui Mali's face was lit up with childish joy as this group of relative strangers performed a beautiful traditional dance telling the story of Vorovoro on his very own beach.

The boys followed, led by Tevita in the vigorous and fast-paced elbow-pointing, thigh-shaking, body-rocking dance, to the sounds of the Fijian men chanting, clapping and playing out the rhythm on the lali. And, as the sun eventually set, a stream of white-clad figures appeared out of the dusk – it was the Mali Choir, dressed in their Sunday best, coming to sing for us and for Tui Mali. The TV crew recorded their perfect harmonies as their songs and faces lit up the night. It was the first time that they would have recordings of their own voices. We ate the barbequed barracuda with fresh coconut miti, taro leaves and buttered baked potatoes before returning to the kava bowl and Fijian songs and laughter.

That day seems as good a day as any to pause this particular story. There were so many perfect days on that island. From May through to September 2007, the village, gardens and tribe grew.

On 1 September, some of the first footers from 2006 returned to the same beach to join thirty-five tribe members and another hundred or so Fijians. A one-year celebration complete with the kai palagi performing the yaqona ceremony and meke dances was followed by tribal summits around the 'digital' tanoa. Only a year on and yet so much had happened, so much had changed. I watched, overwhelmed with pride, as Fijian guests from business and government and other villages looked on literally open-mouthed as this group of 'tourists' entertained them Fijian style. The whole event orchestrated by the now indispensible and inspirational Tevita – the man that had prophesied to Tui Mali it would all happen. But even he surely couldn't have imagined all this? Spontaneous speeches from tribe members and Fijians alike, on their knees beside Tui Mali, recalled an experience in their lives like no other.

But this is only the start of one story, a personal perspective on a period in my life when something extraordinary started to happen. I was fortunate enough to play an important part in

'NOTHING HARD IN THIS WORLD'

building something new and discovered what living on a tropical island was like while realising an internet dream. During it all, I was too often caught up in the day-to-day challenges to appreciate what was actually happening. It really is only now as I write these words that I begin to understand what this experience has started to mean to people both here in Fiji and around the world. The email from a guy called Mark that started an adventure in an English winter and the technology that brought us here via a search engine. There were American breakfast television and magazine cover stories, bloggers that sent us to the edge of failure, fires, cyclones and coups. People who came, those who wouldn't, and those who were here before we arrived and will remain long after we are gone. My good friend Marco sums up island emotions like this:

> You may leave Vorovoro in person, but you never leave it in your mind. For, as you journey away from the little isle all other thoughts are gone. You only think of life on the island. The magical island.

Look, I know you're thinking, 'It's all very well for you to say all this on your perfect little island in the Pacific, but apart from keeping the campers well fed you don't have any real worries.' True, I am awash with high-tide idealism. Wouldn't you be? But I am daily brought back to the reality of life beyond Vorovoro by the journey we had to take to get here and by the journey we will continue to take.

Aaron, our web Chief, said amongst the kava at the tribal summit, 'No island is an island.' He's right, whether it's us as individuals or a place like Vorovoro. The impact of everything we do ripples well beyond the lagoon off the beach. And so this adventure on Vorovoro has, for us, started to become an example of what a lifestyle and a cycle of life can be like if we choose it. Even here, in a remote corner of the Pacific, we are connected to everywhere and everyone at once. It sometimes takes unusual experiences to make us think differently. That's why I love this kind of journey.

And I strongly sense, even without all the science at my fingertips, that if we are to keep our earthly home in good nick as our populations continue to spin out of control then experiences like the one I have had on this tiny island as part of a global tribe are vital. In some ways, Vorovoro is a beacon. If we can start to get it right on an island, amongst the grassy roots and grains of sand, then why can't we get it right elsewhere? It will always be challenging, but it is possible. What has happened since Tribewanted began has taught me that it is possible and, if you want it enough and find the right people who also want it, then it can happen. Nothing hard in this world, right?

Tui Mali took the cigar from where he was holding it between his toes and, after one last puff, stubbed it out on the shell ashtray in front of him as he sat cross-legged on the mat. It was getting late. He turned his head and looked at me with tired, happy eyes. I knew he wanted to say something; you can see his mind working and he never wastes a word. 'You know where we are sitting now?' Well I did, we were sitting on his Chiefly mat, on the sand in front of the Great Bure under the most awesome starry night. But I knew this was not what he meant. I looked up at him and said, 'No, what is this place?'

'This is the place where I met Tevita that morning when he was clearing the grass.' Ah! It all fell into place. Tui continued: 'This is the place we were standing when Tevita said to me that the world would come to Vorovoro. You see, we sit here now and the tribes from around the world meke for the people of Fiji. It is a good story. Tevita was right. We are very happy.' I smiled a big kava- and Vorovoro-induced smile. There was nothing I could say. 'OK, Ben. I'm going to take the lead now, the tide is going back. You know today's story will be in Mali tonight, in Labasa tomorrow, and then across Fiji. It's a big story for Vorovoro.' He chuckled. So did I. The camera crews meant the story would travel a lot further than that.

I stood up with that wise man, helped him roll up his Chiefly mat and turned to say goodbye. As we shook hands I suddenly felt a ripple of fraught, heavy energy rise through my body and stop behind my eyes, ready to burst forth. I knew I wanted to just let everything out, but this was Tui Mali so I held his grasp strongly, swallowed hard and somehow kept the tear ducts shut. I looked my friend and leader in the eye and, bowing slightly as I did so, thanked him for the day. I stood still and watched as he walked down the path, past the firelight and into the night.

Drawing a deep breath, I arched my neck back and took a minute to calm myself. The vastness of the sky and the bright stars looked too perfect to be real. I exhaled slowly. Perfectly relaxed, I turned and looked towards the fire where someone was already twisting flaming poi in giant symmetrical circles around his head and people from Mali and from around the world played guitars and swung in hammocks. I joined them, my tribe, in another glimpse of paradise.

ACKNOWLEDGEMENTS

How many good people and how much goodwill do you need to make a bold idea begin to work?

Answer: lots.

The following people have all played a part in what has become an unforgettable and life-changing adventure for many that promises a potentially greater future.

For your passion, commitment, talent, ideas and humanity, I say vina'a va'alevu. I hope you enjoyed the journey as much as I did. I hope even more that you continue to do so.

At home...

MJ, you are an ideas man. That email you sent me changed my life and the lives of many more. We worked together to get this adventure off the ground, and your passion to make it work was undoubted. Keep dreaming and keep emailing your dreams, and your creative sparks will continue to light the fires that inspire people to change the world.

Andy at 10yetis, thank you for calling us and for your endless

ACKNOWLEDGEMENTS

enthusiasm in those early days and throughout, you were there at a crucial time.

Imal, you educated me in the world of American PR at breakneck speed. It sure was fun.

Andy and Simon at Komodo, you took an abstract idea and created a fantastic online identity and community for Tribewanted. I know it was high-pressure at times but you did it. Congratulations.

Elisabeth Murdoch and Matthew Freud, I never expected to be networking with people like you when MJ and I started Tribewanted. Your support and enthusiasm for the project was generous and gave us huge confidence.

To all at Shine who worked on Tribewanted, your professionalism, cultural and project sensitivity and friendship was fantastic throughout. Seeing Vorovoro on the BBC is a dream come true for all of us. Big vinaka to John Silver, Sara Brailsford, Simon Bisset, Caroline McCool, Anna Boronat, Tori Nelson, Emma Jones, Jon Lloyd, Paul Taylor, Jennifer Linton, Gemma Chapman, Luke Byrne, Holly Lambden, Claire Sweeney and Nicks Bullard (aka Cola).

Dale Vince and Madeleine Carrol at Ecotricity, your support powered Vorovoro and educated all involved about the importance of renewable energy to the future of all our lives.

Michael Buick at Climate Care, you and your team are tackling one of the biggest challenges in the world today. I admire your commitment and thank you for your support. Keep going, there are plenty of us out there who want to find the solutions too.

Helen Lang at Global Sense, it was great to have someone to talk through the potentially complex community relationship we were going to have to manage in Fiji.

Jodi Willis at MTT Sustain, it was good having someone with your experience on Vorovoro so early on. Thank you for hosting the tribal sustainability meets in the UK.

Heather Wilkinson at Striding Out, you lead a network of passionate and talented social entrepreneurs, thank you for your advice and connections.

Dr Sarah Bell and the University College London team, we will always be very grateful on Vorovoro for your work on the Sustainability Plan. We now have a template for really making Vorovoro a totally sustainable existence. I promise we will do our best.

James Vlahos from *National Geographic Adventure*, you have been the most committed journalist to the tribe and you somehow got Vorovoro on the front cover of one of the world's most iconic magazines. I will never forget showing Tui Mali the magazine cover and him saying: 'Oh, it's Vorovoro – good story!'

Tom Griffiths from gapyear.com, you know all about what it is like to run an online travel community and have been a great sounding board throughout. Cheers!

Ben Fogle, Alex Tew, Danny Bamping and Corbin Bersen, you have all added your names and enthusiasm to this project, for which we are very grateful. Now find some time in your busy lives to visit Vorovoro, it's your home too!

In Fiji...

Tui Mali, momo, you *are* a great man with a clear vision for your people and your land. Your leadership, calmness and humanity have inspired me and many others that have met you on Vorovoro. I can never thank you enough for welcoming us into your idyllic home. I hope you feel that it has been as good a story for the Mali yavusa as it has been for the internet tribe. Vina'a va'alevu to you and Anaseini.

Ulai Baya, well, my friend, you are a unique cocktail of talents, traditions and skills. Without you, this partnership would not have happened. Thank you for your guidance, support and helping me with my English! You backed us; you didn't have to. Bula boss!

Peter, you made such a difference to the Vorovoro community in the first year. You were a gentle Fijian giant. We promise to do all we can to support your family. May you rest in peace.

And to the rest of the family Poasa, Francis, Raijeli, Mila, Kesa, Ratu, Mana, Junior Api, Bongi, Va, Semesa, Save, Skipper and

ACKNOWLEDGEMENTS

everyone else in your extensive clan, you have welcomed the world into your home and shown us how to look after people. Vinaka.

Vani, Jiten and Uthroh, you have been a great off-island family to us. Sorry for the late-night wake-ups and vinaka for your endless hospitality.

Brother Apenisa, what can I say? You have been our most trusted friend on the water. Thank you for keeping the tribe safe, as you said yourself you were 'born in the sea'.

Epeli, you are one of many men that helped build Vorovoro. But I think you represent everything that is good about this project; work hard, play hard, embrace people. 'Nothing hard in this world' – if you can say it, you can do it. You have taught the world, a legend you most definitely are.

Tevita, you prophesied it to Tui Mali and it came true. Your passion for Fijian traditions and horticulture has helped make Vorovoro what it is today. I know how much tribe members have loved spending time with you learning mekes and gardening. Fiji should be proud of men like you.

To the villages of Mali – Nakawaga, Ligaulevu, Vesi and Matailabasa – you all helped build Vorovoro and welcomed us into your homes. Thank you for sharing your lives and educating us.

Becky Hunter, you sure played your part in the great adventure and you found your love on Vorovoro. Can't wait for the big day on the beach. Congratulations to you and Ryan!

Sara Jane, well you've been through it all with us and your commitment to this project has been fantastic. Thank you for dealing with all the crap and being a good friend to us all.

Kimbo, mate, you have grown from a Leamington Spa lad into an island man. It's been a pleasure having you on the team. Here's to catching plenty more fish in the water or on land…

James Strawbridge and Duncan Glendinning, I know how fortunate we are to have leaders with your passion, commitment and knowledge to help drive us towards true sustainability on Vorovoro.

Aaron Wheeler, you will be making a big difference to the online experience for tribe members. I hope you and Masayo enjoy your new life in Fiji together.

Jonathan Segal from Oceanic, you and your family have become a good friend to me and Tribewanted. Your ideas, enthusiasm and support has driven me forward. I can't tell you how important it has been.

To our 'island gappers', Murray, Raina, Naomi, Anna, Julia, Craig and Carol, vinaka for all your hard work and enthusiasm on Vorovoro. You were all brilliant.

Giles Dawnay, I needed someone I could rely on to take on the responsibility of leading the project when I returned home. Thank you for being there for Tribewanted.

Mel, thanks to you and USP for early edits of Tribal TV and Suva hospitality. Sham, Hemita and all at Govinda's, thank you for your temporary office and the chocolate cake, you are the front line for IT in northern Fiji. Vini and all at the Grand Eastern, thank you for coping with a neverending stream of tribe members and workers traipsing through your hotel. Graeme & Carolyn at Austpacific for being great neighbours. Chuck for being there at the beginning. Jo Tuomoto and Jane West from the Fiji Visitors' Bureau, thanks for backing this crazy new idea for Fiji from day one.

Tribe members and friends...

Warren, Doug, Kimbo, Riah, Stu, Craig, Micki, Tom, Ryan, Adam, Sam, Chris, Ciaran, Carol and Alice, you have been our Chiefs so far, and you've all taken on the role with pride, respect and passion. And look what you built! On behalf of the tribe, a big vinaka.

There have been many, many other tribe members that have played big and small parts in making Tribewanted a success, both online and on the island. It would be too much to start listing all of you and your achievements here. Those involved in the Dream Foundation, the Tikinas, the tribal gatherings, the online debates, the on-island developments, the thousands of emails and blogs and pictures – all I can say is thank you for taking the

ACKNOWLEDGEMENTS

leap of faith and throwing some of your hard-earned money and precious time at this adventure. I hope none of you regret it, I know most of you are having the time of your lives and it's been a real pleasure meeting and living this with all of you. Here's to the next two years!

A few good friends from before I started Tribewanted have, despite my shocking communication, been there for me throughout. Marco, Joey, Hoops, Trots, Fordy, Jono, Zak, Jen, Bondy, Molls, no.1 boys, Big Gav, Ruth, Pops, Piona, Jake, Jane, Warwick, Toggers and Gilo, vinaka.

Finally, I really do have to thank my family, without whose support I don't think I could have kept going at times. I haven't seen much of them over the last year or so and they are always there for me. Mum, so glad you made it to Vorovoro, you are part of the family here. Come back soon. Dad and Frances – thank you for your amazing support from day one. Looking forward to being by the fire in Devon again. And bro, well, going by the 'When is Taniela coming home?' question I get daily out here, you are the most popular son in Mali. Thank you for being there, I'll never forget it.

See you on Vorovoro soon I hope. Ni sa moce.

Ben

x

ben@tribewanted.com

TRIBE WANTED

BE PART OF
THE COCONUT EVOLUTION

1) Coming to Fiji
and/or
2) Taking the Vorovoro experience home…

ENERGISE	Switch to green power today: ecotricity.co.uk
EAT	Step towards self-sufficiency with the Strawbridges: itsnoteasybeinggreen.co.uk
DRINK	Drink bottled water for the world: belu.org Save water at home: hippo-the-watersaver.co.uk
MOVE	Offset: climatecare.org Travel responsibly: maketravelfair.org, yoursafeplanet.com
SHARE	Contribute to your community: tribewanted.com/dreamfoundation, dothegreenthing.com
STYLE	The future of fashion: stylewillsaveus.com
BUILD	Build it and they will come: lighterfootstep.com
TRASH	Plastic bags are not cool: onyabags.com Keep clean: ecover.com

TRIBEWANTED.COM
What part will you play?